By Any Means Necessary

A Journey With Celtic Bampots

By Paul Larkin

ISBN 978-1-300-09265-0

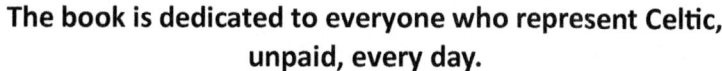

The book is dedicated to everyone who represent Celtic, unpaid, every day.

Also to my brother, Tony Miles.

"We declare our right on this earth...to be a human being, to be respected as a human being, to be given the rights of a human being in this society, on this earth, in this day, which we intend to bring into existence by any means necessary."

Malcolm X

WARNING: This book contains swear words, graphic descriptions of adult situations both legal and illegal, and lots of real life drama. Can't be bad then, eh?

Contents

Foreword

Since I started the Beyond the Waves Celtic Football Show, there have been many milestones we've achieved that have been incredibly humbling. Finding out folks actually wanted to hear our show every week, our first show with 1000 listens, our first show with 4000 listens, being invited to the great Paul Larkin's book launch in the Bronx, amongst many others, but none struck me quite as much as when Paul himself asked me to write the foreword for this book. Sometimes an author will chose someone famous to write a foreword so as to raise the profile of the book. Other times an author may choose someone close to them, who's known them their whole life and can lend a unique perspective to the reader. In me, Paul has neither a famous name nor a childhood friend, but he does have a devoted friend and fan of his work who finds entertainment and education in his style of writing and his choice of topics. Some writers, like music acts, have a particular style that they constantly fall back on, to the point where if you've seen one of their works, you've seen them all. Paul constantly evolves his style of writing while never sacrificing quality. It's a unique trait in a writer and we're lucky as Celtic supporters to have him as a resource and a scribe.

I first came into contact with Paul via Twitter (big surprise, I know) in March of 2011. I noticed that his profile pic was of him in front of the Pentagon in Washington, DC which I found interesting considering how the US government is not well thought of just now. Paul explained how much he loved DC when he had traveled there in the past and given the fact that I live nearby, I now had a link with a Celtic celebrity. Of course,

I had heard about Paul previously from his interview with the LostBhoys where he talked about the book that he had written called, From Albert, with Love but he didn't come off like many of the other high profile Tims. He was extremely approachable and would answer any question I had or just partake in the banter. So much so that it wasn't long before I forgot that he was a Celtic author and just thought of him as one of my twitter mates.

That's the sort of fella he is. It's not about him or his standing, it's about the stories and the camaraderie and the club. I asked Paul one day how I could buy his book and could I Paypal him the funds for said book. He asked me for my address and 3 days later, I not only had a copy of From Albert, with Love but it was also signed by himself and Albert Kidd. I couldn't believe it. He didn't have to do that and I'm not sure why he did to be honest. He could have just given me the link to lulu.com where his book was being sold and called it a day.

He didn't though.

At the time he was living in New York, and I felt that connected us as well. I could tell he understood the struggles and issues and mentality of the American Celtic supporter and with that I felt I could converse with him much more freely than most. This was especially valuable since he was from Scotland his whole life so I almost thought of him as my very own personal Rosetta Stone straight to Glasgow. I wasn't the only one that Paul interacted with nearly constantly. Paul always places tremendous value on the "man of the people" ideal in his writing and he lives it with every second of his life. He helped me better understand some of the challenges we face over here, supporting Celtic, through comparing notes from his experience in the New York CSC's. It's always nice knowing you're not the only one.

I decided to start a Celtic podcast in June 2011 that would have American voices behind it to declare to the world that there are loads of Celtic supporters here that are knowledgeable, passionate and devoted to the club equal to anywhere else on the planet. Paul Larkin was one of our biggest supporters from day one and I can't express how much I appreciate that. He came on our show whenever we asked him to so he could talk about his books and gave his legitimacy early on that boosted our exposure and standing. He also became a very dear friend that I'd trust with my life. I finally met Paul in person for the first Glasgow derby of the 2011-2012 season in Philadelphia where we did a live show from Fado Irish Pub. Sometimes when you meet people in person, they are completely different that the image you have of them from twitter. Paul was exactly the same person but nothing is as conclusive as being able to look someone in the eye. Paul made me feel like he was almost a big brother to me (not just because we are both incredibly handsome) where he'd have my back no matter what. That really meant a lot to me and still does.

He invited me to the Bronx (which can be an imposing place for those who've never been) and took me, the Rev and the Coach under his wing introducing us to the entire crew at the Celtic House, home of the Bronx Bhoys CSC. We did a live show from the Celtic House for Paul's book launch of Wim's Tims and had an absolutely fantastic day out that I'll never forget. I was gutted to hear that Paul was moving back to Scotland but completely understood the reasons why. It's far away and that's a challenge when you have family on both sides. I guess that means I really gotta get my ass in gear and make that first trip over to Scotland to see the bhoys.

I've seen Paul go through the writing process for three books consisting of different topics. Paul has been referred to as the Nick Hornby of Celtic Football Club. Nick Hornby can't light a candle to Paul Larkin. Nick Hornby is the standup comedian that has one great album and tour and then fades away because you feel like you're hearing the same stuff over and over again. I'd say Paul Larkin is more synonymous with George Carlin where time and again he changes, sometimes drastically, but it's always a hit. There's still plenty of material, and still plenty of laughs and plenty to learn.

With this latest book, By Any Means Neccesary-A Journey with Celtic Bampots, Paul takes a look back over the past four tumultuous years for Celtic and for himself. As supporters, sometimes our perspective shifts so quickly we lose sight of just how far we've come. That's exactly why this work is so important. We constantly need to push on and advance and improve, no doubt. But every now and again, it's vital that we take a look back and down the mountain, to see just how far we've climbed and enjoy the gorgeous view. There are dangerous ravines we've crossed and rockslides that have set us back. But we forged ahead, we've wound up where we are today and we've learned lessons that will carry us through what might lie ahead. Paul also reveals quite a bit about himself personally and the struggles that he himself went through during this time, which in many ways parallel the storyline of Celtic from Strachan to Mowbray to Lennon.

Paul's greatness isn't by virtue of being great as much as it's due to the fact that he's one of us. He's been there with us all at one point or another while we've climbed this mountain. He'll continue to be with us going forward. As we, the Celtic supporters, sit now on this beautiful little vista, I hope you enjoy the view that Paul will describe for us here. And try not to cringe too much because it wasn't all that bad. And remember, what doesn't kIll us makes us stronger. And by this point we've all got something inside so strong. Hail Hail and Keep the Faith.

Graham Wilson

Co-Host, Beyond the Waves Celtic Football Show

Preface

The title of Paul Larkin's book instantly conjures up in my mind an image of that famous poster of Malcolm X looking through venetian blinds holding an M1 carbine.

The African American is the epitome of alienation par excellence in the late 20th century.

I was seven when the black power leader was assassinated.

At that age I didn't know about much other than what the loving embrace of my mother's clan bestowed upon me.

I was raised with Irish songs and an affection for Celtic.

A culture is not something you buy at Argos because it is on special offer, it isn't purchased or chosen. It's inherited.

You don't get a choice, it is non-negotiable.

By the time I was Malcolm X's age in that picture I was fully cognisant about what it meant to be alienated. I have no idea what he saw through those blinds, but I am fairly sure he wasn't looking out on a society that valued him as an equal. It was only by accident of birth that I had been deposited in an ex-mining village on the eastern edge of Glasgow.

It never felt like home.

I only ever felt settled when I looked out over Clew bay and knew that this was where my father had cavorted as a boy. I knew I wasn't alone in these feelings of dislocation. My best friend at school had a similar personal history .His father was a Donegal man, but my pal Liam had the advantage on me in that his father was alive.

A dad was something I was bereaved of from day one.

Had we both seen the light of day in New York and not Glasgow then our affection for Ireland wouldn't have been a problem for the wider society. We also would have entered a job market in the mid-1970s that had been a level playing field in the Big Apple since the turn of the century. In Glasgow we would both be 40 before that was achieved for the likes of us.

Thankfully I was well away from the place by then.

Looking around me, the only public place my culture was in any way validated when I was a boy was at Celtic Park. The flag that I knew to be my flag was waved in triumph as Jock Stein's men in hoops swarmed forward. The Celtic family has such a rich narrative that it screams out to be preserved in print for future generations.

Paul Larkin represents a new kind of writer.

This is grassroots literature that is gritty and authentic. It is a voice that isn't usually heard in polite circles and it is all the better for that. Larkin's work has an ability to make you remember how you felt at a specific point in a victorious match or at a low point in a league campaign. That's a fine skill to have and one that I hope he continues to develop.

In this book he puts the recent demise of our toxic neighbours into a social and cultural context for the Celtic family. To do that he focuses on how the death of Rangers was also a defeat for a certain type of cosy sports journalism.

Reporting the terminal illness of the Ibrox club was a victory for a guerrilla media using the epoch changing power of the web.

Futurologist Alvin Toffler in the 1980s predicted that the "third wave" of human technological and social development would produce a "demassified media". The Rangers story was there waiting to be told, but the ancient regime around the sports desks sniffed something that would be bad for Rangers wouldn't be good for circulation.

Perhaps they were correct.

However, the story was a huge one and it had to be told. During this period I inhabited both media worlds - the old and the new. I was busily filing stories to newspapers as a freelancer and uploading posts to my own site.

If they wanted to be, the folks on Planet Fitba were very well informed.

The Celtic people couldn't believe what they were reading because it meant the inevitable demise of their arch rivals. The Ibrox Klan didn't want to believe it because it was so awful and they were being told by people like Paul Brennan from Celtic Quick News, the RTC blogger and little old Fenian me perched on a Donegal hillside. The vast majority of the Rangers chaps chose not to believe.

This was a fatal miscalculation.

One of the factors that contributed to the death of Rangers was the absence of any meaningful mobilization by the club's supporters. They were told by the mainstream media that everything was ok. For circulation reasons they were fed a daily diet of fluffy good news.

Casinos, hovering pitches and star players being flown in on private jets. When those fair stories stopped working then it moved to "it isn't as bad as it is being painted, everything will be ok, don't worry!"

Of course it was THAT bad!

The cruelly ironic thing was that the online Celtic community had a clear view of what was happening and have not been surprised in the least when Rangers' obituary was written.

When Celtic faced extinction in 1993 the fans mobilized.

The Celts for change movement led by Matt McGlone and Brendan Sweeney tipped the balance and the bank moved in on the old board.

The Bunnet landed and Celtic was saved.

Two things were different from the crisis that assailed both clubs. In the 1990s the Celtic fans were very well informed about the seriousness of the situation by the gleeful mainstream media. Basically the guys in newspapers and in broadcast organisations did their jobs and informed the public.

A bad news Celtic story sold on both sides of the city.

The other difference is that Celtic fans do not have any cultural inhibitions to a wee uprising now and then. In the other side of the city, apart from being misinformed by a constant stream of PR generated guff that everything was ok, they aren't good material for an uprising.

When Brian Dempsey said that night "The rebels have won!"

We all knew what he meant.

To be a Celtic fan has been to be on the outside of the power structures. I do believe we are in historical times and that basic reality is altering. Paul's book charts the change in the seating arrangements on the intercity SFA express. These days you can wear your hoops, have an Irish passport in your pocket and sit up behind the driver.

The front of the bus is no longer out of bounds.

The use of new media has been a key to establishing this new zeitgeist on Planet Fitba and Paul Larkin's work is a key part of that.

He is the switched on guy in the pie queue behind you chatting to his mate. You listen in and you think "he talks more sense than those clowns on Clyde!" It was always thus, but a democratised media of blogs, podcasts and self-published books means that the old guard of the media have been bested by guys holding their scarves aloft.

When Rangers were offed the old way of "doing" media in Scottish football was thrown into the grave with them. The reputation of the succulent lamb boys will never ever recover from this. Any society based on democratic principles needs a free press and that can only thrive if journalism remains uncompromised by the powerful.

Clearly when it came to Rangers (1872-2012) the footie bit of the Fourth Estate spent too much time on David Murray's estates.

What this guerrilla media did was to put the story out there in such a way that mainstream organisations like Channel 4 News got in on the act. With the big boys in town it was game over for the thugs and thieves creative writers group. That denouement could not have come if the story had not been developed by people who the laptop loyal wouldn't have about the place.

People in power when they are threatened often define the group that will usurp them. Although it is meant as a term to demean and deride it can be turned round like a judo fighter's trick.

I am not sure who first coined the term "internet bampot", but it summed up what the ancient regime within Scottish sports journalism thought about guerrilla warfare on the web.

Although some preferred to remain anonymous for their own reasons it was people who stepped into the light like Paul Larkin who were difficult to dismiss.

The internet provided the weaponry to fight back against a sloppy and cynical media.

In the hands of someone like Paul the web became something he could use to shoot down the myths that Celtic supporters were paranoid and the game in Scotland wasn't bent.

There is now a model in the country of my birth for an alienated disempowered group to enter the debate on their own terms and re-define the narrative in their world view.

The victory won over the tired old sports media, grown fat on succulent lamb, can be an example to others. The men who founded Celtic would be proud of Paul Larkin because setting up the club was part of a liberation from poverty and racism. It addressed the physical and the cultural needs of a community that suffered hostility and exclusion.

Now the Celtic family have their own media.

There IS an alternative to the PR generated guff of the mainstream media.

In Paul Larkin they have one of their own who can encapsulate the emotions of belonging to this global clan and how it feels in the bad times and in the good.

He is an addictive writer that injects remembered emotion into the reader's consciousness.

I am proud to call him my friend.

The other part of the statement on that famous Malcolm X poster was a call to "liberate our minds".

Paul Larkin can help you on that journey.

He has a rebel heart and it guides him on the page.

Follow him here and see where he takes you.

Phil Mac Giolla Bhain
Ireland
June, 2012

Before we start, let's go back...

Once upon a time there was a young man who loved playing football and going to watch his favourite team, Celtic, when he wasn't playing. Many a Saturday night in the pub was spent cursing a referee who had obviously been biased and cost his team a point or two. After another marathon moaning session he was told for the umpteenth time by his pissed off mates

"Either stoap fuckin moanin or dae sumthin aboot it!!"

"Whit the fuck can a dae?"

"Referee the gemmes yirsel then ye'll only huv yirsel tae fuckin blame!!"

Sobered up on the Monday this discussion kept coming back to him. The reality that he would never play in a "Glasgow Derby" had long since dawned on him but the thought of refereeing one and making sure the bhoys got a fair crack of the whip....... now that did appeal to him. Because that's all they need – no bias, no dodgy penalties or offsides decisions- and then we would see who wins the League.

He phoned Directory Enquiries for the SFA's number – although not so long ago this was in the days before websites, multimedia and mobile phones!

"How dae I become a referee?"

That one question would lead to a career that gave some fantastic experiences but also some depressing lows as he encountered the'secret' influences over refereeing symptomatic of Scottish society in the second half of the twentieth century.

Refereeing was organised on a County basis with Glasgow and Edinburgh having their own Associations. He was given contact details for his local association, arranged to go to the next local class and joined about 20 hopefuls for the 3 month course.

As an introduction to refereeing it was a great experience. The course was taken by two former refs who used stories of their past games to illustrate 'The Laws'. Everything was positive and the hopefuls were told that the only barriers to succeeding in refereeing were the limit of your ability and your commitment. My God, how that statement would be ripped apart in the years to come.

After passing the exam – which had a daunting 80% pass mark – he was invited to the monthly Association Meeting to receive his Certificate and Badge.

When he went into the meeting room he was struck by the number of 'familiar' faces he saw. Current and past Grade1 refs he had abused from the terracing or watched on TV. He was also aware of the number of blazers on view.

The meeting was very formal and, frankly, boring – no lively discussion about that weekend's games – and eventually the new Referees were each called up to be presented with their certificates by the President. He prepared himself for a strong firm handshake but was a wee bit put out by the President's thumb pressing on his knuckle and an awkward repositioning of hands took place – this was a 'handshake' he would meet many times and would become expert in returning 'the grip'.

The new refs were invited to attend the weekly training sessions to improve their fitness and mingle with the more experienced refs. So later that week he got his training bag and headed to meet his new refereeing mates. One of the older refs saw him arrive and took him to the dressing room.

"Get changed here and join us on the track. A few laps a few sprints then shower and into the pub. Not a bad training session, eh?"

By the time he got out, training had started and the rain was pouring down. He noticed quite a few had come prepared with a variety of headgear. He made a note to put something in his bag for next week if it was raining.

The following week the rain was pouring down but our man was ready for it and went onto the track with a tammy on his head. After completing a lap he felt a tap on the shoulder. One of the Grade 1 referees told him that the next time they completed a lap the Supervisor wanted a word with him.

"Must want to make me feel welcome" he thought.

"You wanted to see me?"

"Yes. Get that thing off your head!"

"What? My tammy?"

"Yes. Things like that are not allowed "

It was a green and white hooped tammy but had no wording on it. Simply alternate rings of green and white.

"So what about the guy with the red, white and blue tammy with GERS on the front ?"

"It has nothing to do with you what one of our senior referees is wearing. If you want to continue training here get that off!"

Nice welcome.

He settled into refereeing the Boys Clubs and Amateurs – serving his apprenticeship and carried on attending training, but without the offending tammy.

He enjoyed listening to and joining in the conversations in the dressing room about TV games and incidents from refs games at the weekend.

Discussions about next week's appointments led to advice like "Watch wee so-and-so, dirty wee bastard. Nail him with a card early and you'll be fine."

It took him longer to realise the significance of some comments.

"You going on Thursday?"

"Where were you on Monday night?"

It took a while for him to realise that these other nights were not additional training sessions but Masonic meetings in various places across the County.

He would later realise that referee Association events – Annual Dinner etc - couldn't be arranged till they checked that the date didn't clash with 'other meetings'.

Our man progressed through the ranks and was promoted to refereeing in the Juniors.

Unlike today the Juniors was a mix of players who had reached their level, older pros whose career was on the way down and young talented players farmed out by senior clubs. Notable examples were Tommy Burns at Maryhill and Kenny Dalglish at Cumbernauld.

During his first season in the Juniors he was appointed to a match involving a team considered to have leanings towards the East End of Glasgow. After the match one of the Committee spoke to him.

"Are you new in the Juniors? I thought you had a good game, I'll let the Match Secretary know."

Another Committee man butted in

"For fuck sake don't dae that. If we praise a referee we will never see him again."

"Okay" says the first committee man "I'll phone and say ye were shite"

The next day he was given a game for the following Saturday with the same team.

He phoned the Match Secretary

"I refereed them yesterday."

"Aye and they phoned me and complained about ye. I just told them that I decide who the good referees are and they'll get you every week till they stop complaining."

As he arrived the following week, the Committee man walked past, winked and said in a loud voice "Aw naw no him again!" He always got a good welcome there and did their pre season friendlies and closed door games.

His career progressed and he was told he had a chance of promotion to the Senior List as a Linesman. There were unsubtle hints that he needed to toe party line – eg meetings, training , attend Summer School at St Andrews, blazer and tie compulsory dress for all games etc – but the thought of making the Senior List made all of these 'requirements' seem worthwhile and he buckled down and became a model Association member.

As he made his way through the Junior leagues he was struck by just how often he was greeted by 'the handshake' on arrival at grounds and when meeting Committee men after matches over high class buffets of pies ad Bovril.

Their insistence on giving 'the grip' led to an amusing experience.

Although he had a game of his own that day he was asked to do an early morning mid winter pitch inspection before an important league game. The match referee was unavailable and, as a big crowd was expected, he was asked to check out the pitch at 9am.

He arrived to be met by two Committee men.

"Good morning, gentlemen. How's the pitch looking?"

"How come you're here? You're no the match referee!"

"He's not available but he will be here this afternoon if the game is on"

"Thank fuck it's you. We are at full strength the day and we hear they huv three men missing. We reckon we can do them if the game's on and that Fenian bastard would put it aff just tae spite us"

He said nothing asked for a ball, walked onto the park and booted the ball in the air. It landed "Splatt" He kicked it again and it stuck in water. Lifting the ball he simply said

"Games is off. I'll phone the Match Secretary"

"Fur fuck's sake we thought you wid dae us a turn"

At that they started to walk away.

"Excuse me, gentleman. You forgot to pay me the Inspection Fee"

Grudgingly a cheque was written but he handed it back to them.

"Sorry but that's not my name. My name is xxxxxxxxx."

A look of shock came over them as they realised they had mistaken him for one of the handshake brigade who stayed in the next town.

Taking the new, correctly written cheque he left them with.

"Oh, and I'll let the match referee know you were asking for him. He's a mate of mine"

When the match was played they lost 4-1

There were other Junior refs who would be competing for promotion to the Senior List and he was tipped off at some of the antics they were getting up to ensure they got the high profile games.

The Match Secretary was a well known Freemason and there seemed to be a competition going on to see who could take him to the most Masonic meetings and functions. Referees would detour miles out of their way to collect him from home, drive him to lodges and take him home in the early hours after a good nights drinking.

This was not a new tactic used by ambitious refs and no less a person than Hugh Dallas would use this method to further his career when he was going through the Junior ranks

The season ended and the SFA Referees Committee would decide on his fate for the next season. The final meeting would take place during the Referees Summer School in June at St Andrews.

Although the process was 'secret' – well what would you expect with so many masons involved?- word always leaked out to those 'in the know'.

Early on the Sunday afternoon he got a 'nod and a wink' letting him know he could expect a letter from the SFA confirming his appointment to the Senior List of Referees as a Linesman Grade 3a.

A small group of Senior List referees from his local association took him for a drink to celebrate. A lot of backslapping and a few pints later the conversation got a wee bit serious.

"Right, that's you on the List so we will arrange to get you in to the freemasons."

"Why would I want in?"

"Because it will help you to be seen at the right meetings by the people that matter."

"What do you mean you will arrange to get me in?"

"We will organise it and make sure you don't get blackballed"

"Why would I get blackballed?"

"Because you are a Catholic, but we will get it fixed"

"If that is what I need to do to get on in refereeing, you can stick it up your arse"

No amount of encouragement and badgering would change his mind and he was warned that it could affect his chances of promotion. But he stuck by his principles and reminded them that at the training course he was told that the only barriers to progressing were your ability and commitment. Time would tell who was right.

There were great experiences on the Senior List, none more so than his first appointment at Celtic Park.

The thrill of running out the tunnel and across the park to 'The Jungle' will stay with him forever, as will the sound of The Jungle chanting 'Who's the Mason in the black?' after he had flagged a Celtic player offside.

He is sure one of his mates started the singing!!

If the 'handshake' was commonplace in the Juniors it became even more so at senior grounds.

Meeting referees and linesmen from other Associations brought home how widespread membership of 'the craft' was and he lost count of the number of times he was asked ' How old is yer Granny?' after he had made an attempt at returning the infamous handshake. Although on the surface this seemed like a very polite and friendly question it was another of the 'brother masons' codes to find out what Lodge you belonged to.

Meeting some of the big names from refereeing was an experience and the pre-match instructions, particularly from the more famous referees were an eye opener.

I am sure that it has always been one of the most infuriating things for fans to see what looks to them to be a blatant penalty with the foul committed in full view of the Linesman – or Assistant Referees as they are now called. How often does the referee give nothing and the crowd howl at the Linesman "Did you no' see that?" or "Get yer flag up ya useless bastard!!!"

The truth is that many of our "top referees" are so full of their own importance that they give the following instructions to their Linesmen – sorry assistants.

"All I want you to do is flag for throw-ins and offsides. Everything in the penalty area is my decision. Don't flag unless I look for you. If I've seen it and not giving it your flag won't make any difference!" Having microphone link ups makes it ever less likely you will see a linesman get involved as he can hear the ref say 'no penalty' in his ear so why bring attention to yourself.

Think about that the next time you want to criticise a Linesman.

In every era Celtic fans have always had particular referees they considered to be the most blatantly anti-celtic. Davidson, Syme (father and son),Tait , McCluskey, Dallas, McCurry, McDonald, Collum ... the list goes on and on.

There have been some very public incidents in recent times that have served to confirm the Celtic fans belief that they get a raw deal and it is not all down to 'honest mistakes'

The Reverend McCurry's Simply the Best sing-a-long, Dougie Dougie and the Dallas e-mail all added to the sense of injustice and mistrust of referees.

However, being on the 'inside' brought one or two interesting moments that didn't make the media but opened his eyes and would certainly back up the suspicions of the 'internet bampots'

Davie Syme was a referee who inflamed the passions of the faithful on many an occasion , in fact the late great Jock Stein is reported to have waited at the tunnel after one particularly controversial performance by Syme. As the referee passed him Big Jock simply stated "Your faither would have been proud of you."

Now to the uninitiated this may seem like a compliment but to Celtic fans with longer memories they will remember Davie's father Willie Syme who officiated in the 50s and 60s.

During a discussion among referees about Stein's comment to Syme an older colleague told our man "Davie Syme's Dad used to boast that 'I never gave those people a throw in if I could help it'. He was referring to Celtic so what chance of his son giving them a fair deal.

The first time he shared a dressing room with Bobby Tait his first impressions were of a really sociable and likeable guy who was down to earth and not "up his own arse" like many of the Grade 1 referees. The pre-match chat was very friendly and then they headed to the dressing room.

As they were getting their referees kit on our man noticed that, like many refs and indeed players, Tait put on two pairs of socks before putting his football boots on. No problem there you think. However, while the outer pair were the standard referee socks, black with white tops, it was the other socks that drew his attention.

Black socks with red tops – now where had our ref seen these before?

"Is it not dodgy wearing Rangers socks under your Referee socks?"

"I've worn these in every game since I was a boy and I'm not going to stop now. Anyway, who is going to report me?"

End of conversation

Any time their paths crossed he always got on well with Tait but couldn't forget the 'hidden agenda' and often wondered what the reaction would have been if he had got a leg injury at Celtic Park and the socks had been exposed.

Jim McCluskey was another bogeyman as far as the Celtic support were concerned. This came to a head with the famous private detective story. However, one story the private eye didn't uncover goes back to late April 1986.

The season was coming to an end and Hearts were on top of the league. Celtic had a game in hand at Fir Park on 30thApril and needed a win to take it to the last day.

A typically stuffy game saw Celtic a goal up but under some pressure from Motherwell. An equaliser would finish the title chase but Celtic were awarded a penalty midway through the second half, scored it and held on for a win.

It was now down to the last day. Hearts at Dens Park and Celtic at Love Street. We all know how the story ends – From Albert, With Love – but a conversation amongst a group of referees again shows what Celtic are fighting against week in week out.

The referee at Fir Park was Jim McCluskey. Our referee overheard this exchange between McCluskey and another senior list official well known for his affection for the now liquidated team from Govan.

"I'm telling you, McCluskey, if they bastards win the league it will be your fault."

"What the fuck are you talking about?"

"They were struggling there till you gave them that penalty!"

"But it was a penalty!"

"It was a fucking soft one that you could have got away wi'. I am telling you, if Hearts fuck it up it'll be down to you."

Another wee postscript to 'Love St 86' that shows that there are good decent honest referees but also points a finger of suspicion at the Scottish Football League.

Hearts last game of the season was at Dens Park against Dundee. Win or draw and the title was theirs. They would even become champions as long as they avoided a five goal swing on goal difference if they matched Celtic's result.

Referee appointments were made well in advance. However, the match referee called off for personal reasons, sickness, injury or work.

The Scottish League then appointed Bill Crombie from Edinburgh to referee the match. Now they would have had a fairly long list of possible replacements for the Dundee Hearts game but, in their wisdom they go for Crombie.

Crombie was an excellent referee but it was also common knowledge that he and his family were lifelong Hearts supporters. Post match on a Saturday a lot of Edinburgh based referees would meet in The Centurion in Corstorphine and refs from other areas who were officiating near Edinburgh would join them for a drink before heading North, South or West.

A regular sight after six thirty would be Crombie's daughter wearing hearts scarf arriving to tell him it was time to head home.

As it turned out Crombie gave an almost flawless display of refereeing at Dens and was probably amongst the most disappointed people in the stadium at time up but he maintained his credibility. Indeed he could have easily given a penalty for Hearts.

Why would the Scottish League put Crombie in this position. Well, consider that the Secretary of the League at that time, and the person who would approve the appointment, was none other than Jim Farry, who would meet his fate at the hands of Fergus McCann and you may begin to put two and two together.

Our linesman never progressed beyond that level. He saw others with less ability than himself but who were seen at the right 'meetings' progress through the ranks and he sometimes wonders what the future would have been had he accepted the offer to 'join the masons'.

The thought never lasts long because he would then have given legitimacy to a corrupt system.

Will Scottish Refereeing ever be in a position where referees are promoted purely on the basis of ability and commitment?

Who knows.

Let's hope that day will come.

The Ride

"In my country we go to prison first and then become President"

Nelson Mandela

I heard my name and somehow knew to turn round. It was New York. Queens to be exact, not many people knew me so should it have been someone else being referred to but I knew this was me. I had that instinct. I turned and saw the gun, clean cut law enforcement face behind it and heard the instruction loud and clear "FBI, Put your hands behind your head, lock your fingers and drop to your knees, slowly". As I followed the orders, slowly, I saw two other feds with guns pointed at me, I even saw sweat slowly drip off one of them like morning dew slithering down grass, he was that close. As my knees hit the concrete, already people coming out the subway I was waiting at were giving me a second glance. No more than that though, this is New York, remember? A crowd of smokers from the Off Track Betting shop nearby were looking over but nothing more than a brief glance from what I saw. I then noticed a woman cop, lean with short brown hair and an unsatisfied pent up face, her badge glinting in the summer sun and her gun protruded from her holster as she observed the arrest. Calculating it after the initial shock I regained composure and figured that there are three FBI with guns at my head and this woman detective watching but not moving or talking. My mind went like an Internet connection then, had they expected me to be with a woman? They searched me for weapons and narcotics, I had none, thankfully, my hands were put behind my back, cuffed and then I was lifted to my feet. I saw in fact that they all had badges on their belts so it wasn't a hit, I was 90% sure of that by now. I walked along Queens Boulevard with them, one cop on each arm, past the Georgia Diner on my left, $3.50 a Bud in there, toward the Queens Mall to see there was a car waiting. They pushed my head down to put me in the back, the cuffs digging into my wrists every time I moved, tightening like a junkie pulling leather looking for a vein, and we drove off towards the city.

"Detective Diaz arrest. Coming in with a body from Queens" said the driver on his radio as we drove off. I sat in the back passenger seat, the woman farthest away on my left, one FBI on my immediate left and squeezing me with his shoulder and cheap aftershave with me thinking that I hoped mine choked him, doubtful in this fucking heat. The four of these geniuses proceeded to talk about food, dry-cleaning and people they didn't like in their precinct or unit, they have must have been real cunts if even these pricks didn't like them. One of them, 250 pounds, balding and typical Fed moustache, kept complaining, kind of like American kids do, that he was hungry so they went to White Castle for hamburgers, yeah great taste jerk offs, still no one saying a word to me since entering the car. I thought of that film with Shelley Long years ago where she chokes on the chicken nugget. Scratch that, I fucking dreamed of it. Fed faces fed, we drove off and I glanced at some Met fans, heading for Shea for the last season ever, I used to walk round Shea a lot, exercise mainly and I was going to the new place next week supposedly but that seemed a million miles away right now. For the first time ever, I was jealous of Met fans. We snaked through Sunnyside, still no conversation from these fucks in my direction. My mind raced again, was it a fucking hit? Had some prick just thought "fuck it" and hired The Osmonds here to sing me a lullaby? What fuck were these pricks playing at? Why hadn't they said anything to me and why in fucks name were they not in a hurry to take me to the station?

They chomped their extra burgers, yeah they had gotten take-out too, talked more shit and when we finally entered Manhattan I felt a sense of relief go over me, it can't be a hit, this is Manhattan and I'm Paul Larkin not Paul Castellano. If it was a hit I'd be in the boot now heading for Staten Island to be chopped up.

So I'm told.

We arrived at the Precinct, I wasn't exactly sure where in Manhattan it was at this fucking time, I knew it was around 7th and 33rd but couldn't be sure, I was still in a bit of real shock and ached to wake up and realise this was all a Krueger. As we entered the station my hit fears were finally gone, this was real and these feds and cops were certainly real. I found out the three men were Feds who were brought in especially and the woman was a New York City Detective although she said she lived in New Jersey, I heard her make reference to that in the car. That spooked me because I was sure that wasn't allowed and again my mind was flying like a kite over a wind turbine.

I got booked in at the station, fucking Hill Street by the look of it, quicker than I had in any fucking hotel in New York, cuffed still but then again I had been in a few New York hotels too, taken down for mug-shots, finger prints and still no one had said why I was here. Fucking cops huh, so full of their own self-importance that they lose all consideration the minute they drink their first cup of coffee whilst wearing a hat. I was then taken to an interview room and handcuffed to the radiator by some jerk off who looked like he sucked lemons for a hobby and I was told to wait. Yeah, good one, Rickles job is safe you motherfucker. After around 25 minutes, the woman cop came in and said "Do you know why you're here?" by this time I was fucking raging; "Yeah", I replied, "You brought me here". She was unimpressed, probably not used to being close to a man with wit so she came back with "We have reason to believe you are part of an ongoing criminal conspiracy involving members of the ******** crime family. We are going to be charging you with the following crimes, Racketeering, Illegal Gambling, Menacing, Harassment and Second Degree Assault."

As retorts go, that was one of the best I'd heard.

"Would you like to make a statement so you can start to address this mess and get it cleared up as soon as possible?" Yeah, Henry Hill tried that and ended up having to put out cook books to earn a living and I cannie boil a fucking egg. She went on "If you could supply us with information on the following people **** ****** *****, ******* ********* ******* and **** ****** ***** we could see what could be done about this, you know" Don't beat around the bush honey. Mind you looking at her, you wouldn't beat around her bush, a fucking sniper wouldn't take her out.

I looked at her, I had a feeling that any time a fucking safe was about to drop on my head. "I'll pass" was the only reply I had.

"You think about it funny man" she smiled as she left. Christ her smile made her look like Serpico. Unshaven.

Think about it? Fucking think about it you cunt? All I could think was what the fuck was I doing in this place? I was going to the diner for a burger, Ok The Georgia Diner isn't great but it sure beats the shit out of this place and now I am sitting in a 14 x 8 interview room, chained to a fucking radiator pipe and facing charges that, if convicted, will get me 20 fucking years in Attica eating breakfast with the Latin Kings. And don't mistake them for those guys who sing Hotel California in Spanish.

Diaz, now wearing a name badge, came back in and asked if I had thought about things? No I've been sitting here wondering what the Yankees rotation will be this season sweetie. She looked at me for about 25 seconds then said that as I had an answer for everything except the one she wanted so I would be held there until she could get another officer to accompany her downtown to "The Tombs" with me, the what? Did she say "Tombs"?

I got taken to a holding cell around 10 feet from the room I'd just been in, saw the sun still shining in the room, noticed it was 4.31pm on the clock and Diaz took out a set of keys and handcuffs were removed for the first time. I sat in there for two hours listening to stupid cops talk about how everything they did was right and how everything everyone else did was stupid. Yeah, sure guys, knock yourselves out. They also spoke about a woman they were heading off to arrest who, from what I could gather, liked a guy who worked in Starbucks and had asked the guy out, he'd said no and she had pursued him since. Let's walk through that one again, a guy had been asked out on a date by a girl. Instead of saying yes, or politely declining, he had called the fucking cops to get her arrested? Dude, if you're reading this, you've probably just missed out on the best blowjob of your life and the only chance you'll ever have of fulfilling every wank fantasy you've ever had. How do I know this? Because you work in fucking STARBUCKS Dude, not Rolling Stone magazine. I made a mental note to go into that fucking Starbucks and see this cunt. Fucking prick doesn't know he's born.

I sat down and once again my mind raced through a million different scenarios, all bad of course. Diaz came back about 85 minutes later and said it was time to go. I was cuffed again, taken downstairs by Diaz plus another cop, a fat male who looked a lot like Lou Costello and put in the back of a cop car. After complaints from Lou about the quality of the car, off we went into the New York night. I should say now I never again saw the three FBI guys. Maybe one day I'll hit Posh 405 and catch up with them.

As we approached "The Tombs", which I now knew was the Manhattan Detention Complex, it hit me again, this is fucking real and I'm going to fucking jail here. Diaz took me out the car, told Lou Costello that she could handle it from here but could he wait for her. As we walked into the jail she explained that I was being taken here to be held until I appeared in court the next day where I would either be detained without bail or a bail fee would be agreed upon and I would be released if I, or someone that was in the courthouse for me, paid it. I would be assigned a public defender if I didn't have my own lawyer. Right then I noticed a thawing of her previous jobsworth type attitude. I had no time to ponder that though as she took me down and I was booked in, because I was standing in a queue behind some dangerous looking fucking people, and that was just the guards. I checked out the line, everyone looked like a psychopathic killer from Law and Order. I got to the front and they took all my details again and I was booked in, fingerprinted and searched again. Diaz then left me and said "Good Luck". Yeah, thanks. As I watched her walk away I thought to myself that I probably would fuck her after all. A Corrections Officer (or C.O. as everybody called them) took me down to what I now know is a holding cell. It consisted of, approximately, 25 black guys, five or six Latin looking guys and one Chinese looking guy.

About to be joined by one scared muthafucking white guy...

The Innovator

First they were nowhere, then they everywhere. Podcasts. What the hell were they? I personally had been involved in one for Global Hoops from around Jan 08-June 08 but these were specifically for the members only. Others were for the public and they were good. Celtic Underground started them. Eddie Pearson and co were launching in 2006 with them but for most then podcasts were still a mystery. It wasn't until I grasped what they were and then heard another Celtic podcast that I realised what they were, and I don't just mean folk sitting talking to each other.

I first encountered Chris McGuigan in March 2011 when he asked me if I would like to be interviewed for his podcast, which I now knew as The LostBhoys. I had been a big fan of the show and so to be asked was a real honour. This is when *From Albert, With Love* had just came out. The interview was to take place on Wed March 16th just after Celtic had knocked Inverness Caley Thistle out the cup. I'd had a few beers and was a bit nervous as I sat on my couch in Yonkers waiting for Chris to call. When he did, I'd say about three minutes later I was totally at ease. Chris is one of those guys you love, a humble man with a big Celtic heart. We actually talked for about 15 minutes before recording (something that would grow to be a habit of ours and get longer in time as well) and it was a thoroughly enjoyable experience. After I did it, I took a long swig of Bud Light and got myself ready for St Patrick's Day the following day. I spent it in Manhattan and took my son Jake to see all the marchers and every county was heard from. At that time I started to up my Twitter use to try and promote

From Albert, With Love but still only had 30 followers and at least 15 of them were Hookers. When I came back that night, tired but logging on, I looked at my Twitter and was amazed, I now had 150 followers and had 23 messages of good wishes from folk who had already heard the podcast. The book, which had been out a month at that point and had sold 10 copies had now sold 33 in one day. Now I'd like to think "Hey, what a charmer I am" but the reality is, the LostBhoys launched it all. Chris will never admit that or the impact it has all over The Celtic Family but I'm telling you the truth here.

I spoke to Chris on April 18th 2012, right after Chelsea had beaten Barcelona, and it's weird because the previous times I'd spoke to him I was always in New York, he mostly in Texas, then he moved to Cheltenham in England and now here we were with me in Edinburgh again. I had a strategy with Chris and I reveal it to him now, I asked him for the interview, he agreed, then I told him I wouldn't keep him long and just had some general questions for him. I did this because as he has interviewed so many folk, I knew he would be a tad cagey at first and wanted the Chris I spoke to previous to going on air all the time. So we danced through the questions and then just chatted and that's when the real Chris appears, passionate, dedicated, humble and the heart of a lion with a Celtic soul.

Here is the dancing part:

Where did the idea for the podcast come from?

"It was on a plane three years ago coming back from Vegas, Gerry Dale and I were talking about how we could be a help to the NAFCSC and came up with the idea of a podcast. It was

really just meant to be a platform for the clubs but here we are 137 episodes later"

At what point did you realise that you had a hit on your hands?

"I don't think we ever have! It's a good format with a nice dynamic to it and people seem to like it. We don't dodge the Issues, we cover the main bases having an Irishman, Scotsman and American and although it can be challenging, it's fun"

We talked more on stuff that's been in the public domain for years and you'll already know about, what I wanted from Chris though was to get to the point of the issue.

How do you feel about "representing" Celtic these days?

"Well, it's not something I think about a lot, I don't see it as big deal, it's just a wee show"

Ok, but people who publicly supported Celtic were sent bombs and bullets in 2011, it is a big thing.

"Now you put it like that...ha. I think if I still lived in Belfast I would need to think about my involvement in such things"

Do you think that things have changed now, in terms of the attitude of Celtic supporters?

"Most definitely. Listen, if you'd have told me in the 80's that there would be a Celtic shop in the middle of Belfast, I'd have thought you were off your head. You see Celtic shirts everywhere, bars everywhere, an huge online presence and a complete defiance against and all attacks on the club"

Do Celtic frustrate you at times?

(laughs and then pauses)

"They probably frustrate me less than they used to. I mean a couple of years I felt the club was so far behind in terms of social media and the like that I actually felt we would never catch up but things have changed finally. I've spoken to people at Celtic who had never heard of a podcast and had no idea what one was. That's changing I think. Also like what the club is doing on Twitter, in terms of having a presence there, that's a big step forward"

Chris is one of your own. For someone at the hub of such a successful part of The Celtic Family he is very humble and never blows his own trumpet. That said, he has a fierce passion for Celtic and is nobody's fool. One conversation with him gives you an understanding of why Chris McGuigan is very much at the epicenter of the Celtic fight back.

Summary Dreams and Famine Songs

"He who allows oppression shares the crime"

Desiderius Erasmus

Post Tannadice 2008, things for Celtic moved effortlessly. There was such a tidal wave of emotion around the club that the supporters were genuinely content. We'd done three in a row, Aidan McGeady had rubbed it into Rangers and Dermot Desmond had said on the the pitch at Tannadice post match that Gordon Strachan would be given the necessary funds in the summer to strengthen the team. There was also the fact that Tommy Burns passing united the club in a way that it hadn't been since Martin O'Neill was there. Supporters were expectant that the big signings would roll in, particularly knowing we would go straight into the Champions League stage. We should have known by now.

We brought in a total of six players in the summer of 2008, with Glenn Loovens, a centre half from Cardiff, by far the biggest outlay at £2.5m, snatched from under the noses of Rangers. There was Marc Crosas from Barcelona to wet the appetite and I'd have probably not had any knowledge of him at all had it not been for Barcelona's close season games in Scotland against Hibs and Dundee Utd. Most were hoping for a younger Xavi Hernandez at that time, hmm, we'll see. Shaun Maloney also came back and split the support in half. A lot of people never forgave him for leaving after Celtic re-built his career after injury, whilst others were delighted to see a quality player return. Me? I was happy, I'd met him three times and he had been nice to me so I defended him to the hilt. That's how football works, right?

For some reason Celtic took on a pre season tournament in Faro, Portugal with Cardiff and Middlesbrough and it looked like all three teams had agreed to stage the worst football matches in history. This was followed up by a tournament in Rotterdam, Holland against Feyenoord and Spurs and the team were much better. Where was I in all this?

Under house arrest.

More of that later.

The season started with a crappy 1-0 win against St Mirren that didn't inspire. The following week I was back in Scotland and seeing us draw 1-1 at Tannadice with my eldest son James. I felt like a stranger that day. Simply because The Green Brigade had transformed the away support and I was a novice for their songs and lateral movement. The following week saw Maloney start and The Bhoys play well to win 3-0 against Falkirk at Celtic Park. Being back in Scotland took some time to adjust to, especially when on the third day back I answered my mother's door to two plain suited cops who gave me a "friendly" warning that they would be keeping close eye on me. After about three weeks back in Scotland I got my own place after a tortuous time at my mother's house. The visit from the cops made me fear every time I heard the gate outside and I started to live in a state of perpetual fear. Not only that I was having night terrors that were making me fear falling asleep as well. There was also the small matter that I was skint, had no possessions and a lot of friends turned their back on me. Of course I was only realising that. At the time you don't think about it but as the weeks go on you start to realise some folk never did get back to you.

The one distraction to this was the fact that Rangers were coming to Celtic Park. I went through with James and met a few guys before the game who knew of my predicament and had a good laugh before it. I had a bad feeling about the game and this was confirmed when Kevin Thomson committed a shocking tackle on Nakamura and wasn't red carded and Rangers went on to record 4-2 victory that was most down to our own ineptness on the day. The air was filled with even more hate that day, not having won a title since 2005, Rangers came in defiant mode and their supporters had a new song to play with:

"Why don't you go home?

why don't you go home?

The famine is over.

Why don't you go home!"

I've probably said this in every book but the only thing worse than a Rangers fan is a Rangers fan.

I left Celtic Park that day totally disgusted, not just with our awful performance, but with the level of bile emanating from the Rangers end and absolutely sod all being done about it.

Welcome back to Scotland.

Omaha Steaks

"People in the United Kingdom and outside the United States share my bemusement with the United States that America doesn't share with itself"

Bill Hicks

So how did that happen then? How did I end up in jail. When I left you I was on top of the world, we'd just won the league at Tannadice and clinched three in a row. How could I be in that situation less than a month later? Well, to be honest, I still don't know, so I'll tell you now my version, exactly what led up to that arrest and see what you think:

It was Sunday June 15th 2008, and I was heading for Gary Haley's work. I often did this on Sundays as it was quiet and we could watch a film or have a beer. He started at 3pm so I gave him a couple of hours and headed in on the F train from Queens, got out at Radio City, checked the Blackberry as usual then text him that I'd be there in a couple of minutes. As usual, he told me to go to the loading bay, it was getting too familiar going in through the front door and he didn't want an incident with the cunty woman security guard who was on the front desk increasingly more and more.

We went down the escalator, turned left along the long white corridor and then right into his huge office space. This was the hub of the building, where any problem in this huge storied block would be reported directly to him and he would have to deal with it. Nothing untoward was happening today though and we sat shooting the shit for ages before he suggested we go to Hawaiian Tropics, a restaurant of scantily clad women, as my birthday had just passed and he hadn't seen me since.

We got in there and were seated by this stunning girl in a bikini and many sexist comments later, Gary was asking what plans I had that week, I told him I had tickets for the Mets later that week, I was going to see a speech by Bill Clinton on Tuesday and I also had tickets for Talk Radio, the show with Liev Schrieber. He asked me who I was taking and I said it would be my regular girl I was meeting her after this too.

We had a great meal and it was a great time to be alive. I finally was starting to feel established now in New York, it fitted me. Guys seemed to like me, I had a terrific relationship with women here, great apartment, money rolling in and I had Gary. He had become like a brother to me and I had never had that before in life. When I first came to New York looking to change my life and hopefully be happy, I did not know then that what I needed wasn't the money, success, girls or vacations, it was a Gary.

I'd always been someone who didn't back down but that had cost me a lot of friends and he made me realise that it doesn't have to be like that. Confidence shattered, I'd came to NYC more in desperation than anything else, realising that in 30 years on this planet, I hadn't gotten anywhere. I'd been lots of places but what did that matter? If you had no one to share your experiences with when you got back, roll over all the incidents and the like what was the fucking point? Gary was always like that, he was cagey about his own life but always wanted to know about mine, how I was doing and he seemed to take great pleasure in hearing all my stories. That felt good. Felt like I belonged.

The club he took me to in Queens made me feel part of something too, I could call any one of the guys there and be lined up with anything I needed and had stopped there before I came into the city to pick up some white. All was great there today too, a Sunday, by definition much quieter and more laid back, few guys reading the paper, a couple watching TV, two playing cards, all seemed right in the world when I went to the club. I was taking pleasure in life and it was brought into focus by that waitress in Tropics handing over the cheque and showing enough cleavage to guarantee a good tip. In a previous life I'd have spotted that a mile off and complained to whoever I was with, now I was delighted to tip 50%, especially as Gary was picking up the check. I looked up and down the check, Shrimp Tacos, Thai Chicken Lollipops, Filet Mignon, Teriyaki Seared Salmon, Caramelized Apple Tart and Warm Flourless Chocolate Cake. That all made me feel good reading it for some reason. I drained my Heineken bottle and we left.

Walking into the cool air of 7th and 49th Street I had a nice glow about me. I walked Gary round to his work to kill a bit of time, walking past Ted Turner's place and thinking about Rachel the barmaid in there I'd been out with a few nights previous. On a platonic basis. I was also down to play golf with Joe Pesci that week, $500 it cost me. I told Gary I would call him tomorrow and made for 6th Avenue.

It was a beautiful spring night and one of my favourite places in New York, Bryant Park, was coming into focus so I set down just before and waited on my regular girl. I was maybe there five minutes when she appeared and she asked if we wanted to get dinner, I said I had already eaten and she flipped. This kind of shocked me as I'd never seen anything other than contentment in this girl. I told her to calm down but she was almost hysterical at this point and I had no fucking idea why. So I raised my voice to tell her to stop fucking shouting and she looked around, wild-eyed, and then said "So, you won't watch me eat?" I said no and she stormed off. What the fuck is going on? I tried calling her a few times but nothing. I sent her a text saying I'd wait at Bryant Park Subway until 10pm but she didn't show. I had a walk looking for her but couldn't see her anywhere so thought fuck it, and went home.

By the time I got out of the subway I was pretty livid that she had ruined an otherwise perfect day but at the same time she meant nothing to me really, as harsh as that sounds, so I didn't want to let it bother me too much. That said I didn't want to go home so I walked up to a club to chill out for a few hours. Still going over in my head what the fuck that was all about I noticed that there were no lights on in the club at all. As I reached it I realised there was no one in there and I thought about it, couldn't recall ever a time when this was the case and about-turned. I called a few guys but all phones were off. It was almost midnight at this point so I didn't think too much more about it. I walked back down Cooper Avenue, crossed at Woodhaven Boulevard and onto Yellowstone. The streets were quiet as I reached my apartment block, nodding at the concierge as I went in. Up the elevator, into the apartment, no calls or messages, nothing seemed out the ordinary, Although I did ponder what a strange end to the fucking day that was.

I woke early the next morning, restless sleep that I normally only had when I knew an alarm had being set, called the regular girl a few times, nothing, emailed her more and still nothing. What the fuck was she playing it? I was sitting there in a kind of dazed bemusement when the buzzer went, it was the concierge saying a special delivery had come for me, so I got dressed and went down.

On the way down I got filled with a little trepidation, paranoia had set in a little but this went when I found out what the package was a huge box of Omaha Steaks from Gary, for my birthday. What a fucking stand up guy. I struggled back to the elevator with the box, it was huge, and eventually got them back into the apartment. I checked the phone and blackberry, no messages. It was still early, I couldn't call any of the guys or Gary without an ear-bashing so I thought the best thing to do was sit tight and someone would be in touch soon.

Thing was it was regular girl's birthday the following day and I had splashed out because she had helped me a lot I guess, just that it never really entered my mind until then.

I watched HBO on demand, Sopranos and Entourage, then Bill Maher but my mind was elsewhere. Fuck it, I called Gary, got him and explained what had happened last night after I left, he was as equally stunned, and then I threw in the story about the club. He said he'd make some calls and get back to me.

Two hours passed, I'd emailed and called her again and again and still nothing. I tried a few of the guys again but their phones were still off, had these bastards gone on a trip without me? Gary then called back, he had tried her work but there was no response there either. Gary was always on the money with these things and he said to me to sit tight, wait until tomorrow morning and then see where we are. So I did, although my mind was flying always, maybe I appreciated this girl more now that she had disappeared, maybe it made me re-evaluate some shit, maybe.

Another restless sleep and I'd had enough I was going to her work to see why she wouldn't take my calls. I flew down the street to the subway, got there as quick as I could, she worked in Midtown Manhattan, and I went through the big doors of the block. I went to the desk and explained the situation to the security guy there. He sounded concerned and went to call her floor. At last I would be able to speak to her and find out what the fuck she was playing at.

I looked around and watched the workers go to their parts of the building and the normality of their day made me jealous. I saw the guy come back and I knew there was a problem, he said I had to leave the building right away, "what?" I asked him what he was talking about but he wouldn't budge, he said I had to go. I said "Look, I've been trying to find this woman for two days now, as far as I am concerned, she is missing so I have to go to the cops now" and he said that's what I should do, go to the cops right away.

The red mist descended and I felt like killing the inconsiderate prick but was able to control myself and left. I walked out the building and wondered what the fuck was going on with this cow? Why was she doing this? What the fuck had possessed her to start ranting and raving the minute she saw me on Sunday?

I called Gary, told him what happened and he sounded gravely concerned "Listen, go home, wait for my call, something's going on" then he put the phone down. I sensed right there that all around me the walls of Jericho were collapsing so I went to go home. I ran down the subway stairs on Lexington and went to get a ticket, stupid machine rejected my credit card. Tried another, rejected, and the other, rejected. Fucking machine. I got the dollars out of my pocket, slid them in and out for like three minutes and went for the train. Then it hit me, no not the train, fear.

Gary sounded very concerned, that fucking security guard knew something but wasn't saying and the machine had rejected all my credit cards. Something was going down. So when I got out the Subway I made straight for the bank and withdrew $2000 I had in an account I kept for a rainy day and right now, on this day, it felt like it was fucking pouring. I'd tried my other account but the card got chewed but at this point I was too frantic to wonder why. I went back to the apartment, no messages, sat there and thought "Fuck it, I've had it with this shit" and packed a case to go home to Scotland. Whatever the fuck was happening, I wanted no part of it.

I went online to book a flight and once again all the cards were rejected. Fuck! I had two grand so resolved to buy a ticket at the airport. Then the phone rang "YES!" it will be her and I'll sort this out, I walked briskly to it, took a deep breath and picked it up, the voice startled me as it it was not the voice I expected, I also didn't understand what was being said. It was a friend Chris asking for fucking dating tips. Not having the time to explain I just said "Chris, you know the secret? Fuck them face to face and they always come back for more" and with that I pushed the button and hung up.

I sat down on the chair in my living room and realised that I hadn't eaten anything for almost two days. I couldn't order so I walked into the kitchen and saw the box again, Omaha

Steaks, so I got the really sharp knife out, opened it up, pulled two fillets out and cooked them.

Just for a moment things seemed normal again, I'd overcooked them and the smoke was everywhere in the kitchen. I just flung them on the plate after that, washed the sharp knife to cut them with and munched them down which did make me feel better. What it also did though was make me feel tired, the emotional strain of the last two days was finally catching up on me. I sat down around 10 minutes more and was about to leave for the airport when my Blackberry started buzzing.

It was her.

Regular girl.

I was so relieved that she had called all my anger dissipated right there and then. I picked up and said hello, she said "Hi, I think we need to talk"

Absolutely, once I spoke to her face to face, I'd find out what the fuck was going on, smooth things out and all would be good again, then I could help out Gary and whatever problem he was having. She then said "Ok, meet me at the Subway station in 25 minutes".

Perfect, a place we'd met a thousand times. I laid out all her birthday gifts on the sofa, freshened up and got ready to go. A text came through "Hi, running a bit late, wanna grab a bite at Georgia? see ya soon",

No problem, things were looking up again. Then I called Gary, told him what had happened and he sounded relieved. Very relieved. I asked him if he had got in touch with any of the guys but he said he'd try later, ok cool. I wanted him to know that I wasn't as frantic as I had been so I told him I'd take a walk up to the club later once I'd smoothed everything out here. I also told him that I'd ring his phone three times at 4.30pm to let him know all was good and that if I didn't, there was a problem. It was a precaution we always took if we knew one of us was walking into a difficult situation. I didn't expect there to be but it would let him know I was back in control and thinking again. "Alright, cool" was the last thing he said to me.

I made my way out the apartment, down the elevator, past the concierge and out with much more of a spring in my step, glad to finally have the chance to get things back to normal again.

I stood at the Subway, sent the same text to a few people saying I'd be out of contact for the next couple of hours. Things felt normal again, I'd be back in business shortly. Some people came upstairs but she wasn't among them. One girl that was heading upstairs was beautiful, long dark hair, pert breasts, white pantsuit. I looked at her and she smiled, I smiled back. It made me feel good and also made me think about her out of that pantsuit. Reminded me why I loved this place, the women were phenomenal, New York, Queens to be exact. It was because of that I didn't even see the cops approach me and as you already know, before long, I was in "The Tombs"

Bad enough but things were about to get worse, so much worse.

The Voice

Graham Wilson does not fit the profile. He's not Irish, he's not Scottish, he's not Catholic and he doesn't live in an Irish area in America. Of course people like me would pour scorn on any suggestion that you need to be from a certain type of background to support Celtic but the reality is most of our support does come from a certain type of background. Graham Wilson does not. So how did he end up a huge Tim and the voice of the American Celtic support.

Graham picks up the story

"I started getting into Celtic around 1998. I was always a fan but it took a while to start taking a serious interest. If I'm honest it was wavering a bit around 2006. All my buddies support teams like Arsenal and Man Utd and I could easily have swung that way too. It would have enhanced my social life immediately if I had switched but then Nakamura put that free kick in against Man Utd and I never had any doubts again. After that I was online more and the advent of Twitter was a huge thing for me"

For it was there you got in touch with two of your sparring partners, Rev and Coach, right?

"Yup. I guess it was January 2011 and because we lived relatively close to each other, in an American sense, we got chatting and became friends soon after. I'd met Seamus(Seamus Cummins, I-Celtic) the previous summer at a tailgate at the Philly-Celtic game after he had advertised it online"

How did these meets evolve into a show?

"A couple of things happened. We got together for the 2011 Scottish Cup Final and we started talking about it and I told them I would get things moving if they would come on. They all agreed buy Coach(Jim McGuigan) did say he had nothing to offer. I knew then I had to get him on. "

It didn't happen right away though did it?

"No. Family life took over and such but one thing triggered it. I heard Tam Donnelly say on the LostBhoys podcast that Peter Lawwell had said to him that Celtic supporters in North America didn't do enough for the club. I was enraged by this. That's why the show started in July 2011. I felt that Celtic supporters in North America were being misrepresented by Peter Lawwell and wanted to do something positive to fight back."

How was the reaction?

"Unbelievable. I launched the Twitter feed and got 100 followers in an hour, 250 by the end of the day and 400 the following day. I was floored by this. I must also say I got great encouragement from Harper (David Harper, HomeBhoys) and fantastic technical advice from Chris McGuigan. Without that and the boost we got in audience figures when you came on to talk about Wim's Tims in August 2011(Cheque is in post Graham) I doubt we would have a show still"

When did you know you were onto a hit?

"Are we a hit?"

Yes you fool.

"Ok, well I guess when I got tweets at 5.30am EST asking if the show could come on"

Do you feel a responsibility now?

"No question. Since we joined Hail Hail Media our accountability goes up. That's good though, I want people to take me to task, the callers are the show. Guys like Deco in Toronto or Tony Cassidy calling in to tell me where I am going wrong are the lifeblood of the show"

You have done shows in Philly and The Bronx, what's next?

"Scotland. We have to get the gang over to Scotland. It's a dream for us."

Finally Graham, sum up your co-hosts in a sentence?

(long pause)

"Rev, looks can be deceiving. Coach, silent but deadly. Seamus, passion."

One part of the interview is not in what you just read. It's the part where Graham talked about the night, July 4th 2011, when Seamus house was hit by a car and burnt down. Graham quickly set up a fund to help Seamus get over this monstrous tragedy and told me that he could not believe the urgency and kindness from The Celtic Family to help a stranger to most. He said that produced a bond that will never be broken. He also said that he felt accepted by The Celtic Family after this. Well, I know Graham Wilson well. Anyone who did not accept him as a member of The Celtic Family needs their head read. Graham is as passionate a Tim as you'll ever meet. More than that though, he's a brilliant guy, funny, intelligent and entertaining. We even once shared a hotel room in Philadelphia.

That story will be on the directors cut.

Living Like Elvis

"Adversities such as being homeless and going to prison has made many people stronger"

Philip Emeagwali

Walking into that holding cell was probably the scariest experience of my life. Up to that point. I'd have taken on a hundred drunks, faced a thousand doctors or forgot to buy Frankie Fraser a drink rather than be here. The first things you notice are the lights and the horrible cream meets beige colour everywhere. Institution decor. The cell gate was slammed behind me and being the only white guy in there all eyes went on me. In a look that said "you must've done something really bad to be here, you're white" I looked to my left and saw an empty space on the metal bench that ringed the cell. In the opposite corner was a toilet with a three foot wall around it. If you were looking for privacy, you'd come to the wrong place. As I planked my ass on the bench and noticed that the guy next to me smiled. I looked at him and he had a kinda smart Latino look about him. This was around 8pm at night and he quickly made me aware that I'd be in here a good 15 hours minimum. It was the same night the Boston Celtics would complete the largest single season turnaround in NBA history and defeat the LA Lakers to win their 18th title. I watched almost every game in that season and went to see them six times, yet on the night they clinched the Championship, I was in this fucking holding cell.

There's not much to do in a holding cell once you establish that if you don't bother anyone, they won't bother you. So you sit there and listen. There were your usual comedians, the guys bitter at everything and everyone, the quiet ones who looked like they could take your eye out and the one who looks like he thought this was part of an NYC tour. Discussions ranged from where people were from, who did they know, what scams were good, who was a rat and there being no chance of Barack Obama winning simply because his they would need to change the name of his residence as President.

Then of course there was all the people who should not have been there. That's pretty much everyone. If you believe them. One guy said that he woke up that morning and his back was sore. He took a half a pain killer to help it and off he went to drive his truck for the day. About four hours later his back was sore again so he pulled into a bar in Harlem to get a glass of water to take the other half of the pill. As he came out he was arrested. Why? Well, the cops say that he left his house and all morning went round dealing MDMA in pill form. That's Ecstasy to you and I. He made a drop in the bar in Harlem and when they arrested him found 16 Ecstasy tablets on him. Which he said they planted.

If you're lucky you'll get put in a cell with a phone meaning you call friends and and try to get them to make bail for you. With the rates of bail, then mostly this means getting your friends or family to go to a bail bondsman and put down 10% of your bail and they supply the bond to get you out. I wasn't in a cell with a phone and was glad as folk went crazy trying to use it.

After you listen to this for a while, you begin to relax, you're not going to be killed, take it easy. Then it hits you, the people you've let down, the ones you want to see right now more than anything, you're at the lowest point of your life and you're completely aware of this. Adrenalin keeps you going but the enormity starts to hit you. What the fuck is going on? Why am I here? How the hell will I get out? After a long night, sprinkled with an argument over a cigarette lighter, food comes. I say food, it was a see through bag filled with the tiniest milk carton you've ever seen, stale peanut butter and jelly sandwiches and an apple. I took the milk and apple and gave the sandwiches to a homeless guy who looked like he hadn't eaten for a week. I got chatting to him and said he couldn't wait to get up to court. "To get out?"was my obvious answer but he replied "Na man, get to Rikers. TV, warm cell, three meals a day"

Outside it's America.

Eventually I was part of a group taken to another cell which I later realised was literally a door off the courthouse. After about an hour my name was called and I realised it came from one of the booths in the cell. I opened the door and there was the usual glass between you and the other person. That other person was Kevin Morgan, public defender. I admire public defenders, they are like Doctors who take their skills where they are most needed, and you if you're willing to go through law school for five years to then give your skills to the people who need them most, I take my hat off to you.

However.

If you're an incompetent fool who gives off the same amount of confidence as drunk pilot then fuck off and work for

McDonalds. I sat down expecting to be asked what happened but instead the first thing he asked me was "How much money do you have?" At the time I had $87 on me and $2000 with Gary. I had cards and accounts that gave me access to $175,000 though. I left that last part out and he said "Ok, we will go for $500 bail" and then he got up and left.

What the fuck.

See that may sound cool and professional to you but to me, who hadn't a fucking clue what was going on and was expecting someone to come in at any second and say "This has all been a huge mistake" a mixture of anger and dread came over me. I'd been talking to a guy John, black guy from 108th and Lexington, and he had been a far better prison tour guide than this cunting lawyer. I don't know anything else about John other than he was around mid 40's and I know there's probably as much chance of him reading this as there is Kevin Morgan curing AIDS but John, thanks man, you were a cool head when I was losing mine and I'll never forget that.

About 35 minutes later I was taken into court. I scanned the courtroom and didn't recognise anyone. I took my place on the bench, delighted that this nightmare would be over soon. There were four guys in front of me who all got low ball bail and this relaxed me. My name was called and Morgan advised not to speak just confirm. I did this with my name and date of birth and watched Morgan stumble and stutter his way through my side of the case and ask for $500 bail when this snooty prosecuting District Attorney, for book purposes we'll call her "The Devil" completely destroy Morgan and demand $200,000 bail. You know that expression "My heart stopped" ? So I'm standing there in a moment that makes purgatory looks like a beach resort and the judge looks at some papers, looks at me and then says "We'll make it $100,000, do you have the means to pay?" I nodded and said I had cards and he replied "Cash only"

What is this, a fucking Bodega in Washington Heights?

Clearly I wasn't carrying $100k on me so I gave Morgan Gary's number and told him what to do to get it. I went back to the cell and the enormity hit me, I'm not leaving here any time soon. Remember, my cards didn't work yesterday, something is going on here. What? I don't fucking know.

Back to the cell and it felt like the walls were closing in on me. It was now 5.30pm and slowly we, the guys not going home, were going to be shackled and taken back to The Tombs.

Then came another cameo from Morgan.

Lifting my spirits for a brief second thinking he would tell me I could go, he delivered the immortal "Ok, due to severity of your alleged crimes and the bail figure, they're going to take you to Rikers"

Thanks.

The Wikipedia entry for Rikers Island says the following:

The Rikers Island complex, which consists of ten jails, holds local offenders who are awaiting trial and cannot afford, obtain, or were not given bail from a judge, those serving sentences of one year or less and those temporarily placed there pending transfer to another facility.[citation needed] Rikers Island is therefore a jail and not a prison, which typically holds offenders serving longer-term sentences.

Facilities located on the island include Otis Bantum Correctional Center (OBCC), Robert N. Davoren Complex (RNDC, formerly ARDC), Anna M. Kross Center (AMKC), George Motchan Detention Center (GMDC), North Infirmary Command (NIC), Rose M. Singer Center (RMSC), Eric M. Taylor Center (EMTC, formerly CIFM), James A. Thomas Center (JATC), George R. Vierno Center (GRVC) and West Facility (WF). The Bantum, Kross, Motchan, and Vierno house detained male adults. Taylor houses sentenced male adolescents and adults. Davoren primarily houses male inmates who are of ages 16 through 18. Singer houses detained and sentenced female adolescents and adults. North Infirmary primarily houses inmates who require medical attention from an infirmary. West Facility houses inmates who have diseases that are contagious.[6]

The average daily inmate population on the island is about 14,000.[7] The daytime population (including staff) can be 20,000 or more.[8] On average, the inmate population is 52% Black, 41% Hispanic, and 7% White and other. An overwhelming high number of inmates are of either African American, Puerto Rican, Dominican or Jamaican descent. Inmates tend to segregate themselves, with Puerto Ricans and other hispanics on one side of the facility, and African Americans and other non-hispanic blacks in another part of the facility, to prevent racial riots. Major gangs in the facility include Bloods, Latin Kings, Crips, Trinitarios and Folks among others.

The only access to the island is from Queens, over the unmarked 4,200-foot (1.28 km) three-lane Francis Buono Bridge, dedicated on November 22, 1966, by Mayor John

Lindsay.[9] Before the bridge was constructed, the only access to the island was by ferry. Transportation is also provided by the Q100 limited stop bus service, which runs around-the-clock. There are also privately-operated shuttles that connect the parking lot at the south end to the island. Bus service within the island for visitors visiting inmates is provided by the New York City Department of Correction.[citation needed]

The North Infirmary Command, which used to be called the Rikers Island Infirmary, is used to house inmates requiring extreme protective custody, inmates with special health needs, mentally ill inmates, and inmates undergoing drug detoxification, as well as some regular inmates. The rest of the facilities, all built in the last 67 years, make up this city of jails. There is also the Vernon C. Bain Correctional Center, a floating barge (described below). New York City's jail system has become something of a small town. There are schools, medical clinics, ball fields, chapels, gyms, drug rehab programs, grocery stores, barbershops, a bakery, a laundromat, a power plant, a track, a tailor shop, a print shop, a bus depot and even a car wash. Rikers Island has been referred to as the world's largest penal colony.[10][11] For comparison, Europe's largest correctional facility,[12] Fleury-Mérogis Prison sits on 180 acres (0.73 km2) and houses 3,800 prisoners.

What stood out to you there? It's near Queens? It has a Gym? No, it has a 7% white population. Now I would regard myself as pretty much as anti racism as you'll find. That's all that needs said on that.

However what you must understand is that this has fuck all to do with race, this is about survival. I'm a white guy that thinks black people and hispanics, in fact any non white person, has the absolute right to hate any white man given how fucked they have been by the white man since time immemorial. I don't really think people of this generation appreciate or understand that. I can speak with a tiny bit of authority on this and explain why I am not claiming to have been born with the mind of Martin Luther King jr.

The reason I don't have a racist bone in my body is, at present, eight members of my family are either black or mixed race. That's my Uncle Rudy, cousin Kim, her kids Brittney and Mackenzie, my cousin Tony and his kids Cameron, Kyra and Annah. They are all American. Also if you were to meet Tony you'd realise that if I'd been born in America , then he is who I'd be. He is so much like me and I am him, it often spooks the life out of me. I spent a lot of my life with them, whether it was Chicksands in England or in various parts of America or when they made annual visits to Scotland.

In the late 80s myself, Mark O'Neil and his brother Steven started getting into Gangsta Rap. The first album of this genre I ever bought was Straight Outta Compton by N.W.A. After this I bought, borrowed and taped albums like Ice T-Original Gangster, Fear of a Black Planet-Public Enemy and AmeriKKKa's Most Wanted-Ice Cube.

Then in the early 1990's there was a feature on The Word about gangs in L.A. (Crips and Bloods) who were starting to come together and wear one colour, black, and primarily the gear from the L.A. Raiders, that N.W.A. had often been seen wearing. In the summer of 1992. when I was barely allowed to use the house phone, Tony came over to visit and had asked what, if anything, I wanted brought over. I told him and when he appeared there was a Raiders sun hat and a Raiders t shirt. They were very rarely off my back and head then. At most, the best anyone in Scotland could hope for would be a Raiders baseball cap and they cost a fortune. So just remember in future if I say something you don't like or you hate on a blog, I'm O.G. you cunts.

Anyway.

So knowing and loving all my family, there was never a chance I'd be racist, primarily cause a lot of them are Air Force and Cops and would blow my head off. Seriously though, by the time I knew what racism was, I already was as far away from the mindset as possible. The other reason I'd like to think I can speak with a tiny bit of authority is that I've read tons and tons of stuff on black culture, I've studied speeches from my hero Malcolm X(and his book *The Autobiography of Malcolm X with Alex Haley* is by far the most inspirational book I've ever read), I've been to where Malcolm preached in Harlem, I've stood on the spot at the Lincoln Memorial where Martin Luther King Jr had a dream and gone to the recently built memorial for Martin as well in Washington DC. I've even gone to the Muhammad Ali Center in Louisville, KY to marvel at another of my heroes. I'm fascinated by the struggle but even more by how these people fought back and changed the world. Reading about Rosa Parks refusing to give up her seat on December 1st 1955 on that bus in Montgomery made me so angry. I extended my reading to people like Chester Himes and Iceberg Slim, whose writing and turn of phrase is up there with anything Shakespeare has done.

Of course none of my knowledge or tolerant views meant jack shit in jail. I was a white and seen as the enemy of a lot of the people with me. Larry David does a fantastic skit on Curb Your Enthusiasm where his manager, Jeff, asks him why he just nodded at a black guy who just walked past? Larry replies "to confirm I'm one of the good whites". The scene is brilliant because it's real. I couldn't be sitting on the bus to Rikers and then stand up and go *"Ok everyone, I'm not racist, I'm a good white guy, I know who Eldridge Cleaver is, I know E.D. Nixon probably should have been who Martin Luther King Jr became, I know that the closest white society has come to the acceptance of African-Americans is to buy Beyonce records, please don't kill me or rape me in the showers like you see in all those films"*

I'd be dead before I reached the gates.

I'd love to be able to tell you lots of Shawshank Redemption type stories, well apart from the rape scenes obviously, in fact I saw nothing remotely like that in Rikers. The reality is being locked down for 18-21 hours a day and sometimes for 23, there's not a lot that happens. Fear grips you the minute you're booked in and I must say the booking process was a lot easier than booking into a fucking Jurys Inn. The worst night is the first and what you quickly realise that the one thing that is completely unattainable in jail is silence. People left me alone and some were really kind to me. One guy told me to eat food really quick. When I enquired why he said "Sometimes the brothers in here start shit when they're all together at a meal, it's a lockdown, and you may not eat in 48 hours, so always eat it quick" Another guy heard my accent and could not believe it, he had never heard anything like it before. After talking for a bit he said to me "You like Fiddy?" I had no idea what he meant. After a long discussion, and hard one it has to be said, I realised he meant the rapper 50 Cent. After much hilarity had died down I replied "No" and he was crestfallen until I said "I love Wu Tang though?" and he cuddled me.

Of course my entire focus was on getting out. About 15 days in a depression hit me and I started to realise I wasn't getting out. One day there was a count for the whole prison and the C.O.'s (Correctional Officers-Screws) shackled up my whole wing, hands and feet, and walked us out to the basketball courts. It was then I earned the nickname "Dot", I'm sure you can work out why.

Anyway as we passed another group of inmates I recognised one. I shouted his name and he said "Hey Paulie, yeah they got me too, don't worry, we'll be living like Elvis again"

A day later I got word that I had a new lawyer, organised by Gary and at a rate for the whole thing that was 50% less than normal. Did I tell you how much I love Gary Haley? He came to see me and straight away "Ok, my name is Don. You have to go back to court on July 21st, but I hope to have you out of here the Friday before that"

That's the heart stopping again.

"You see the police department did not inform the British Embassy of your arrest and due to the bullshit nature of it, the set up, the charges and asset seizure, I'm going to argue what is called the Vienna statute that was made law after World War Two"

I was excited then he explained that everything I owned had been seized. Apartment, all possessions, bank accounts cleaned out, everything. I had the $2000 Gary was holding, $1500 of which was going to the lawyer, and not a penny more to my name.

Suddenly jail didn't seem too bad.

I shook his hand and told him thanks.

The rest of the time was ok, I kept my head down and read three books that got sent in, all Henry Miller ones, even got to send some emails but they were a disaster as no one could get their head round what happened and then I got word I was to be released on Friday July 18th.

See when you're in jail and they tell you you're getting out, it's like time standing still, and worse when, when that day came, they let me out at 10.50pm. Cunts. I was lucky, I had $87 on me, the other guy getting out was released with a train ticket. On a fucking island. He said to me he only lived in Hazen Street in Elmhurst which is just across the bridge and only needed five bux for a cab that I later realised sat outside Rikers all day and so I gave him the five and he left.

I should have phoned Gary who, unbeknown to me, was waiting on work on my call, but I wanted to talk to someone else. I had no phone on me and no numbers so I got a cab to Connollys on West 54th st, where she worked, only to be told by Graham the Barman that she had just left. FUCK. Luckily another waitress overheard and offered me her number and phone to call. I did and quickly I was on my way on the metro north to The Bronx to meet the woman who would become my wife.

First though, the rats weren't done yet.

Jersey Shore

"I want the people of New Jersey to jump off a cliff like Kurt Vonnegut so I can show them how to fly. This way, nobody needs to grow any wings, which would be impossible anyway because we're humans and not some kind of bird"

Richie Sambora

I got up to The Bronx and made my way to her house, it was after midnight now. This was Trisha. See for the past seven months we had been in a pretty full on relationship. We were not a couple, we just really loved each other. In that jail I knew then I had to tell her I really loved her. So, with Gary going crazy wondering where the hell I was, I made for The Bronx and told her. She repeated it back and that was that.

A condition of my bail was that I had to stay at Gary's house. So the next day I made my way to Ringwood, NJ. There was one slight problem. Gary and family had gone on vacation. Thankfully Ringwood isn't The Bronx so it was easy to get a way in as he told me how to do it. I arrived on a searing hot day and bought a pack of Marlboro Lights. I'd quit smoking three years before but picked the habit up again inside. Of course Gary being Gary he calls me five minutes later saying "Grace room needs decorating, the paint is already there" Some might say that that is a liberty but I know Gary, that made me feel like I was earning my keep just a little.

So I wired in straight away only to become aware of the fact that someone had entered the house. Armed only with a paint roller, I crept toward the noise in the kitchen and was about to give the intruder a lick of pink paint when I realised it was Gary's neighbour, Jim. Gary hadn't told him I'd be there so he came over to check all was good. Or he was being nosey as fuck, you decide.

It wasn't my first encounter with Jim, that was back in November 2006. I'd been off the rails a bit with drink and women and was trying to keep a low profile in Gary's house, where I was staying then, when Jim called Gary and asked us if we fancied a drink, locally, they did 3 for 2 on Thursday nights. I thought it was a good idea and not for the reasons you probably imagine. After the debauchery of my previous weekend, I needed to screw the nut and get back to the normality of a couple of pints, quietly, amongst friends. No need to ask us twice of course though, we were changed and ready to go within 12 minutes of the call, I checked the clock alright? Then Gary produced some cider he said he'd been waiting to open. "When did you buy it like?" I enquired, "Oh, at least a couple of hours ago". I suggested we mix it with beer to have a few "Snakebites" and before long we had the music on in his kitchen and Gary was dancing to Pon De Replay by Rhianna, something to this day he does not remember. As our party was now in full swing we remembered about the invitation to the local bar from Jim and we were soon on our way and bizarrely Gary drove the half mile though I wasn't complaining at the time.

As we arrived in the bar, a kind of steak-grill place with lots of tables and a small raised platform acting as a stage. Jim was there nursing a beer, holding a menu and enquiring immediately about what food we are going to eat? We looked at him as if he'd just asked us to go down on him and replied in unison "no food, beer". Not sure if at this point Jim realised how drunk we were, I certainly fucking had, but on Gary's arrival back from the bar, he gave Jim a double whiskey and told him to "catch up". After much protestations (Jim:"I need to teach schoolgirls music in the morning", us:"You lucky bastard" Jim: Fuck off you two, please!") he eventually scooped it up and slowly caught up, dispensing with any nonsensical "food" thoughts. Was $5 a beer in here, pretty expensive for NJ but with the 3 for 2 deal, it was game on.

As the night wore on, a young guy, tall, skinny and fresh-faced maybe 23, went on the small stage and started singing. He'd been hired to do that like; he didn't just fancy an impromptu one. He was good, had a great range but given that this was New Jersey, and the local yokels wanted a bit more with their beer before they got up to milk their pigs or whatever, the scene started getting a bit more ugly, and not just the women, and before long it was akin to the scene in "The Blues Brothers" where Jake and Elwood are confronted by red necks and abate them by singing the theme tune from "Rawhide".

The young guy was struggling, there was only one person in the whole place seemingly enjoying his act and it was a crazed girl, albeit very fuckable, at the bar who hung on his every word and danced like she had just met a generous Ecstasy dealer. Several times. We quickly established that this was the singers girlfriend by the process of elimination, "what fucking else could she be?" So Gary walked over to the guy during a break and said "Sing Sweet Home Alabama" "Why?" the guy replied "Just do it Ok?" Gary retorted in that Queens twang that always came back when he meant business. So he did and the crowd whooped. The atmosphere changed and all was well, even though I couldn't now get the song out of my head. I was pissed, Jim was patting me on the back after being told by Gary I'd been laid twice already and I sauntered to the bathroom happy and nodding at cunts for some reason.

I went in, pissed like a race horse onto a silver trough, shook, zipped up, walked out past some guy wearing a Nets shirt and somehow got talking to a woman, who was the double of Barbara Walters, outside the bathroom but that's all it was even though we talked for ages about, I think, Texas. So by the time I got back, the night was almost ending. The scene now was different. I looked over and saw Jim, barely able to stand; scooping up another double whiskey but it wasn't that. A lot of the locals were now dancing away and happy but it wasn't that either. It wasn't even the fact that I'd noticed some cunt had picked up my half full pint from the table. It was the singer. He'd gone from a "happy-go-lucky" young guy to a look a fury as he encored "Sweet Home Alabama" through gritted teeth. "What the fuck is going here" I mused.

I scanned the room and saw the problem. Gary, by now rip-roaringly pissed, was talking the singer's girlfriend at the bar.

Time to go.

Anyway, that was my first encounter with Jim.

Did fuckall for my nerves though. Similarly that night, after finishing the cunting painting, I managed to get the computer in Gary's kids play room working and began looking at normal things again, message boards, hotmail and so on. For the first time In over a month my arse cheeks weren't clenched and I began to relax. I was sending emails, keeping friends like Joe Clark and Tam Donnelly, who worked wonders for me, updated. Then BOOM. The whole house goes dark. All electricity goes off. Arse cheeks clenched once more. I would become accustomed to these power cuts caused by the weather but at this point only two words went through my mind "Home Invasion".

The power came on again in an hour but the nightmare was only gearing up.

I started to spend more time at Trisha's house in The Bronx, I wanted to give Gary and family as much space as possible. They came back and settled back in and I was away a lot. I'd just got off a train at Grand Central with Trisha, heading for a day out to try and get a few hours respite from the fear and madness, when Gary called me. He said that detectives had been sniffing about his house when he wasn't in and had left a card.

Never a good sign.

He called them and they confirmed they wanted to see me. Then I got a call almost immediately from the lawyer saying I was due in court on the Monday as part of the process of my arrest. The world was falling in on me. I called the detectives and they said they were investigating new charges on me, they said no more.

A worrying 48 hours later I was back in court and hoping for all this mess to end when I was hit with it, as my lawyer was about to speak the prosecuting D.A. said to the judge they wanted my bail increased and were filing new charges against me. What were they? That in the four days I'd been out, I'd gone round to a house in Queens and tried to throw a guy off a building from six stories up.

I stood there dumbfounded.

My lawyer was dumbfounded.

The judge said to the prosecuting D.A. "New charges? where is your arresting officer?"

For the first time The Devil was flustered. She fiddled with her papers and said "Ah, um, we don't have one, but we still want bail increased"

At this point confusion reigned and we broke for lunch. I sat on the corner of Duane and Reade and contemplated the prospect of supper on Rikers Island. I called Gary who was flabbergasted when he heard. The night in question, the night I was supposed to have gone round and attempted murder, I was with him, in Ringwood, New Jersey. The insanity of all this was too much for me but Gary never wilted once. Not a thing you forget. I smoked about 12 cigarettes in the 90 minute break and nervously made my way back to court.

When I was called again, the D.A. wasn't for backing down. The vindictive cunt.

This infuriated the judge, he replied to her "You have new charges, you need an arresting officer, you don't have one, the charges are dropped. You want to increase the bail? Bail was set, the guy showed up, what else do you want from him? Next court date is August 18th, you can leave Mr Larkin"

It may have seemed like small victory but this meant I was heading back to The Bronx and the warmth of Trisha, not on the grey goose heading out to Rikers.

Thanks Judge.

The One Stop Shop

With blogs and pods everywhere, it was hard to keep up, step in James Cameron

"The idea of the Celtic Network was born out of anger and frustration. Like any Celtic fans I was dismayed at the pro Rangers anti Celtic news in Scotland's main stream media. Being involved with the internet since 1995 I had watched the growth of the Celtic online media which became stronger and more impressive as the years went by. By around 2010 there were a multitude of blogs, podcasts , sites and forums. For some reason the Celtic fans online community was growing faster than any other club in the UK.

I personally had stopped buying newspapers in the mid 2000's when I realised I could get better quality news from a multitude of sources on line so I was very internet savvy. I had also built and administered several web sites. So basically that's my background out of the way.

As all Celtic fans know season 2010/11 was a year filled with on and off the field controversies.

We ha d the Dallas sectarian email scandal, the Dougie, Dougie liar scandal, bullets sent through the post to Niall McGinn, Neil Lennon and Paddy McCourt, Neil Lennon physically attacked at Tynecastle and Celtic going to war with the corrupt SFA.

However for me matters came to a head in the aftermath of the so called shame game on Wednesday , 2nd of March 2011. During that game then now liquidated Rangers FC had three players sent off. Also during the game the Sewer rat that

RF had signed ran from the centre circle to have a verbal go at neil Lennon and Alan Thompson who were standing in our technical area, another Rangers player Manhandled the referee who for some reason forgot to mention it in his match report and on three occasions Mr Alistair "Dignity" McCoist encroached into the Celtic technical area on three occasions to shout abuse at our staff. At the end of the game which Celtic won 1 – 0 the aforementioned Mr Dignity provoked Neil Lennon by whispering something in his ear which enraged Neil.

The following day I expected to read out right condemnation of RFC, their players and manager for the shame they had brought upon the game in Scotland. How daft was I? Celtic message-boards, Facebook and twitter were awash with links to Laptop Loyal articles concentrating on demonising Neil Lennon for standing up for himself and our clubs name being dragged through the mud by associating us with the thugs of RFC including us a being equally to blame for brining the game in Scotland into disrepute in front of a worldwide audience of millions. For me that was the last straw.

As I mentioned the Celtic online community had grown at a very fast pace not only that but some of the blogs , pod casts etc were actually producing an unbiased and higher quality news and debate than you could find in the main stream media. However the problem was although many of them were up in arms over the events of that season there seemed to be no cohesion or central focal point to bring all these new media outlets together in one place. And that was when the idea of the Celtic Network was born.

I sat down the evening after the so called 'shame game' and drafted up a basic list of what would be required to bring all these media out lets together and they were as follows:

Celtic fans media hub analysis by James 3rd March 2011

·	Portal for gathering and displaying news feeds from partner sites on the www on a 24/7 basis

·	Encourage more open interaction between cfc fans sites and other bodies such as CSA, NAFCSC etc

·	Discussion forum to coordinate and organise joint responses and campaigns (closed forum for partner site admins or reps)

·	A directory of Celtic partner sites including CFC media outlets like CFC web site/facebook players twitter accounts.

·	A directory of useful contacts for all Celtic fans including press, football bodies, politicians

·	A live guide to online Celtic fans podcasts and events

·	Portal to provide a platform for positive news on Celtic fc and challenge negative or hostile media outlets (blog)

·	Promotion of good causes and charities which are in line with the ethos of CFC and our support

·	Offer encouragement and support to groups or individuals who would like to start up forums, blogs pod casts etc.

·	Offer Celtic fans a viable free alternative to mainstream media.

So that was the basic idea.

The next thing I had to do was get the message out and invite sites to form a partnership rather than just a site filled with links. At the time I was running a forum called G40 Celtic Chat with Jacky Campbell who was based at that time in Turkey. We had some followers on twitter and Facebook as well as our forum members but there was no way that would be enough to generate interest in a new project. For a few months I had been tuning into Over and Over radio hosted by Housey on a Friday night so I emailed him and asked if he would let me on the show to explain the idea of a central Celtic fans site media hub. Housey generously agreed and before I knew it I was on his show explaining the idea and asking people/sites to get in touch if they were interested in joining and helping to develop the site. I also set a dead line for the site to open on the first day of the new season which was the 24th of July. The initial feedback was incredible which left me thinking 'what the hell have I just started'?

To get the project up and running I set up a private forum for interested parties to discuss the development of the site. It also allowed me to upload development documents as the site moved through the design and development stage. It was decided that the site would be built on the wordpress platform. I had no experience of this so I handed the development process over to another person and I concentrated on the project management side. Unfortunately a few weeks later the person who had assured us that he was a wordpress expert and would have the site ready within weeks walked away from the project for no apparent reason and to compound problems further he had left no documentation on how he had produced and coded the partial site that he left behind. With only one month to go the pressure was on. I decided to take over the site development myself so I pretty much learned how to build a wordpress site as I went. Fortunately I got the site to a stage where it was in a position to launch on the dead line.

There was a bit of tension at this time between myself and the person responsible for site branding. He felt the site needed more work done design wise before it was launched. I was of the opinion that if you promise people a deadline then you deliver on time. While he had a genuine concern that the site could look better I was happy that we did have the content we promised and I took the decision to launch the site on time.

So on to launch night. The site was to go live at 12.01am GMT on Sunday the 24th of July. I remember being a bag of nerves so much so that I decided a bottle of 'fortified' wine was the order of the day. My wife asked me how many visitors on the first day we make me happy. I told her I would be delighted to get 500 and then hopeful around 1,000 per month after that. So you can imagine my shock and delight when after the first 24 hours the site had been visited 4,126 times.

The first ever blog on the site was written by Phil Mac Giolla Bhain who had kindly agreed to write the article.

On launch day we had 17 partner sites. Now I use the word partners as to me it was crucial that those sites/blogs/podcasts who had links on the site were there because they wanted to be part of an true online independent fans media site. It was important that it felt like an actual media community and not just a list of links. One of the main principles behind the Celtic Network was that we would follow the ethos of the clubs founding fathers of the Club and provide a free platform for Celtic related charities to promote their mission statements and also use the blog to announce charity events. Therefore we are proud to partner the KANO Foundation, The Good Child Foundation and The John Hartson foundation. We have also provided a platform for individual Celtic fans to highlight charities and charitable events that they are involved in.

As I write now the site has grown massively we now have over 60 partner sites which range from Blogs, forum, pod casts to supporters clubs and the site now averages 35,000 visits per month. This is really the highlight for me. The sheer success of the network and the great support and feedback we get via our followers on the site and social media platforms.

Another important part of the Celtic Network that most people and some partners don't realise is that every partner site has blogging permissions on the site. The idea behind this is that if a partners site is ever down for whatever reason they can use the Celtic Network to let their followers know what has happened and to publish article that they may have wanted to publish if their site was up and running.

As with every project there have been some low points. The first was the fact that the site's database was deliberately hacked and when that problem was resolved the site itself was maliciously attacked with files and pages being removed from the server within weeks of the site launch. To resolve this I basically had to work through the night and totally rebuild the site from scratch. Fortunately I had a back up of the last test site I built before the final site was built so I was able to get most of the original site back up and running. The sad thing about these events was that it was a Celtic supporter who carried out these attacks. I later found out during a discussion with Seamus Cummins of iCeltic that his site was also taken down by the same person. The shameful thing about Seamus experience is that his site was attacked on the very night he and his family suffered the tragedy of watching their family home burning to the ground. I could name and shame this person but I would not dignify them by having their name published in this book.

Another low point at the beginning was a fall out with the guy who designed the original Logo for TCN. I was happy with the design however from the minute the site was launched I was getting a lot of negative feedback regarding the logo ranging from the fact that people thought it was more suited to a construction company through to those who did not feel the colour scheme properly represented Celtic. I made the decision to advertise for new logo designs for consideration. Unfortunately the original designer sent me an email instructing me to immediately remove his logo design from TCN and all our social media outlets. I found that very childish but then again I could see his point of view.

Other than those setbacks things have gone from strength to strength. The network seems to have been fully integrated as part of the Celtic online community and that makes me very proud.

So what does the future hold? Hopefully there will be a new version of the site in the second half of 2012 which will be accompanied by Android and i Phone apps. The site will continue to evolve and the ultimate dream would be to have a truly 24/7 Celtic fans media online channel including independent fans TV.

The site will always remain free to use and will never in any way be affiliated to Celtic Football Club. I have great respect for Tony Hamilton the head of Celtic FC media he has worked tirelessly both during work hours and in his own time to engage with fans and answer their queries however I do not believe it would be healthy for TCN and Celtic to form a close relationship after all TCN is a fans network and the fans don't always see eye to eye with the club therefore I feel it's better that we have a healthy relationship in as much as we support the club but we are also free to criticise the club on matters we do not see eye to eye on. The final thing I would say is that TCN will never agree to a partnership with fans sites who are invitation only or behind a pay wall. No disrespect to these site but we believe in free open access to all Celtic fans regardless of their views."

Revelations (Part 1)

"Nice like Van Halen, seen him at the tunnel with his skin palin', did two days thought he was jailin"

Wu Tang-Clan

I had about three weeks between leaving court and going back again. My lawyer said this was good, I just wanted to go home. Then another bombshell, I was standing in Gary's kitchen when a law officer came knocking one Friday at around five o'clock. Gary answered and gave me the summons. I was being taken to court for unpaid rent of my apartment. Let's get this one straight. At this point I was banned from the borough of Queens, I'd had everything I owned taken from me and was told if I set foot in my apartment again I'd be arrested. I'm supposed to keep paying fucking rent on the place? Yeah, right. My lawyer said it was all a government tactic of intimidation. I said it was fucking working. It was clear to me then that I was a marked man and I had to get out of America. Gary suggested a water park with the family to take my mind off shit, I love him but I'm more a strip club guy, but I went along anyway. Jim Stanyck, the good neighbour/nosey fucker came too and I ended up going in his car. As we drove up to Mountain Creek my mind started to wander to this mess I was in. It seemed to spiraling out of control and I started to think I was going to burst into tears. Then Jim said "I've been listening to this Radio station, giving me a lot of good ideas, particularly this guy on now, in terms of who to vote for November"

It was Rush Limbaugh.

I figured then that things would never be that bad.

The day actually turned out quite good save for one incident that shook me to the bone. Gary, his young son Aidan and I queued about an hour for a popular ride where you went down some rapids on a dinghy. I'd never done that before so had agreed to give it a shot. As we queued we talked over my predicament and looked at girls (hey, I'm in the shit, not dead) and so by the time we got to the front my mind was elsewhere. We took our places in the dinghy and strapped in. We went down a couple of corners nice and steady and the next thing we knew we were in a cave and hurtling down water at a ferocious pace. So much so that Aidan flew out of the dinghy but I managed to grab him, in the pitch fucking black, and hold on for grim death with my other hand. Gary was sort of above us and and as we moved toward the light, still at the speed of fucking light, I saw him look at me like "WHAT THE FUCKING IS GOING ON!!!!", finally we slowed down and met the light after around 90 seconds of sheer terror. As we were about to congratulate each other on still being alive, we suddenly went down a ramp, then up one and were propelled 30 feet in the air before coming down in an almighty splash.

This was probably the one time where I wasn't thinking of all the shit that was happening. Fucking cunts though.

I began to relax a hell of a lot more when one day I was visiting Trisha and got a call from the lawyer saying most of the charges were going to be dropped. There was a deal in the making that meant if I plead guilty to a lesser charge, I'd get community service. That wasn't great but it also wasn't jail. I'd take it. New court date, August 8th. Fuck me, I might be home for the start of the season.

The rest of the time was spent with Trisha, a rock throughout and with Gary. It should have been a time for keeping the head down, but then if you think that, you haven't met Gary Haley.

First there was a softball game. Well, two. In the same night. Although things had started to look better my head was up my arse still as the multitude of the whole thing was almost too much. Gary's wife, Anne Marie was fantastic and often took time to come down to the basement where I was sleeping and living then to talk to me about things and that was a huge help. So when Gary suggested, one Monday night, that we take in two of her softball games, whilst reluctant, I agreed. Of course Gary, being Gary, had a cooler full of beer so big that it could have taken a body. 102 bottles of beer got in it and we were off to the first Ringwood Tailgaters game. We sat in a tiny ball park and watched a pretty good game of softball, drinking and me smoking too, although never in front of the kids which was easy given my skill of hiding a cigarette had been trained perfectly in jail. The Tailgaters lost but we had no time to spare and all jumped in cars and were off to the next game. I'd say we were maybe 10 beers in at this point.

We arrived at the next ball park and it was situated down the way from the car park and you walked through woods, with the aid of stairs, to get to it. There was a decent crowd there and once Gary and I had hauled the cooler down I began to relax a little. I pulled a cold beer out the cooler, lit up a cigarette and took in the cool night air. It was still about 70 degrees but it was comfortable for July. I made acquaintance with an older Italian guy who was there to see his daughter play, I offered him a beer but he refused then relented about three seconds later. We shot the shit and it felt really good to be talking to someone about subjects not pertaining to court, lawyers and fucking cops. I could feel the weight lifting my shoulders and with every drag of the smoke I was chilling. Then I became aware of a noise. It was distracting at first, as me and the guy talked, then it got louder and louder and I snapped into focus as to what was going on.

Gary had taken over the softball team.

At some point in the last 15 minutes he had effectively "Stood down" the coach of the team and was now on the sidelines booming out orders. Anne Marie, at second base, was giving him a look that could strip paint but on he went and you know what? They won that game.

After it was finished we all made our way to the car park to tailgate. Most of the women were great and I had a good conversation with one who was fascinated by Edinburgh and how haunted it was, that's as far as it went though, I had Trisha.

After we got home that evening Gary and I sat and finished off the beers and had a long chat. The measure of Gary as a man is that at no stage ever had he asked me "Did you do any of these things?" That night though, I told him my side of the story.

The Medium

The global effect of Celtic rising meant that supporters wanted more, especially ones who couldn't actually get to games, step forward Krys Kujawa:

"What's your first reaction when Celtic score a goal? I'd imagine for most Celtic supporters it's sheer elation, and I'm not going to pretend it's any different for me either!

What's your second reaction when Celtic score a goal? I suppose it depends on the goal. On some occasions it might be to turn to opposition fans and get it right up them in any way possible. For others, it might be as simple as trying not to fall over the row of seats in front of you as you bounce about like a lunatic. Maybe it's to turn to the guy next to you and hug him. I've done all of them in the past, but for me now it's the same thought at every game for every goal.

Hit "record".

I've been doing "as live" match reports for the LostBhoys podcast for the best part of eighteen months now. I'm sure it looks very strange to anyone that sees me speaking into my phone every so often... or yelling depending on events. Well, I say I'm sure of that. It can't be all that strange though, because in all the time I've been doing it I've only ever been asked what I'm doing once. It was a game at McDiarmid Park and the attractive young blonde lady standing to my right asked why I kept talking into my phone.

"I'm recording for a podcast", says I.

"Oh, what one?" she asks.

"LostBhoys."

"Oh, I follow them on Facebook!"

I'm not convinced she could have told you who I was even if she did follow on Facebook, but it was nice to hear anyway! I didn't press her for much more, although she did seem happy to know that her excited squeals might be on the next podcast. I'm fairly sure they were as well.

Why didn't I press her? Well for one thing she was an attractive young blonde lady and my wife was standing on the other side of me! But more than that, I'm not really comfortable when it comes to the praise I've received for the recordings. She may not have given me any, but I wasn't going to go looking for it.

Don't get me wrong, this is a personality failing of mine rather than anything else. It's always great to get positive feedback, I just never know what to say in response! It's even great to get constructive criticism, although I'm happy to say I don't get that as much. For the most part I've had some terrific reactions to recordings. Some of the comments come from people who go to the games themselves which is brilliant, but for me the people that really seem most appreciative of them are the guys who can't make the game.

They vary from people in London who can't get up to Glasgow, to folk in the US who maybe come across once a season if they're lucky. There's even one or two people in the Middle East who went there for work and miss the action they left behind. I've had reactions from around the globe and it's all the same comments. They love to hear the atmosphere and the passion. For some, it gives them a sense of being homesick. A sad but welcome reminder of what they might have left behind. For others, it's a connection to something they experienced just once or twice, or maybe something they hope to experience for the first time some day.

As with everything Celtic, it's all about the fans. But it's not just those fans listening and being appreciative of what I've recorded, but also what I'm picking up from the fans at the games. I've heard on several occasions how people love the guy next to me at Celtic Park. I mean lets face it, in the time between me reacting to an event on the park and hitting record I've had a bit of time to compose myself and think about what I'll say. It doesn't always happen of course, but for the most part I'm relatively calm and manage to keep the swearing to a minimum! The guys around me don't have that moment, or even the inclination, to calm so they're still in full on rant and it gets picked up. I should point out that it's not just the guy next to me, but a couple of guys behind me too.

There there's the atmosphere itself. I'm fortunate to be near enough to the Green Brigade at Celtic Park that you can hear them in the background whenever I'm recording. They do a terrific job of keeping things going throughout the match, but also to kick start most of the things where the whole stadium joins in. Then of course, because I'm behind the goal, you get the full effect of "Come on you bhoys in green" being called across the length of Celtic Park, before the delay in the speed of sound finally gets the response from the other end. I'll be honest, they're the bits I enjoy the most because I don't need to say anything!

There are some who don't listen for the atmosphere though. They listen for my reaction to what I'm seeing at the time.

That's probably the hardest bit. Most of what I'm saying is immediately after the event and I'm trying to remember what I've just seen and who was involved. Depending on the complexity of the move or a crowded penalty area or action at the opposite end of the park that can be quite difficult. Then of course it's not so bad when it involves people you see most weeks, but on occasion I get it completely wrong and Andre Blackman becomes Rabiu Ibrahim!

Sometimes I get lucky and I happen to be recording as a goal is scored. I generally get penalties as they are hit, but sometimes it's a goal from a corner or from a free kick. There was even one occasion - again at McDiarmid Park - where Celtic broke up the park after a St Johnstone set piece and scored at the end of it. It's always a good feeling when you know you've captured the goal itself, crowd roar and all.

I record at pretty much every game I go to now. It actually seems odd if I don't! Of course, not everything recorded makes it onto the podcast. Lets face it, no one wants to hear back some of the games we play. There's always that poor game where we took the three points and that's about the only positive you can say about it. Then of course we've had two years running where the League Cup final recording has been "left off the podcast" shall we say! But while some games are best left off, I've also been fortunate enough to record some absolute gems.

Probably the best reaction I've had to any game was our New Year visit to Ibrox when Samaras scored twice in the second half to haul us back into the title race when many had feared it was about to come undone. There was just something about that day where everything clicked. If you listen back, you can hear my optimism and belief growing over the course of the match. Even when it's 0-0, I keep commenting that if we can just do this and that then we can win the match. The goals eventually go in, we win the match, and three stands at Ibrox empty as we celebrate a brilliant result. More people thanked me for that one recording than all the other recordings put together, and so many people told me that I was saying exactly what they were thinking at the time.

There's been some other great moments too. Proclaiming that I wished people could see what I could see as the whole of Celtic Park did the huddle for the first time as we beat Rangers 3-0. Screaming "we are level" into the microphone as we clawed things back at Rugby Park to 3-3. The almost hour long recordings for the parties at Easter Road after Rangers went into administration and the return to Rugby Park when we won the league. But this whole idea started on another huge day, and out of what pretty much amounted to a guilty conscience!

It was the day of the first Celtic Graves Society event and they were marking the grave of Dan Doyle. It was time to coincide with Celtic's birthday, 123 years to the day of the meeting at St Mary's in November 1887 which kick started the club we all know and love today. Thanks to David Harper suggesting I get an app for my iPhone earlier that year to try and record the "Dog and Pony" show - something I annoyingly didn't manage as my phone didn't let me download the app that night - I decided it would be good to record the event for the LostBhoys podcast to let others hear it.

What I hadn't counted on was the Celtic Underground guys spotting me recording the whole thing and asking if they could get it before I had even got the chance to listen back and offer it to Chris McGuigan! Well I was hardly going to say no to them. So, sitting in my car in the car park at Celtic Park, I had the mad idea to try and record my thoughts during the game. I figured it was worth a try, no one else out there was doing it, and it would at least give me something I could send to Chris. One SPL record setting 9-0 thrashing of Aberdeen later and I had recorded a fairly historic match at Celtic Park! I sent it on to Chris, he loved it, it went on the podcast the following week and the rest is history.

I don't know what the future holds for these recordings. Maybe someday the 3G signal at Celtic Park will be decent enough that I could stream commentary directly from the stands. I'm not convinced I'd be the best person to do that, but then eighteen months ago I wouldn't have thought I was the best person to record my thoughts at the game. Maybe I'm still not and someone out there would be better at it. That's the real beauty of the fan produced material - if you think you can do better or differently then go for it. Everyone's take on things is different, everyone has different ideas, and there's a place for them all.

But as long as there's people out there who think the recordings bring them that little bit closer to the action and Celtic, I'll be doing my best to supply them with that."

The Fucking Great Escape

"So why did I do it? I could offer a million answers, all false. The truth is that I'm a bad person, but that's going to change, I'm going to change. This is the last of this sort of thing. I'm cleaning up and I'm moving on, going straight and choosing life. I'm looking forward to it already. I'm going to be just like you: the job, the family, the fucking big television, the washing machine, the car, the compact disc and electrical tin opener, good health, low cholesterol, dental insurance, mortgage, starter home, leisurewear, luggage, three-piece suite, DIY, game shows, junk food, children, walks in the park, nine to five, good at golf, washing the car, choice of sweaters, family Christmas, indexed pension, tax exemption, clearing the gutters, getting by, looking ahead, to the day you die"

Mark Renton

By the time August 8th came round, I was ready. Not for the Beijing Olympics that were starting that day either. The lawyer had worked wonders and had worked a deal with the prosecuting D.A. that if I plead guilty to menacing (phoning up to see where she was!!!!) I'd get community service and could almost certainly go home in a few months. It wasn't ideal but it massive Neil Armstrong leap from a long stretch in fucking Attica.

The only worry I had at that point was if any bullshit would be further flung at me when I got to court. I stayed with Trisha the night before. I never asked her to come to court at any time, never asked anyone, this was *my* problem. I smoked a cigarette and got on the train. Considering I had no idea where the court was two months ago, I could now direct a blind guy to it. It was a scorching hot day and I smoked one more before going in.

You never know when you are going to get called so you just sit there waiting on your lawyer, watching all the other cases. There I spotted "Mr White House" from The Tombs. He had been on a motorcycle and being chased by the cops. He had jumped off and took them for a run before realising his ankle was fucked. The judge, basing it on his record, offered him 42 days in jail. He refused. A shiver went down my spine, jail for speeding?

My lawyer came in and I was called, ready to do the deal. The judge heard from the prosecution, The Devil keeping her side of the deal, and then my lawyer said we accepted this. Remember though the judge still had to agree... The judge looked over the papers and started to look incredulous and my arse was making buttons. He looked at me and then said to the prosecutor "You want a guy, who has someone close to him disappear for two days, to do community service for trying to call her?" The Devil stuttered again. The judge went on "I'm going to dismiss these charges, Mr Larkin you can leave here without a stain on your character, you're free to go"

Let that one sink in.

I wasn't ready for this. I shook the lawyers hand and I asked him how I could get my passport back that the cops had taken? He sent me to the building next door where the cops held all that shit. In the meantime I called Trisha and Gary. Neither could believe it. I can still feel the genuine elation in their voices and it makes me feel so humble. Both stuck by me that summer, along with Tam Donnelly and Joe Clark, who I'd be in touch with soon, and I'll never be able to thank them enough.

I stepped out into the sunlight and made my way left to get my passport. I walked in, did the security check and glanced right to the Brooklyn Bridge as I was patted down. I got to the part of the building where it should have been held and they had no record of it. FUCK. If I get this cunting thing today, I'll be seeing the league flag go up on Sunday. It was 1.30pm and I was told to call the police station that arrested me. I did and got some prick who was as helpful as a sharp spike on a park bench so I jumped a taxi and went to the station. I got in and asked the desk sergeant about it and she looked at me like I'd just asked for a three way with her and her daughter. She gave me a number to call and so I went outside and called it, only for her to fucking answer!

Eventually I got the number for Detective Diaz only to be told she wasn't in until Sunday. Pity she hadn't taken the day off she fucking arrested me. I collected my thoughts quickly and thought "British Embassy" , called Gary, got the address, then walked up there. By now it was 3.33pm and it shut at 3.30pm. FUCK. It didn't open again until the Monday.

I wasn't seeing any league flag.

This was fucking horrible. Now a free man, I was trapped here until Monday. I let out a yelp of frustration and more cunts took notice than when I was being arrested. There was only one thing for it.

Beer.

I went up to the bar Trisha worked and she was happy to see me. I told her what had happened with the passport and she was enraged immediately. I offered that there was nothing I could do until Sunday so there was no point worrying, I pulled up a bar stool, chatted to some girls who had no idea where China was and settled in to watch a spectacular opening ceremony.

Saturday passed in a blur of bewilderment and bevvy.

Sunday came and the first thing I did was watch the league flag go up. Albeit 3000 miles away on a dodgy laptop. I wasn't in the frame of mind to socialise. After the game I called the cops again and got some fucking thumbsucker who told me Diaz wasn't in yet. I called back an hour later and got the same prick who then told me Diaz was on holiday for the next fortnight! I called Gary and he, like me, thought the cops were at it after a humiliating result and I had no chance of getting my passport back from them. I resolved to go to the British Embassy the next day.

I got down there early and told them the script. The woman went into her computer ad said "You have a case pending on August 18th, can't do anything" I told her was resolved on Friday and showed her my bail receipt to prove it. Not being American, she accepted this and said "When are you traveling?" I told her that as soon a I got a new passport today, I was going to book a flight, to which she replied "I can only issue replacement passports to UK citizens who have travel documents indicating they are leaving the country in the next three days" "So I'm screwed then?" and I resigned myself to never getting a break again when she said "What you're going to do is forget this visit, go and book your flight, come back in, show me your documents and I'll give you a new passport"

I could have kissed her.

From there I called Gary, who arranged for me to go to his work to book the flight, his boss Charlie was great in that respect, then I booked a flight to leave that night for London, not ideal but a damn sight better than looking over your shoulder New York. I than called Trisha to ask her to bring my meagre bag with me.

I then made a big mistake.

After getting my passport, I was so excited about this nightmare finally being over that I did not take into account how devastated Trisha was that I was leaving so abruptly.

That was stupid of me and I feel terrible about it.

We said goodbye at Grand Central Station and I jumped a bus to JFK and saw her in floods of tears.

Through my own.

I got drunk at the airport to stop my paranoia of being stopped and as I sat on the plane and the doors were closing I text Gary "Sayonara" and left America, leaving the nightmare behind me.

Aye, right.

Home James

"For almost thirty years I repeatedly saw one and the same dream: I would arrive in Vienna at long last. I would feel really happy, for I was returning to my serene childhood"

Alfred Schnittke

Arriving at Heathrow was a sobering experience. I was in the first stages of a major hangover after nine pints of Stella and several plane red wines. It was grey and rainy in London and I called my Ma to tell her I would be home tonight. From there I got the tube to Kings Cross and felt a bit relaxed but absolutely shattered. In a funny way, people reading the Metro on the tube was comforting. This was the first time I'd been in the UK for 14 months, since a trip home for 2007 Scottish Cup Final and the simplicity of it, even in London, was welcome. What wasn't welcome was the fucking fare from London to Edinburgh on the train at Kings Cross. I'd gone to an automated ticket machine and thought when it said "£156.40" I'd mistakenly pressed First Class. I had some money, thanks again to Tam Donnelly, Frank Martin and Joe Clark, but not much and this was a major hit.

I slept most of the way back to Edinburgh and was down at My Ma's for around 1pm which was a lot earlier expected. Completely under dressed and feeling vulnerable, I picked up the key she had left and let myself in. I had no idea what I was going to do or what on earth was going on but I knew one thing, I'd see my son James again.

When he came in, this was the first time I'd seen him since February, he came over and gave me a cuddle and it was hard to keep emotions in check. I felt a complete failure as well.

Over the next few weeks relations were not good with My Ma and I had to get out soon. Also only Paul O'Neil and Allan Hosey got in touch to go for a drink, some others I've still not heard from again, and then the guys from Global Hoops arranged a wee get together before a game and it felt great to be doing normal things again.

The fear was still there though.

After the two polis had visited I just couldn't shake the feeling that a safe was going to drop on my head at any time.

I felt isolated, alone, paranoid and absolutely terrified.

I got a house after a couple of weeks, thankfully, and in a stroke of luck, it was in Buchanan Street in Leith, a stones throw from Allan Hosey. I still couldn't shake the cunt off. I moved in and was happy to be away from the constant arguing with my Ma and to get some solace at last. The first night I slept well and all was well until the post clattered through the door. I almost jumped out of my skin. All thoughts of court letters and summons came back and I pulled the cover over my head.

The only communication I had with Trisha up until that point was email. The Bhoys and Ghirls in the club had a whip round for me and I was able to get a phone and quickly after talking to her a few times she agreed she would come to stay with me in Scotland at Christmas. For good. I had a goal. Except this was early September and it would be three months til she came over. I had to get to that point. The new house meant that James could come and stay and I lived for those weekends. We'd go to the football on a Saturday and watch it all day on a Sunday. I'd also managed to get him in a football team, Dunedin, thanks entirely to my good friend Steven O'Neil and those weekends were my life. I then got some money I was due from America and that would get me to Christmas at least. Trisha and I were saving as well. It all sounds good doesn't it?

It wasn't.

I spent days in total isolation, rarely using the Internet, going for walks to kill time, not going out to see people and spent a lot of time scared. I tried to organise a bevvy session in Glasgow in the October, no one could make it. I used one of those invite sites to have a house party but cancelled it as there was no real enthusiasm for it. By November I was reaching out to people to talk but only the same names as always were interested, and I'd go out and put on an act and forget all about it. Frank Martin was fantastic at this point but he has a wife and family. Jamie O'Neil came through twice, once where we had a great laugh in Rose St, Edinburgh and another where we saw the film Hunger on the Saturday night and saw Celtic beat Hearts at Tynecastle 2-0 on the Sunday but these occasions were few and far between and the darkness was descending on me. A heavy depression washed over me like a tidal wave. Come the middle of November I was in a terrible place, no not Leith, and one night I lay on my couch and thought about how I'd kill myself. I could not stand the fear and isolation any more, I had no life and Trisha should stay in NYC, not bother about a cunt like me. On TV that night was the film The Krays, awful film, but I saw Frances Kray kill herself with pills. I then watched The Sopranos on DVD and heard a line from Johnny Sack that was "You wanna commit suicide? Pills are a lot easier" So I got up, put my coat on and walked up Leith Walk to the Tesco at the corner of Brunswick Road. I bought three packets of paracetamol and three packets of Ibuprofen, pretty cheap as well, two bottles of Evian and went back home to take the lot. On the way back I got a text from Frank saying the club were sending me to Celtic Park on Saturday as their guest. Don't think so Frank. I got back in from the cold air and looked at my couch as I put the pills on the bunker and opened the water. Evian tastes divine, always does. I looked up at the picture I had of James up, it was about two years old and was from his first week at school. I thought about how I'd tried to move to help him have a better life and it had all collapsed, that he would be better off without me.

Then I thought about how I had let him down.

I'd love to be able to say some divine intervention stopped me taking the pills that night. It didn't. What stopped me was the thought that James would get one final let down and have to live it with it the rest of his life. So I didn't do it. It didn't change anything except that I'm still alive.

I also never told a soul until right now.

Merry Christmas (Drought is Over)

"Anybody who believes that the way to a man's heart is through his stomach flunked geography"

Robert Byrne

Things got better in December. Trisha was flying home to Ireland on Dec 16th, I was going to see her Dec 19th. Four long months without her. It also has to be said, four long months without sex.

Celtic were doing ok. After the humiliation of the 4-2 Rangers defeat we settled down to play well together and go on a good run with Samaras excelling. I also went on two trips in this time, one a weekend in Inverness and one a two day jaunt to Manchester. In the same week. You may be wondering how the hell I could afford this? Well, Joe Clark had been putting on the Irish lottery for me, that's the kind of guy Joe is, and the previous week he emailed me to say my three numbers had came up on the Wednesday draw and I'd won over £600. I was over the moon. On the Saturday I came home from the football late and logged on, Joe had sent me another email that said "There it goes again, £600, well done pal" I looked it at again and it took me about a minute to register (and check) that my numbers had come up again. £1200 in four days. So a few calls later and we were going to Inverness for the Friday and Saturday, with Celtic playing there on the Saturday, and I paid for the hotel for Joe and Rab Tait, both of whom had been incredibly supportive, and although I could never repay what they did for me, it was nice to be able to do that. Joe then went on to drink most of Scotland's whisky that weekend.

Driving back hungover on the Sunday, we already knew we were all going to Manchester on the Tuesday for the Celtic game at Old Trafford and we decided "Fuck it, let's go on the Monday instead" I got dropped off at St James Centre in Edinburgh and was walking past the Elm Bar when I heard a roar. Hibs had scored v Hearts in the first minute. Was a great feeling that day going home and relaxing knowing Old Trafford was beckoning.

Getting down there a day early meant we had the chance to hook up with Patricia Ferns, Ricky Fearon and co. We all pitched up to a pub called The Hare and Hound where wee Ricky had assured us Patricia would be singing that night. Arriving in this pub, on Shudehill, let's put it this way, it wasn't the sort of place you'd expect to see an Irish rebel singer. Ricky being Ricky though took over and a superb night was had. Plus if you ever bump into Big Joe Clark, ask him about Big Tracy...

The following day we all were back in the same boozer. There was a pest in the night before who wouldn't leave Patricia alone and kept bugging her for songs. The next day we discovered said pest had collapsed in the toilet and fallen asleep, staying there all night. When we emerged in the morning we gave him a nice chorus of "Please release me...."

I didn't have a ticket for the game but managed to lay my hands on four before giving them to others. Wee Ricky came to the rescue though, he had one for me and one for Gray O'Brien. That name may not ring a bell but at the time "Tony Gordon" was the biggest name in the UK. As the baddie on Coronation Street, everyone knew him. We knew he was one of us as well and we all spent a great afternoon with him that day. Singing, of course, "OH Tony Gordon, The Corrie Psycho, He hates the huns..."

The game itself was crap.

Celtic kept winning though right up until a dull 1-1 draw against Hearts with only a late McManus equaliser saving us from total disaster. A crunch period was looming over Christmas with away games at the Falkirk Stadium and Ibrox. I had a crunch time then too, seeing Trisha for the first time in four months. I left on the Friday, Ryanair Edinburgh to Shannon and was a mixture of nervous and excited. It had been a long four months, where I'd been in the depths of hell for most of it, and this was the place I had been desperate to get to. I tried to compose myself on the plane, be cool about it but inside I was churning, especially when, on a clear day, the plane took about 40 minutes not the 1 hour and 20 advertised. I got off the plane and it was a brisk day in Limerick, slight drizzle around and only having hand luggage I was in arrivals in no time. No one was at customs. I knew I'd turn this corner and she'd be there. The woman who stopped me from losing it completely, the woman who brought me chicken salad rolls at 1am when I was hungry, the woman who always took a dash of lime in her Corona, the woman who bought me the best Yankee jacket I ever had, the woman I saw The Dark Knight with, the woman who would bring wine when meeting me in Manhattan, the woman I first kissed on 6th and 54th St, the woman who sat in Faces and Names with me oblivious to the fact that an ex girlfriend glowering at us from over the bar, the woman who answered a stranger number the night I got released, here she was....

No she wasn't.

There was no sign of her. I looked round the tiny airport and couldn't see her anywhere. I admit, I panicked, I got paranoid, was this all a set up? All I could do was stand and wait. I wanted a cigarette but didn't want to leave this spot. Then I turned and saw the blonde hair bound through the front door, she spotted me and ran over. In a way that dispelled all my fears about her not linking me four months on. Whatever else happens in the future, we will always have that moment. And it was the traffic that made her pal Denise, driving, late!

I was there until the Monday and we spent a great weekend at her parents house, just being together, chatting, laughing and eating. That was it though, it was her parents house after all.

Trisha moved over to Scotland on Dec 26th 2008. The day before I spent two hours with James before going home to an empty house to eat a Chinese takeaway for my Christmas dinner. It didn't matter though, my present was coming the next day.

Dec 27th came and The Bhoys went to Ibrox to preserve a four point lead at the top. We had won 3-0 at Falkirk, in the midst of an overblown argument with Aidan McGeady and Gordon Strachan, and gone to Ibrox in decent form. It was a crap game with no one giving an inch and Barry Robson excelling. Scott McDonald scored an absolute peach to win us the points and set us up seven clear.

Speaking of not giving inches, Trisha arrived on what some men call, in the parlance of our time, her "bad week". Fortunately though we had a week in London booked the first week in January and I can tell you now the walls and ceiling of the hotel room looked great.

For three of us...

How Twitter Killed the Tainted Media

By Eugene @the_eriugena

Like Neil Lennon I grew up in a part of Northern Ireland where supporting Celtic was an act of defiance, an expression of Irish identity as well as an appreciation of a great European football and sporting institution. There was just something about those green and white hoops even on a flickering black and white TV set that set them apart.

Seen so rarely on local TV the Celtic team became even bigger, mythical legends as you were never likely to meet them in the flesh. The Lisbon Lions cup victory, the great battles with Leeds United and the disappointment of defeat to Feyenoord were already in the distant past, but Celtic still had a special aura for a young and impressionable sports loving Irish boy looking for heroes.

I don't remember ever seeing Celtic in a full Scottish league game on TV until much, much later and as a kid you depended on what you got in the media. And what you got in Northern Ireland wasn't very much at all.

My parents were not football fans, boxing and Cassius Clay was my dad's passion, so when I came home from school one day suggesting a trip to Scotland to watch the famous Celtic play they feared for my safety more than anything else. Glasgow was a long coach and ferry ride away and in the 1970's Glasgow was a remote, dark and highly dangerous place for a young lad, especially when Celtic were playing Rangers. My parents had watched the Play For Today 'Just Another Saturday' on TV and were not inclined to let me visit

Glasgow any time soon even though Northern Ireland had it's own religious tensions.

So even though Bobby Lennox was still playing in for the first team I never got to see my him play at Celtic Park and had to content myself with third hand match reports of big games in local papers with the occasional glimpse of the famous old team on the BBC.

For a long time too my adult passion to see Celtic at Celtic Park was often blighted by bad luck as, moved away and working in London, Paris and then the South of France, I missed big mid-week European games due to fog at Luton airport or yet another overrun deadline or missed connection, and had to be content with a long-wave radio commentary or the late night TV goal only highlights.

In short my passion for Celtic was moderated by the media.

Remote and with limited time and resources, I had nothing but the newspaper and TV's words and images to rely on. No other way of knowing anything about Celtic except what the media told me. And so, like everyone else, I believed what they said and got on with my hectic, deadline-driven life with Celtic football club turned down and crackling in the background.

Then towards the end of 2010 I was working on the launch of a new company and had built a fancy new website and decided to try out Twitter in the hope of promoting our new business service. Thanks to my iPhone I had long been downloading and enjoying the Celtic Underground podcasts, where 'Eddie' and the guys were already trying to lift the very heavy lid on some of the dark practices of the Scottish media and Scottish football in general.

Like most newbies when they join twitter I looked around for things that interested me and stumbled upon some Celtic sites like @CQN @TheLostBhoys and @Celticrumours and started to follow some of them.

And then the referee strike happened.

It was clear to even the neutral observer that something was putrid at the heart of Scottish football. When @CQN and @Pmacgiollabhain started blogging and posting about a sectarian email sent by SFA Head of Referees Hugh Dallas on the SFA email system and how he was using the threat of strike action to try to salvage his job and reputation, I was convinced it would be only a matter of time before the full story came out and even used some of my own media contacts to help the story get out there.

Radio 5 Live had nothing about the Dallas blackmail. The Guardian's Football Weekly podcast wheeled out Ewan Murray to blame the entire shocking episode on Neil Lennon and Celtic's hysterical paranoia. All of the mainstream media seemed deaf and blind to the issue and collectively agreed to paper over the cracks of something that to me seemed a deep rooted, far-reaching sporting scandal.

Without blogs, without podcasts I would have known nothing. And most of all without Twitter I would have had no channel to air my views about what I thought was going on. Twitter became a powerful outlet and since the referee's strike I have never listened to Radio 5 Live or the Football Weekly podcast. Twitter opened my eyes to the truth and opened the eyes of lots of others too.

Of course since then there have been many more such damning incidents in Scottish football where twitter and social media have helped expose the truth. The 'Shame Game' where Rangers coach McCoist attacked the Celtic dug-out, threatened Neil Lennon at the end of the game but it was Lennon himself who was widely vilified in the media. The bomb attacks on the Celtic manager and other high profile Celtic fans and the agenda-driven way the media reported it. The attack on Neil Lennon by a fan in the dug-out at Tynecastle even prompted arch troll Graham Spiers to criticize Lennon for attempting to defend himself.

Too many of course to go into detail but all of them reported with an all too apparent agenda in the mainstream media while social media and Twitter was giving me the inside story, and by this stage I had also started to contribute to that narrative.

Which brings us of course to the ultimate Twitter moment – the death of Rangers. Where would we be with @rangertaxcase and other blogs and Twitter accounts that have given us solid facts using sources and tools available to anyone with wifi and a laptop?

Anyone on Twitter can clearly see how the tainted media failed on every level to report what had been happening at Rangers for many years – the two contract scams, the incestuous collusion with the SFA, the failure to tackle financial doping and mismanagement and the history of sectarian signing policies to name just a few.

The tainted media, so incompetent and blinded by their own agenda, failed completely on the Rangers insolvency story. Even when they went into liquidation they largely attempted *to present it as if it were a must-have fashion accessory for every football club and totally ignored the human, sporting and social consequences of an institution involved in systematic financial cheating to continue it's own existence. With of course the BBC north and south of the border was the main cheerleader for the establishment team. As yet only Twitter and social media and maverick journalists such as Channel 4's @alextomo have dared speak the truth.*

In the age of Leveson mainstream media is viewed by many as tainted. In the age of Leveson journalism itself has been shown to be at best unreliable and agenda driven but often little more than a propaganda tool with Scottish football journalism one of the worst examples of the kind.

Without social media, without Twitter I would know nothing.

Twitter is a very powerful search tool that when combined with other applications and good skills can become very powerful. Powerful enough to bring down some long lingering barriers.

Twitter makes you feel part of the game. Makes you feel part of Celtic. It uncovers and tells the truth when others driven by their own agenda won't. It's hard to hide your real character on Twitter. The limitation of those 140 characters lays your soul bare.

And Twitter is of course a social media where Neil Lennon and Celtic football club can speak directly to the fans. Who needs mainstream media?

So just the other week I went up to Glasgow to catch a midweek game at Celtic Park and thanks to a Twitter pal found myself in a seat in the Main Stand right beside the Press

Box. New media staff journalist @_LauraBrannan was working hard covering the match and posting updates as the game unfolded to @celticfc while the Green Brigade danced and sang in the cold crisp air.

While in another corner wily old dinosaur @RoddyFor plugged in his headphones and tapped inexpertly with one finger on his laptop ignoring the game to catch up on the latest Rangers news – like his tainted tartan colleagues he takes everything from the game and gives nothing back.

So Twitter killed the old media but let's not shed a tear. Really they killed themselves.

You can follow Eugene on Twitter @the_eriugena

One Weekend in Letterkenny

"Going back to Ireland involves at least six to seven emotional breakdowns for me per day."

Anjelica Houston

The lift of Trisha coming back, winning at Ibrox and going to London for a week definitely was with me for a couple of weeks. Trisha though was finding it hard to settle. Who could blame her after five years in New York? A girl she met in NYC, Jemma, was going to be in Manchester the last weekend of January and, coincidentally... there was a Celtic weekend in Letterkenny the same weekend. So she went to England, I went to Ireland.

I should say now I almost didn't. I picked up really bad flu the week before and felt awful. I made it worse by going to a midweek game that I hoped Celtic would wrap up sharpish and I could get back to my sick bed. The game was Celtic 0 Dundee Utd (AET, Celtic win 11-10 on penalties) Bastards. Still, it was worth it to see Artur score.

A very early start on the Friday to hotfoot it to Prestwick Airport for a flight to Derry. This was the start of the real rip off Ryanair where boarding passes not printed saw £40 fines and folk were charged £25 for checking a wheelchair with causes consternation everywhere. On a good day any flight from Prestwick to the North of Ireland hardly seems worth it, you're up and down quicker than a weight watcher and it always makes you think "Why don't I do this more?" We had a bus waiting on us and made the short hop to the Clanree

Hotel to commence a weekends bevvying. I should say at this point that accompanying us where none other than Bobby Lennox, Stevie Chalmers and Joe McBride. Also accompanying us was Brad, a Gorbals legend. I volunteered to share a room with him on the basis that there was absolutely no chance any other cunt would. To give you an example, on the Saturday we had a fairly heavy sesh in The Wolfe Tone Bar. A few of us went back to the hotel to freshen up for the main dinner dance at night. Brad stayed out. When we took our seats at our table for dinner, Brad bounded in announcing he wanted "fuckall to eat". As the dance got down to the dancing part Brad was in a state of disarray. So much so that about 30 minutes later a bar woman came up to me and said "Is that your mate sleeping on the couch outside?" I looked and confirmed it was, so Jim Martin and I got him up and in his bed. Job done we went back to the night which was in full swing. About ten minutes later the same bar woman came up to me and said "You really will have to move your friend I'm afraid, really sorry about this" I protested we already had moved him but upon walking back to the lobby I saw the cunt lying on the same couch again.

The following morning Brad woke with the immortal "I'm choking on a drink here" like he'd just staggered in from a three week hike of the desert not spent the whole of yesterday drinking lager. Not only that I realised the cunt had arsed 34 of the 48 cans we had for when were in the room and the bar was shut.

We also watched a dreadful 0-0 draw in Inverness that was so bad some of our company actually fell asleep without the aid of drink.

The Sunday came and that meant quiz night. Now a certain Mr Lennox isn't called the Buzzbomb for his incredible pace on a football pitch, it was actually because of the number of times he was first on the buzzer in the show *Quizball*. His team had won all the previous quizzes but I'm partial to the odd quiz and our team went on to win an array of bevvy that had Bobby beeling. So much so that when I put the drink we had won on the hand luggage part of the plane the next day, Bobby tried to slip it into his bag! This followed an exchange on the plane where I jokingly referred to him his a bad loser and he replied, for the benefit of the entire plane, "JUST CAUSE I BROKE INTAE YER ROOM LAST NIGHT AND STOLE THE PRIZE!!!"

Don't kid yourself though, I was still in awe the whole time.

Before the quiz though I took the time to have a few hours kip in the room with that cunt Brad nowhere to be seen. I was just dozing off when I got a call from Trisha in Manchester.

"I've done three pregnancy tests, all positive"

BOOM!

That's what I meant by the three of us in London, you dirty-minded bastards.

On the train up to Glasgow on the Monday, fresh from a 20 minute conversation with the man who changed the world, Stevie Chalmers, Brad and I made sure Joe McBride got back ok.

Joe was telling some great stories, resplendent in his Celtic jacket, when the train guard gruffly demanded tickets. No prizes for guessing who he supported. Brad piped up and said "I'll get this" and brandished a twenty pound note. The guard looked at him incredulously and said "Where are you going?" Brad, without breaking stride said "Hame". The guard was raging and said "Look, I've no time for your pathetic games"

Brad leapt up and said "Here you, that's Joe fucking McBride sitting there ya cunt, any mair ae yer shite and I'll tell the fat controller"

Full steam ahead.

Raging Bull

"Don't think. Thinking is the enemy of creativity. It's self-conscious, and anything self-conscious is lousy. You can't try to do things. You simply must do things."

Ray Bradbury

We had it confirmed soon after and it was real, we were expecting a baby. A boy. This was to be Trisha's first and my second. I was genuinely delighted. It was another part, with things like Trisha, London and Letterkenny, in staving off dark feelings for the time being. With kids names(and books titles too) one of the hardest things ever to come up with, we wracked our brains constantly. I do it with book titles too. You want something some snappy but clever, something that folk will smile and nod at, preferably that explains the book and what it's about. I've probably only achieved that with *Wim's Tims-The best thing to hit Scottish football in 10 years* I reckon. *Poles 'N' Goals and Hesselink* stumped most people. Apart from fans of the Madchester scene which I need to get my head round was over 20 years ago. Hopefully I've done it justice for this book. It was going to be called "Fear and Loathing on Captain Correllis Mandolin with The Catcher in The Rye" but...I'm joking.

Celtic were a bit eaksey peaksey at this point. There were great games, good games and some fucking awful games. Probably the worst ever Glasgow derby draw took place in February that year, with a spineless boring 0-0 that saw managers Gordon Strachan and Walter Myth laughing and joking with three minutes to go that went down as well with all supporters the same way a proposed merger would. There were great games like a 7-0 trouncing of St Mirren at Celtic Park but they were then followed up by awful 1-0 defeats at, eh, St Mirren.

Of course January 2009 is thing that Peter Lawwell would later say would be on his tombstone. Which made me think "Has he bought a plot as well as lost it?" The backdrop being David Murray had announced at the start of January that not only would Rangers not be buying any players, they would need to sell on of their top ones with Kris Boyd being the guy touted.

It was obvious that Lawwell took the bait.

I should say that most of you who know me know I've been highly critical of Peter Lawwell. I make no apologies for that. I will say though that this was probably the one and only time he was outsmarted by David Murray. Lawwell had Murray's number big time. The signs were starting to come through that Murray's empire was crumbling. Peter Lawwell did anything and everything he could to ensure Rangers were kept beneath us (if you overlook joint sponsorship deals of course...), so I don't criticise him for that but I criticise him for many other things, some folk agree, others don't. What everyone agreed on though was that in January 2009 Peter Lawwell should have signed Steven Fletcher from Hibs.

The first game I attended when I got back to Scotland in 2008 was actually not a Celtic game, it was Hibs v Falkirk at Easter Road. Reason being Celtic weren't playing until the Sunday and I just wanted to go to a football match again. So I bought a ticket for the west stand and sat and watched Hibs and Falkirk play out a 3-2 win for Hubs in which Steven Fletcher made

Colin Nish look like Gerd Muller. I exaggerate of course but the difference in Fletcher since I last saw him play live was staggering. So when it looked like we would sign him in the January, I was delighted.

Instead we got Willo Flood.

I guess the only people who know what really happened are Peter Lawwell and Rod Petrie but it has been said that there was a deadlock of £200,000. Peanuts compared to the price Fletcher is now worth.

Whatever, it meant we were looking increasingly toothless up front at a time where every goal would be crucial. It fucking showed as well and none more so than that at New St Mirren Park as we meekly exited the Scottish Cup. After the game Gordon Strachan was asked by a female reporter how a team could beat another 7-0 one week and then lose to them 1-0 the following week? His reply went down in history "I can't explain it, it would be like you trying to explain childbirth to me" Later Gary Caldwell said the players were delighted when he said it, saying it took the pressure off them. Great. Most supporters just cringed again.

Of course that flu ridden semi final did end in victory and this meant a cup final at Hampden against Rangers. It had been 20 years since we had beaten them at Hampden in a cup final, when Joe Miller latched onto Gary Stevens back pass to right foot away any hope they had of a treble, and most of us agreed it was far, far too long. I took James to Hampden that day, this was his first Celtic-Rangers cup final, incredibly it was also Walter Myth's first as manager, and after a dour 90 minutes Darren O'Dea bulleted a header past McGregor to put us one up.

After the celebrations of that goal died down, nerves kicked in. We were close. Rangers pressed but looked about as threatening as a balloon on a stick. Still with the clock at Hampden in constant sight, the minutes dragged down. Then one of those moments happened that make it worthwhile all the shite you have to put up with in football. With the clock showing 120 minutes, Aiden McGeady went on a run to take the ball to the corner flag we thought. Then suddenly he skipped passed Broadfoot, who looked like the egg faced cunt he is, and was in the box. Big Kirk could only adopt the usual tactic of fouling him and a penalty was given. With us well into injury time by now the game was done. Even if McGeady missed, they had no time whatsoever to launch any kind of attack and I distinctly remember bouncing up and down with anticipation that the cup was coming back to Celtic Park. Of course Aiden did score and a headline was born.

Ireland 2 Rangers 0. Haw haw haw.

The week after this game, a cinema in Edinburgh was showing *Raging Bull* and I took the opportunity to go and see one of my favourite films on the big screen. After watching the performance of De Niro and being inspired by the story of Jake La Motta, I knew then we had my second son's name.

And it wasn't Robert.

Stolen Chips, Polo Mints and the Red Hand of Ulster

"He is now rising from affluence to poverty"

Mark Twain

Living in Leith was a new experience for me, relatively. When I'd lived in Edinburgh previous I'd lived in the Muirhouse area in almost all of it, save for a month or so when I did live in Kirk Srt in Leith with a mate and we were so poor, we had to share a room, a single bed, steady, and order chips from the chippy then run out the door with them unpaid. One day we had a packet of polo mints to last us an entire day. The next day we got money and went straight to the Supermarket to get stocked up. Or we went straight to the Volunteer Arms to stock up on bevvy and play pool. You decide.

Actually that day we were in The Volly sparked off a weekend of events from bizarre to fucking mental. It was March 1992 and for once Celtic were playing well. I'd got my giro through as did my mate, Dav, and we got a rent cheque as well. We had about £300 on us and the rent was £120. We paid that and hit The Volly early doors. Scratch that, I'm talking pish. The rent money went in the bank and we withdrew it on Leith Walk at one minute past midnight on the Friday. Then in the morning we took the landlord, Colin, over to the bank with the intention of giving him the rent money we knew we had already taken out. Hey, I was 17, Dav was 18 and we were both fucking brassic and daft. And young. So after a week of stolen chips and polo mints, where was the first place we hit? Boots. To get aftershave. It was the weekend fur fucks sake.

After buying our Armani splash on, we hit the Volly at 9am, and settled in for a game of pool. This cunt called Mel latched onto us and before we knew it, he was wearing Armani too. Aye see you judged us before eh, now look, good samaritans ya cunt.

Several jars later we were in a house drinking 100 proof vodka.

I've no recollection of whose house it was but one incident I recall with great clarity. There was a football programme on TV, probably Scotsport Extra Time, and well pished with this vodka, we watched intently. No one more so than Dav who kept getting closer and closer to the TV. I'd almost lapsed into a coma when, for some unknown reason, Dav started kicking the telly in. I hauled him off but at that point we knew we'd outstayed our welcome.

The following day we woke up in our room, him one end of the bed, me the other, completely fucked but still in plenty funds so we thought we could divvy up some of the rent money. I peeled off £70 and was about to enter the landlord's room where I could hear talking. I listened closely and looked through the gap of door and wall to clearly see the landlord wanking off the old guy who also had a room there.

The £70 went right back in the tail.

Dav went off to see his bird, I went off to see Celtic and we arranged to meet that night in Morrisons Pool Hall, now sadly gone, on Leith Walk. Hosey came along too. We played pool and drank all night, eventually latching on to these three girls in the corner and I'm not talking *All Saints* here. We were hitting them with the usual pish and it became clear they were from the north of Ireland. As one reached for a drink we gasped, she a pair of of school woolen Rangers gloves on. Not being daft cunts we made no mention of this.

A game of "Killer" was on the go and the rules are basic, you get one shot at pool, you miss and you're out, last man standing wins. Dav wasn't in as in a brief moment of morals he had decided he had to apologise to the folk from last night after seeing them in the street that day.

I came down to the second last ball in the game but fucking missed one on the cushion. You can tell 20 years on I'm not bitter.

I had been so engrossed in the game I didn't notice Dav had came back in and was standing at the bar with his back to me. I walked over and realised the cunt had a flower vase in front of him. Half full of 100 proof vodka.

I went back to the table and the Rangers glove wearing woman asked me if I wanted to go for a walk? Sure. We walked round the block and had a snogging session before she wanked me off. After I insisted the gloves came off of course.

Nowadays Leith is a different place, a huge migration of Polish people has changed it. Plus you never see girls with gloves or cunts standing at the bar with a flower vase in front of them.

When I were a lad...

Wish You Were Here

"A friend is one who knows you and loves you just the same"
Elbert Hubbard

As season 2008/09 was drawing to a close I started to get pangs of fear again. It was happening so often that I was living with it as opposed to doing anything about it. As usual though I was so wrapped up in Celtic that I put it all to one side just in the hope I'd see us stagger over the line for the title.

The other thing on my mind was the fact that Gary Haley was coming to visit. I'd had a routine with Gary where I'd call him every Sunday at work. Our club was having a dance in April 2009 and through talking we both agreed it would be good if he came over for it. Thing for me was though I just wanted to see him again normal circumstances. He arrived a couple of days before the dance in April and, in typical Gary style, he told me he would call me when on the way but what he actually did was called me to say he was in Edinburgh. We arranged to meet on the High St and I just arrived there when I saw him walking up. It felt weird. All other times I'd seen him was on his turf, now he was on mine and something didn't fit. I think it was me, I really missed him and I didn't want to fuck anything up. We went for a beer and a burger in The Filling Station and it was good although I was still tense.

We saw Celtic beat Hamilton 4-0 on the Saturday then the dance came and went and on the Sunday it was Trisha's birthday. Gary came through and I met him at the station before we walked down to Leith on a beautiful day. Halfway there I suggested we stop in the Conan Doyle for a quick one and Man Utd were playing Aston Villa on TV. It was the game Macheda scored the late goal and it was good to be having a few beers, watching the action unfold. It was that day I realised I missed New York but more importantly I missed Gary and missed that buzz of being out with him in Manhattan on a Saturday night knowing that anything could happen and plenty did. I've written in the past about the telepathy of the relationship between Jackie McNamara and Simon Donnelly, and that's how I felt about Gary, we just clicked, right away. Not in a gay way of course, he prefers blonde men.

Something happened that day for me. I went home with Gary to see Trisha and we all went out for a great Indian meal. After Gary left I said to Trisha I wanted to go back, fully expecting her to say "Are you mad? After what happened? Have you noticed I'm pregnant?" but she didn't. She said "Yeah, me too" and I felt good.

We set a small plan to head back Summer of 2010 and I focused in on four in a row. The crunch was coming on May 9th at Ibrox. If we took anything from this game they wouldn't catch us. So what possessed Gordon Strachan to drop Aiden McGeady and bring in Shaun Maloney for his first game in four months is beyond me. Strachan had been highly successful with Celtic but at this point supporters were convinced he'd lost the plot. Davis got the only goal for them and my abiding memory was Samaras losing the ball and going through the theatrics of punching the ground continuously. This defeat meant we fell two points behind in the title race with just three games left. We looked dead.

The next game was a midweek game against Dundee Utd at Celtic Park on the Tuesday and the strange thing for me was that Trisha came with me. She's not even a football fan never mind a Celtic supporter but I thought now was as good a time as any to take her as it was roasting hot and I had no one else to go with. Kidding. We won 2-1 that night in a tense game that put us one clear with two games to go but Rangers were at Easter Road the following night. Being pretty close to the ground I thought up loads of things I could to derail them but settled for "Watch the game and pray" Things were going pretty well up until the last minute of the first half when Derek Riordan put Hibs one up. My heart sank. This game had 0-0 written all over it and now Riordan had just awoken the beast. The expected onslaught came and so did equaliser when Maklamby decided to throw ratface Novo's shot into the net. Incredibly, Hibs held on and we were still top, albeit on goal difference, with two games to go and the next game at Easter Road. We could fucking do this again.

Gary stayed for five days on his visit. I've known him over 10 years now and despite a multitude of provocation, a lot of shit and an incredible amount of alcohol, I've never once fallen out with him. That's why I always wish he was here.

From Albion Road to Wembley Way

"Who are you

Who who who who

Who are you

Who who who who"

Pete Townshend

Things always seem to happen when you least expect them, right? There I was on another sunny day (Why is summer in Scotland now in April and May) in Leith, heading round with James to hopefully see Celtic beat Hibs at Easter Road and take a giant step towards four in a row when sitting next to me was a guy I hadn't seen in years. I think he would admit that he's not the most positive chap at the best of times so if you think you had a bad day that day Easter Road that day, you didn't have to sit listening to this dour faced cunt say for 90 minutes "We're never going to score here" and I say that with respect. Every time I think of that game I always think back to two things, Lee Naylor missing from an inch and post match walking up Albion Road.

There is a story that after Rangers won the league at Easter Road in 2005 several Hibs fans applauded the Rangers team bus post match because Alex McLeish was on it.

After the 0-0 game, living just a goal kick away, I didn't turn left to the Bothwell Bridge, James and I waited with the disabled people until Albion Road was free to use. As we walked past the Albion Bar, me, James and about six wheelchair users with carers, we were subjected to a torrent of abuse. One guy in particular reveled in screaming "Why don't you go home, why don't you home, the league is over, why don't you go home!" This led to three other supporters of No Identity FC singing the actual "famine" song. The red mist was descending on me. It was roasting hot day, we'd just blown the league and I had the dawn of man in my ear, I wanted to push the big cunt right through the Albion Bar window. I knew I'd be battered senseless but what stopped me was James who was crying at this point. I've many friends who are Hibs supporters and do not blame them for this, nor do I suggest all Hibs fans are like this, but your complete lack of identity leads to behavior like this. Too many folk go to Easter Road and have no idea who they are. Irvine Welsh created an image of Hibs that never existed and bams try to live up to. More than that, the level of hate Celtic experience at Easter Road is both unfathomable and very sad. It's not a two way thing and there's never been a Rangers-Hearts type atmosphere at Celtic Park any time Hibs have visited. Don't get me wrong, some Celtic supporters are as much to blame when going to Easter Road, from the cretins who threw the CS gas canister, to the moronic "Feeder club" jibes, they're not welcomed by the majority of Celtic supporters. Folk on both sides need a wake up call.

Fuck me all the feelings form that day just came back, see, method writer me ya cunts.

Anyway.

We'd blown it. There was still one game left but you knew they were going to win at Tannadice. Primarily because the SPL and SFA spent the whole week trying to ensure they did.

The previous day before Easter Road, Rangers beat Aberdeen 3-1 at Ibrox. Two players were sent off, Majdid Bougherra for maiming the entire Aberdeen team and Charlie Mulgrew for not touching Kyle Lafferty. The ref was Stuart Dougal who spent most of the week getting Bougherra off, no jokes please, before retiring and speaking at an Orange Lodge. All of that is true apart from the first part, Dougal knew he was retiring and wanted to ref a Rangers game before he did.

So the Sunday came and it was awful. Rangers won comfortably at Tannadice and we were hopeless against Hearts in a 0-0 draw. The Hearts fans in the stadium that were amongst the worst ever experienced at Celtic Park. Pro Rangers songs, loyalist anthems and chants about child abuse were the order of the day. After the game quite a few Hearts fans got a sore face yet , as is always claimed, none of the ones singing. Funny that, eh?

Gordon Strachan resigned soon after. A season that promised so much delivered a league cup and a lot of angst. Supporters say different now but I didn't hear many complain when he did go. Most I spoke to felt he should have gone out on a high at Tannadice the year before.

Thankfully Gordon did go out on a high, coming back the week later for the Tommy Burns Testimonial match. By this time a lot of dark thoughts were coming back to me. I didn't want to talk to people, didn't want to go places and had a sense of hopelessness about me. I turned 35 that summer and had a very real feeling on my birthday that this is how it is, this is how I'll always feel. It had been a year since I'd left America and I had re-built parts of my life but I hadn't re-built myself.

As usual though, in my own stupid selfish way, I went on as normal and went through to the press conference to welcome new manager Tony Mowbray. I'm not wanting any pats on the back but at no stage did I ever think Tony Mowbray was the man for the job. I remember distinctly having a bevvy with Hosey in The Iona Bar on Easter Road one Thursday night, right at the time West Bromwich Albion were getting around £2m from us, that this would be a disaster for Celtic.

Still, I bought into Tony Mowbray's spiel at his press conference, I'm a sucker for an underdog, but I went away that day from Celtic Park convinced that Mowbray thought he was taking on the club he left in 1995. He simply had not grasped how much the club had grown nor I think did Peter Grant who had a bizarre press conference which included talk of how he had phoned Ally McCoist a few times but had no reply. Psychologists would say you were one down already. Supporters who don't need a weather man to know which way the wind blows cringed. The mood wasn't helped when Mowbray spunked over £3.5m on a striker not known for scoring goals. The world of football is flooded with guys like Marc Antoine-Fortune. Forwards who want to float about, drift wide, sit in behind the front two, just anything to ensure no one bothers about the fact that from the 100 chances they got in a season scored six goals. These guys are ten a penny and so you don't spend pretty much all your transfer budget on one.

Tony Mowbray did.

Still, one thing to look forward to was a pre season trip to Wembley. I'd been to Wembley three times previously for the football and Wembley Arena once for the Snooker but was looking forward to seeing the new Wembley. I was either pretty young or pretty skint on my previous trips there for the football but the snooker one was a memorable one. It was 2005 and I'd gone down with my mate Jamie, another big snooker fan, on the Wednesday for three nights and we were staying in the Hotel Ibis, a mere miscue away. Unbeknown to me, Jamie hadn't actually told his work that he was going and told me that he had to phone them just as we left the tube at Baker Street to hit one of our favourite haunts, The Globe. So there there he is belling his work that he's sick and his bed when like a sonic boom all you hear "The next train approaching is for High Wycombe" quick as a flash Jamie says "Hold on please, Mum, turn that film off will you". We had a few scoops in The Globe and this female tagged along. Mini skirt, leather jacket and face that looked like it had just been embalmed. When it comes to women, when Jamie and I were single like then, if we were a moral compass, we'd be pointing DOWN yet if even we were looking at her and thinking "Na". We legged it to the Wetherspoons across the road and settled in for a cheap bevvy. Out the corner of my eye I saw a girl, Lisa Stansfield thing going on, crying and holding a unlit cigarette in her hand. We had been eyeing up the four women at the table next to us but a wave of confidence came over me and I whipped over to Stansfield's table a bit lively and offered her a light which she accepted gratefully. Quicker than the flash of the lighter I asked her what was wrong? She told me a long story about how her boyfriend had cheated on her and that she was meant to go back to her parents tonight but couldn't face them just now. He who dares Rodders, he who dares my son.

I was close that night but not close enough. She swithered with coming back to my hotel with me but in the end she thought better of it. We had a kiss and I saw her to the train. I made my way back in and Jamie was relieved to see me, he wanted to move on the four girls at the next table and I was ready, I gave them a line and they started blankly.

Not the first time I've had that reaction it has to be said.

After 30 seconds or so I realised they were all Polish and none could speak a word of English.

See what happens when you knock back women like her in The Globe?

Jamie and I travelled back to our hotel and were delighted to see the bar was still open. The receptionist warned us a group of German bikers were in and a bit rowdy. A few jars and a few rebel songs later we cleared the place. So much so that when a beautiful woman walked in to go to the lift, we serenaded her with *You've lost that loving feeling* ala *Top Gun*.

We were fucking drunk ok?

So I was looking forward to another Wembley trip, this time with my mate Rab Tait. Rab is one of these guys that steams in anywhere he goes, not fighting like, just with his personality. We took in the first game on the Friday, against Al Alhy, and were delighted with the 5-0 win. The incredible thing was when I got to my seat, who should be sitting in the next one? The same miserable cunt from Easter Road.

Come the Saturday, no games, Rab and I decided we needed a major sesh. We had a good scoop the night before and some good banter with some Spurs fans in a curry house which had wetted the appetite. We hit central London and a boozer I always take a look in on Whitehall, The Lord Moon of The Mall. I used to always go to The Red Lion closer to parliament but it was always full of spooks. One night back in 1999 I was in there and Mo Mowlam strolled in. She was the life and soul of the boozer and was happy to chat away. I should also say, I definitely would have.

We settled in for a good bevvy and food in the moon and before long were having banter with the manager who was a loyal one from the occupied six but, to be fair, was good craic and as honest enough to tell us they had to shut any time Rangers were in town. We were scooping all day and realised that most of the staff were Polish. One smiled at me and I started winking over, being the shy, retiring type. Of course it was only banter, I was miraculous. So I says to yer man from the north, by now my best mate in the world, "One of your staff fancies me, you better tell her I'm taken!" he was pissing himself laughing and said "which one?" I pointed her out and his face dropped

"That's my wife"

Time to go.

The Sunday saw us beat Spurs 2-0 and win "The Wembley Cup" and I don't give a fuck what anyone says, I saw my team win a trophy at Wembley ya cunts.

Post match, myself and Rab found a boozer that wasn't to far from our hotel which in itself wasn't too far from Wembley. After about, oh, two minutes, we realised it was, in the parlance of our time, a gypsy boozer. After about an hour a huge fight broke out amongst a big crowd in the bar. When it finished they all came over an bought everyone a drink as an apology. Fucks sake mate, hit him again. Rab being Rab had the landlord eating out the palm of his hand and a substantial lock in was secured meaning the hangover on my flight back was hellish.

Not as hellish as the passenger next to me though, it was that miserable cunt again.

I should have read the signs then.

Medication Time

"No one ever told me that grief felt so like fear"

C.S. Lewis

By the time season 2009/10 started, I was really struggling. Events, like Wembley, took my mind off things but ever for too long. Jake was due in early October and Trisha was going to finish up work mid September. She had handled the pregnancy well and thought she'd be driven mad if she finished work too early. I was fine with the pregnancy too, Jake would be my second and things seemed more routine this time. The problem was that I just wasn't right, something was deeply wrong.

I'd been living like this for over a year now and it was my life. Then one night I opened up to Trisha and she told me I had to see a Doctor. I reluctantly made the appointment and was glad to get an early one. Sitting in the surgery that morning, surrounded by all those notices that make you think you will drop down dead any minute, I looked at all these people around me, these people were sick, I wasn't, I shouldn't even be here. Then my name was called by an average height, well dressed guy and I would come to know him as Dr Russell.

He offered me a seat, checked his computer and then turned to me and said "What can I do for you?" I had no idea what to say so told the story of what happened to me in NYC and went on to describe my life just now "I get scared going out, I sit at home and think every footstep in the stair is going to end up kicking my door in, I get frightened when the post comes, I have about three or four panic attacks a week, I get night terrors, my tolerance is low and my temper is high and I can't handle seeing or watching anything that reminds me of New York"

I half expected him to say "Aye, Sex and The City, pish eh?"

Instead he looked at me in absolute horror and said "How long have you felt like this?"

I replied casually "About a year or so" and he stopped and started at me.

"Look, this is serious, I cannot believe you haven't had this dealt with by now, these things can lead to suicidal tendencies"

I then said "Well, I did contemplate it last November"

And that was that. He started scribbling prescriptions and grabbing leaflets and then said "Look, what income do you have just now?"

"None"

"Ok, you need to claim Employment Support Allowance, it's designed to support you whilst you get better, you'll get the form from the DSS"

So after I left, armed with prescriptions, I went down to Commercial Street Brew and got the forms.

I handed in my prescriptions and waited about ten minutes, before coming back with four different types of pills.

The main was Lorazepam. I was to take one after lunch and this meant I sat like a daft cunt on the couch all afternoon. Who'd notice the difference? It slows down the nervous system. It's highly potent, short acting and fucking mind numbing. From around 1pm to 7pm every day I could hardly do anything. Celtic, after a bright start in the league, had drawn Arsenal in the Champions League and that would normally be the holy grail for a guy like me, instead I gouched on the couch.

I didn't read books, I stared glumly at daytime TV, ok I know every cunt does, I lost all sex drive and appetite.

I had become a completely different person.

As I said, I'd went down to the DSS at Commercial Street in Leith and shown the guy my sick line. He gave me a form and I got a number to fill in. A couple of weeks later I got a letter saying that I was entitled to Employment Support Allowance.

I was quite happy with that. In the constant visits to the Doctor he outlined that I may never get over PTSD but that I need breathing space to get beyond panic attacks, night terrors and thinking the door would be kicked in at any time.

I thought about the things he told me, tell people, write it, get into a cathartic process. I arranged a couple of days in London with Paul O'Neil to have a wee break away from the norm. I could see a clear path ahead of me.

I was wrong.

#Team Samaras

An example from the Celtic world on the impact of Twitter came one horrible evening in August 2011.

I am Steph, and I am a Twitter addict. I freely admit this. Also known as chibchenko, more recently as chibnewco, and also occasionally as "yon Team Samaras arsehole". The Team Samaras thing in particular is possibly something that will haunt me until the day I die. If you've not heard the background, I'll briefly explain. After we were beaten 3-1 away in Sion last August (Christ, that seems a while ago now), I sat on Twitter, and was completely astonished at the level of vitriol directed at one man in particular. Not Daniel Majstorovic, whose first minute show of lunacy left us with ten men; not Ki, whose inexplicable gift led to the third Sion goal and who also gave away the free kick which led to their second – but Samaras, or "Jesus CHRIST Samaras", to give him his full title. I decided I was fed up with the unwarranted abuse directed at a man whose only crime was to play and look like a bit of a jessie, so I decided to wind people up. After all, that is the main purpose of social networking sites, is it not? My post was something ridiculously daft along the lines of "#TeamSamaras – retweet and we shall take over the world". It was retweeted a lot in the end, including by a couple of the more followed Celtic accounts. In fact, #TeamSamaras ended up trending in the UK by the end of the night. This enraged people further – which of course I found hilarious. The following night I wrote a blog entry explaining my defence of him, which I've found and have replicated here.

"Last night, I spent a highly amusing few hours encouraging people to join Team Samaras. Obviously, this was started as a bit of a laugh, however inevitably I did get some comments from those who were astounded that anyone could actually appreciate him as a football player. I promised an explanation, and this is it.

Giorgios Samaras is a highly frustrating player, of that there is absolutely no doubt. The reason for this frustration, for me at least, is down to the fact that, under that mess of hair, there is a player of some ability struggling to get out. When he signed initially on loan, he scored that fantastic debut goal in the 5-1 pumpfest at Rugby Park, darting down the wing and casually finishing. I immediately thought to myself "here, we could have a player here." Sadly, as we all know, it hasn't quite worked out like that. His talent has flickered here and there, but all too often he, for want of a better phrase, makes an absolute arse of it.

And here, we get to the crux of my Samaras defence. If you were to take someone who knew nothing of football and played an audio of some of the abuse Samaras takes from his own fans, I'm sure at times you'd think he played for our biggest rivals. Errors that other players may get away with are just not acceptable when it comes to Samaras. And for me, the reason he is always so noticeable on the field is because, and I must apologise profusely for this cliché, he always gives his all. He is always looking to get on the ball and never hides on the football pitch, which is something he should be admired, not pilloried, for. The likes of Hooper and Stokes can go missing completely at times, which - some may say unfortunately - Samaras very rarely does.

Yes, Samaras makes aimless runs into players, refuses to release the ball, and is very often the definition of the "forward's challenge." However, let us not forget that with his frustration, at times comes genius. His delayed pass to Izaguirre to set up Hooper's second in the 3-0 game against Rangers at Parkhead last season. His entire performance in that game was outstanding, despite not troubling the scorers. And of course, who will ever forget the New Year game at Ibrox when we were all expecting a trouncing. The latter game showed Sammy at his best - up front on his own, with McCourt playing just behind him. Samaras is a forward who does not work well with other strikers. This has been evident on several occasions, most recently against Sion. And who do fans blame for this? Samaras, for the most part. The question I pose is this - does Samaras really deserve the blame for tactical decisions which don't allow him to perform in his preferred way?

That, my friends, is essentially it. I recognise Samaras is average as a football player, who often runs up blind alleys and borderline refuses to score goals. However, he's also a player that thrives on confidence. Is it any wonder he struggles when the fans are on his back for the slightest error? Jump on the bandwagon. Support Team Samaras."

Having read that back, it's not the best thing I've ever written, and I've even been proven wrong on one point – Samaras is probably best on the wing, rather than up front himself with someone playing off him. However, I did get some great feedback on that blog, from people I really respect. Since that night, #TeamSamaras seems to have worked its way into popular Twitter vernacular. The guys at Rhebel Rhebel made a

Team Samaras t-shirt. It still trends sometimes, for example on the very rare occasions he actually manages to find the net, at the time of writing most recently in Greece's game against Germany at Euro 2012. It's an easy phrase that caught on, and I guess it's just stuck. Of course, it coincided with him "coming good" – he had a fantastic second half of the season, and folk got off his back and started actually supporting him. And I'm claiming full credit for his form.

As a football fan, Twitter has changed the way in which I hear news, gossip, rumours and slander. What I like most about it is the ability we now have to hear news as it happens, from the horse's mouth, before it is pushed through the spin machine of the mainstream sports media. Pick and choose who you follow in order to get the news you want from the people you want. There are some people out there doing fantastic work and without Twitter and messageboards, many fantastic bloggers could go unnoticed. Similarly, with the official Celtic FC account now on Twitter, news from the club is immediately accessible. I'd never pretend what they're doing is perfect – the fact they have an account called "Celtic FC Commercial" gies me the boak, a bit – but it's a far sight better than what we've previously had. Twitter users also have the opportunity to interact directly with journalists, the club, and the players, and see first-hand how many times Niall McGinn goes to Nando's in a week. Sure, that might not be to everyone's taste (no pun intended) but it gives the illusion of a more personal touch, which I think is one of the reasons Twitter is continuing to grow as it is.

Of course, my favourite aspect of Twitter is being able to debate things with fellow fans I might not have encountered *otherwise. Believe it or not, I don't actually have many Celtic-supporting friends. My brothers are fans of Aberdeen and Partick Thistle (a mystery), and most of my friends – well, they supported a club that no longer exists. Twitter has allowed me to debate players; the way the club is run; individual games and the like, with fans who share my passion. I love a good debate, which is why I persisted with the Samaras thing, and I love hearing the opinions of others and thinking of ways I can shoot them down, preferably in 140 characters or less. This is the crux of why I am a Twitter addict – there's always something to discuss, and it never gets boring.*

The Game Changer - Part 1

Phil Mac Giolla Bhain has gone through a transition. The name that that is. First very few folk knew how to pronounce his surname, then everyone did, then no one needed to. How did that happen then?

I first became aware of Phil back in 2008. Not long after that horrific 4-2 defeat to Rangers at Celtic Park, where the Rangers fans belted out their bile all day and mocked An Gorta Mor, I became aware of a blog that was doing the rounds on the messageboards. It told a story of a man based in Donegal flying over to Edinburgh and attending a match at Tynecastle between members of the press and some ex pros. Included in the team was one Billy Singh, the top man of Show Racism The Red Card. The man from Donegal asked questions that I, and probably most Celtic supporters on the planet, wanted asked of Billy Singh, namely "Why have you done sod all about The 'Famine' Song?"

I liked that.

I put the blog into my favourites and started to check it regularly. The impression I got of Phil Mac Giolla Bhain was that of someone that most people in authority would not like. He reminded me a lot of Bill Maher. For those not aware, Bill Maher is left wing comedian in the US who won't stand back take the shit of right wing America. Bill Maher asks awkward questions of people in authority, he puts out those sort of facts that blow away arguments and he does it all knowing that lots of people would love him to shut the fuck up.

Similarities.

The next blog that struck me was when Phil attended a Hamilton v St Mirren game and sat in the away end, listening to the vitriolic abuse James McCarthy would be subjected to. This was an issue that had been boiling away in Scotland for a while regarding McCarthy and it was coming to a head now that Hamilton were in the SPL. It seemed like no one was doing jack shit about it. This was the kind of journalism I wanted to see.

It was becoming more and more evident that there was a sinister vibe creeping into Scottish football. We had hatred and bigotry since time immemorial but racism of this nature was starting to become rife and, dare I say it, accepted. We heard Keith Jackson of the Daily Record the ridiculing of An Gorta Mor as "banter"

I've been to a few memorials to An Gorta Mor in my life. The one in New York is huge, and has rocks from each of the 32 counties in Ireland within it as well as names of some of the people who perished. The most impressive I've seen is in Philadelphia , PA. A huge structure made from copper and iron, it depicts what a an immigrant from Ireland would have to go through, from the horrible boat journey that far too many perished on, to the arrival in Philadelphia where they are welcomed with open arms.

Welcomed with open arms.

That's a phrase that would not have been known to anyone who took the boat east for the far shorter journey to Scotland. Indeed the people who fled An Gorta Mor to come to Scotland were the ones who would need the help from somewhere. A few went to Protestant Soup Kitchens and this didn't go unnoticed. As poverty ravaged the east end of

Glasgow in the late 1800s, something would have to be done. A Marist Brother, Andrew Kerins, decided that a football team should be formed, after seeing the impact Edinburgh Hibernian had, and in St Mary's in The Calton on November 6th 1887, it was.

Celtic were born.

Not only were the club a source of food, shelter and money for people, they were a beacon of hope in an otherwise grim existence. From that hope grew something that would go on to take on the world's best.

And beat them.

To think that those people were being mocked by residents of Scotland more akin with Montgomery, Alabama and laughed it by journalists who can barely string a coherent sentence together was not acceptable.

As Phil probed and blogged, it would soon become an offence to sing The "Famine" song and a prosecution was gained against William Wells, in February 2009, when he was arrested or singing it at a Rangers match. It was held on appeal and Lord Carloway said the following:

"the song calls upon persons of Irish descent, who are living in Scotland, to go back to the land of their ancestors, namely Ireland [...] they are racist in calling upon people native to Scotland to leave the country because of their racial origins. This is a sentiment which, once more, many persons will find offensive."

The significance of this was enormous. A song derided as "Banter" by leading journalists in Scotland was now declared illegal. A song that had been chanted with gusto all over Scotland could now get you arrested.

Would this have been possible without the man in Donegal? well, Show Racism The Red Card were doing sod all about it until Phil put pressure on Billy Singh, their head. The Irish Embassy in Scotland got involved because Phil asked them to get involved. It got into the Celtic mainstream because Phil blogged and talked about it everywhere.

There is no doubt that what this proved was that was New Media could be used to influence that higher echelons of Scottish society. Although some may not have realised it, and probably even Phil who had no idea just how many people were hitting his blog on a daily basis.

Things would never be the same again.

Labour Pains, London Calls and So Do Many Others

"And all this effort, all this loss of comradeship, all this prostitution of idealism and manhood, to assist the capitalists of this country to defeat the proletariat!"
Harry Pollit

The Labour Party, when I didn't know any better, would have been the party I assumed I'd vote for all my life. I remember as far back as Michael Foot and how people called the Labour party manifesto on 1983 "The longest suicide note in history" . I always thought Labour stood for the people, whilst the Tories stood for everything to be despised, then and now. I remember Labour having huge support in Muirhouse, the area I grew up in. Allan Hosey (snr) was a big campaigner for them round the area and I can visualise him now, flowing red hair and brown blazer, delivering leaflets for the 83 election. Funny thing though, I couldn't actually cast a vote until 1997. In 1992 I was still 17 when the election happened and even though Labour were in vogue by 1997, I voted Socialist and have done so at every election. In fact, I've only ever voted for two people in my life, Willie Black (Socialist) and Margo MacDonald (Independent). See in between thinking Labour would be my party and actually voting, I was politicised. Funnily enough Allan Hosey (snr) was part of that, but mostly it was Jim Slaven and The James Connolly Society. Jim was the first guy who alerted me to the fact that it was the Labour government who sent troops into the north of Ireland.

He also made me aware of the fact that when James Connolly was executed in Dublin, Labour MP's cheered in parliament.

Why am I telling you this?

So folk realise that the current persecution of the people in the UK, on benefits, old, young, sick, disabled and so on, was started by a Labour government.

It was probably about 10 days after I received the letter saying I would get ESA that I got a call from a place called Ingeus. The woman explained I was to attend an office in Festival Square where I would be given help and advice to get back into work.

Eh?

I didn't get it but went along anyway. I was supposed to be there for three hours, I lasted 15 minutes. A very nice girl explained what they did then asked me why I was on ESA. I told her my story, glad for a continuation of the cathartic process Dr Russell had advised, and at the end she said "Oh, you shouldn't be here, there's nothing we can do for you given the extent of your problems"

I left the building and had a cigarette, baffled as to what had just happened and why I was there. It was November 2009 and I was going to London for two nights at the end of the month, so I thought about that as I made my way home via Princes St on a crisp, bright morning.

I got home and told Trisha what had happened and from that conversation we decided that a positive thing to do would be to press ahead with a baptism for Jake. I wasn't keen at first.

As I said before, a lot of folk used what had happened to me basically rubber ear me whilst some people, whom I had regarded as good friends, turned their back on me completely. I wasn't sure anyone would show up if truth be told. We did go ahead with it and was a decent day but in my weak state I felt some folk couldn't be arsed with it at all, even being there. Maybe that's the way my mind was at the time but I felt my mind hardening quicker than normal to certain folk that I would have laughed off previously. By the time it was finished, I couldn't wait to get away.

The Monday after the Sunday christening, another letter came in, this time it was from place telling me I was to come in for a medical exam on February 8th. I hadn't a fucking clue what was going on, so I went back to Dr Russell and he told me the government were no longer taking the word of doctors and that they had their own examiners now, not from medical backgrounds, to assess people. It was based on a points system and you needed 15 to be eligible for ESA.

I took all this in and was flabbergasted. I told Dr Russell that at this point I felt like telling them to shove it up their arse but he implored me to see it through.

I left his office and the morning felt even colder.

London was coming at the weekend. Tony Mowbray's Celtic were a fucking disaster, capitulating at Tannadice after going one up and Tony uttered the immortal "We'll just take it on the chin" and at that moment you knew his career at Celtic was all over bar the shouting.

Paul and I went to London the following weekend. All hopes of relaxation were spoiled by Paul's dress sense and the fact that our digs couldn't accommodate us in the first night and we were sent to a place Terry Waite would have turned his nose up at. Pissed on the Saturday night, we watched The Jonathan Ross show, where guesting was Peter Kay. Paul went into a drunken rant about how he didn't think Peter Kay was funny before proceeding to laugh like fuck at everything he said. The purpose of the trip, as well as saving me from suicide, was to go to Arsenal v Chelsea. I had one ticket and would get another down there but at £55 for the cheapest, I gave Paul the ticket I had, he being a big Arsenal fan, and I watched Didier Drogba, and Chelsea, destroy Arsenal 3-0, from the comfort of a north London boozer.

Something funny happened to me that day, for the first time in my life I didn't mind sitting in the pub all day on my own. I'd never felt like that before and it dawned on me that my social and communication skills had reached such a low point that I didn't want to talk to anyone. More though, I didn't want anyone talking to me. Paul was fine, he came back in like a drowned rat, because he is a low maintenance type of friend, if you discount his constant worrying and need to text his bird every 10 seconds, and I could handle that. Normal, every day, social situations were becoming a big problem though and I knew it.

Still on came the mask and I said nothing, even managing to laugh when Paul approached and repelled various women and even appeared to have the facial expression of a stroke victim by the end of the trip.

The only things keeping me going were Trisha, Jake and Gary Haley.

Oh, and the fact I decided I would definitely go back to America in the summer of 2010.

The Waiting Room

"If you see oppression of the poor, and justice and righteousness trampled in a country, do not be astounded"

King Solomon

The minute I thought about going back to America, it fitted. I felt a weight come off, it gave me a purpose again. Obviously I had an enormity of loose ends in America, I still had no idea what had happened or, more importantly, why it had all happened. I knew this though, I missed New York. I had spoken to Trisha and she immediately agreed to it, saying that whatever problems we had, we would overcome. You know, small problems like having a baby with us, having no work to go to, or a house, oh and wondering if we would even get back in the country, particularly Public Enemy No1 Larkin.

Before all that though there was a Glasgow derby and an appointment with these fuckers re the ESA. It has to be said that Tony Mowbray's Celtic battered Rangers in January 2010 but he made one fatal error, dropping Scott McDonald. This was exemplified beautifully when Scott came on, at 0-0 and Celtic having missed a hatful of chances, and scored with his first touch. Still, we didn't care, we had gone one up with 12 minutes to go. Rangers equalised a minute later and that was that.

I don't know if Tony Mowbray had decided to break up the team before that game but, soon after, Caldwell, McManus. Robson and McDonald were gone. A raft of signings and loans came in and the biggest was last. I was sitting in my house in

Leith and it was a dark night even though it was only 5pm. I had Sky Sports News on as it was transfer deadline day and Jim White came on, I thought, to close the day (That's his job isn't it), when he said "And right on the deadline we have the biggest transfer of the window, Robbie Keane is on his way to Celtic"

I almost fell off the couch.

Sober.

This was exciting, no doubt about it. Robbie Keane had been a player I had admired since his Coventry days when he scored a goal against Arsenal that made a laughing stock of the biggest cock, David Seaman. He had scored over 50 goals for Ireland and was a top player, no doubt about it. There was also the fact that there was a Celtic connection and the fans loved it. maybe we could still drag this league back to us?

We got beat 1-0 the next night at Kilmarnock and, even though it was his debut, Keane was hopeless, no doubt about it.

My mind was on my appointment with the ESA people and the appointment was February 8th.

It was a dull morning when I went up to York Place for the appointment. In a way I was happy it was happening now as I could get it over with and get on with my recovery. Some of the methods Dr Russell had given me were working and there was a target of a year to get off the tablets.

I got in and took my place in a waiting room full of worried looking people.

Death Row would be chirpier.

I was called after around 20 minutes and I was ready. It would be a good opportunity for me to get my story out again and look at options from here on in.

Aye, right.

I was shown to a seat and a woman in her mid 40's sat down and asked me what my problems were and I proceeded to tell her my story when she stopped me mid sentence and said, in as cunty a way as possible, "I'll stop you there, I'm not interested in why they are happening, just what they are"

Ok.

So I told her about the anxiety attacks, the night terrors, my fear of going out, the horrors I felt when someone came to the door, my suicidal thoughts, my high temper and low tolerance.

She said, in a confused way, "So there's nothing physically wrong with you?"

I may be dumb but I ain't no dumb ass and at that point I genuinely considered punching her in the face. I could see what was going on and what her game was and I was exasperated. She ticked a few boxes on a clipboard of paper as this level of pish went on and on before she said I'd hear in about a week and looked at me as if to say "Get the fuck out"

Walking out that building, a massive panic attack came over me. So much so that I had to sit down as I thought I was going to have a heart attack. I got home eventually and Trisha asked me what was wrong. It was freezing outside but I was sweating like I was in a sauna. I told her and she reassured me that all would be ok. After wanting to go up and batter the living fuck out of the woman I had just spoken to.

It takes a special type of cunt to be someone who tries to scare the shit out of someone with mental health problems. Like a grass for the social or a tax inspector. Ok, maybe the latter is ok now... but it was obvious to me that the plan was to tell every cunt attending these interviews that they had to "Pull yourself together" . I had agreed a plan with Dr Russell, things were bad just now but slightly better, now I was plunged back into a black hole of fear and paranoia.

The next day I booked flights for the three of us to America.

I did it on a whim. I'd had enough. I was going to get fuck all help here and had to face my demons.

See I must tell you that after I came back from New York, I couldn't hear about it. Couldn't watch anything on TV about it, didn't want to talk about it. I wouldn't even watch American films, that's how bad I was.

Then a film came out that I fancied. Primarily because it had De Niro and Pacino in it. Righteous Kill isn't a great movie but when I saw it in the cinema that day I was watching the police station I was taken to and the jail I ended up in. Scared the shit out of me.

I began to realise that I'd spend a life of longing and wondering if I didn't try to get back to New York and I had to face it again. Or die.

So flights were booked.

To Chicago.

Mobbed Up

"Persecution produced its natural effect on them. It found them a sect; it made them a faction"

Thomas Babington

There were a number of issues about going back to New York. The main one being, how could I face anyone after the 4-0 mauling Tony Mowbray's last Celtic team took at St Mirren Park.

Neil Lennon was brought in to steady the ship and it worked, save for a 2-0 defeat to Ross County at Hampden that had "inevitable" written all over it, to the point where won every league game from there on in.

I think I've been pretty honest with you so far in the book and have to keep it real to get the whole story out there. The charges I had faced in New York were very serious. I was told the day I was arrested I was looking at seven years minimum. This made me a marked man. As well as jailing me, taking everything I owned, harassing me on two different continents and generally painting me as Al Capone, there were many other things that went on. For example, since I had came back from New York in August 2008, I'd flown to Limerick(three times), Derry, Munich and London. On every occasion, there and back, I was pulled in and questioned. At one airport, every single person on the flight I was on used the new fancy passport readers with ease, all going through no problem, except, guess who? On three occasions in Leith and one at my Ma's I was visited by plain clothes police.

Word was reaching from The Big Apple that shit was happening also. As a birthday gift, I'd got tickets for Gary and his wife for Don Rickles. When they got there someone else was sitting in there seats, with the exact same tickets. I wrote previously how I used to send stuff to folk all over, gifts, from NYC, all of a sudden those people were getting customs bills for hundreds of pounds/dollars. My Red Bulls season tickets were inexplicably cancelled, despite the fact I'd paid cash up front for both. A Christmas holiday in Orlando I had bought and paid for was cancelled without explanation.

There were many other things happening too, and they were bad, but nothing compared to the worst aspect of all the shit.

The day after I was arrested, my son James was supposed to be coming over to NYC. I'd paid for his flights, and for his Mother's flights, plus a week in a hotel for her so she could take him back. James was supposed to be staying a month and in that month we were going to Los Angeles for a week so he could go to the David Beckham Soccer camp.

Making that call to him to, in the situation I was in, was one of the hardest things I've ever had to do in my life. It broke his heart.

Mine too.

I learnt later that it was a common Government tactic to fuck with "Known associates of organised crime" Did you read that there, I'm a known associate of organised crime.

That's what they say, but why?

Well.

All this comes from something known as the Rico Act. I'm sure you know it or at least can Google it, but John Gotti summed it up best "Let me get this straight, this means that if anybody, anywhere is caught doing anything, then everyone up and down the line can be arrested for it. This is a law?"

I should say at this point that John Gotti's HQ, The Bergen Hunt and Fish Club, in Ozone Park, was five minutes from my house in Queens. This was the main headquarters for The Gambino Family. There and the social club in Mulberry Street, Little Italy, Manhattan.

How does this all affect me?

Down with the LCN (Part 2)

"A rumour that followed me forever was that my family was in the mafia. For years I had to live with it. They'd call me the mafia princess, so I rolled with it for the rest of high school. People even joke about it today"

Giuliana Rancic

As I said in *Poles 'N' Goals and Hesselink* (Did you know that PGH is available on Kindle now!) I know Mob guys. I have friends who are mobbed up. I'm not going to deny that. I've not seen or heard them talk about killing people or any that bullshit you see in the movies, The Mob is about making money. I know all this seems alien if you're not in NYC but people in NYC grow up with these guys, they influence everything and they can get you anything. Some people in NYC think they have never had any association with The Mob but I guarantee at least once their garbage was picked up by them, they bought a meal in one of their restaurants, drank in one of their bars, bought some of their clothes, bet from one of their bookies or even bought tickets from them for Shea or Yankee Stadium.

If the above are my charges, I plead guilty now.

Of course, those weren't my charges. Mine were:

Racketeering

Illegal Gambling

Menacing

Harassment

Second Degree Assault.

Doesn't look that good when it's on paper, huh?

Let me try and explain the FBI/NYPD thinking behind each charge.

Racketeering-

This basically when someone demands money for "protecting" a business. I was accused of doing this with four different businesses.

Illegal Gambling-

Fairly self explanatory. I was accused of being part of running a book on the NFL.

Menacing-

This is like threatening someone. The difference is you use a weapon. I was accused of threatening someone with a weapon.

Harassment-

Threatening again. Except repeating it. I was accused of threatening the same three people repeatedly.

Second Degree Assault-

GBH to you and I. I was accused of beating up someone.

Of course, as you're now aware, these were nothing compared to the attempted murder they wanted to charge me with but fucked up not having an arresting officer.

Now, I think I know you well enough to think that you're thinking right now "Well, did you do it then you fuck?"

Patience my friend, we need a good ending.

The Revolution Will Be Blogged (And Tweeted)

By Sean Walsh (Digital-Football.com)

The radio phone in, the back pages, the TV studio pundits and the heated debate down in the pub – if you're a football fan then it won't have taken you long to understand how important these aspects are to the life of a supporter. Football fanaticism goes so much further than catching the match highlights on the TV or getting to the odd game here and there. Instead, it's the in-depth insight into every aspect of your club – the AGM, the financials, even critique of the marketing department. The problem has always been that the journalists or board members hold all rights to access and fans have been subjected to their agendas and opinions. Not anymore.

The dawn of the social media age ushered in an entirely brand new way for fans to consume everything there is to know about their football club. With what started as mailing lists, soon became message boards and very later transforming into highly influential online social media networks that could command thousands of fans with the a keystroke.

The digital age of football gave football fans the access and platform they so long yearned to have, free of arrogance of the mainstream press and control of their own clubs. Fan influence has always been an important factor for the success of a football club, after all a wise man once said "football without the fans is nothing". So with a new found "online voice" and a network of likeminded fans ready to be mobilised, it became apparent that the digital fan could dictate everything from transfer policy to kit designs. If there's one thing football fans are good at, it's complaining.

Celtic has long been a club with a very vocal and active internet presence. Many of today's larger message boards such as CelticMinded.com or The Huddleboard can trace their origins as far back as 15 years, which may not sound much to the ordinary man, but in the social media world this is impressive.

Celtic has always been "more than a club" in that it very much positions itself as a family rather than a set of supporters. It's no surprise then that the Celtic family took to the internet like water of a ducks back. Message boards quickly became the new family dinner table on which the family could sit around, debate recent games and often entertain into the wee hours of the morning. The internet meant that no longer did Celtic fans need to be restricted to Paradise, Celtic Supporters Clubs or any pub down the Gallowgate in order to talk all things Celtic, they now had a common location where geography and distance meant absolutely nothing. The first step into understanding the widespread growth of Football Social Media is a simple one – connectivity. With millions of fans across the globe, many never getting to walk into the famous Parkhead arena, the internet was a bridge to bring the already tight-knit Celtic family closer together. Combined with the level of fanaticism that every true football fan harbors, you suddenly have an incredibly powerful and multi-national online presence.

So what are the benefits, and consequences, of this online football presence and what does it mean for the future of the game – politically and commercially?

Politically: As already mentioned, the freedom to debate on an accessible and uncontrollable platform creates influence. Social Media like Twitter, Facebook and message boards have enabled thousands of fans to communicate very rapidly and easily. The speed at which messages are shared across social media channels has meant that traditional media can no longer keep up in a world where being second to the punch means nothing. More importantly, the viral nature of social media has massively raised the profile of normal fans to positions of power where they enjoy the same (if not more) levels of influence and authority around footballing matters than some of the game's most senior figures including CEOs, journalists and football association officials. Social media sites give them a platform to make themselves heard as well as spread their message across the globe – all that matters is the quality of the content.

A very recent example of the power of Social Media amongst football fans has to be the ground-breaking investigative reporting of the demise of Celtic's former rival Glasgow Rangers. Rangers were millions of pounds in debt, facing a huge tax bill from HMRC, potentially going to court regarding legal matters and almost certainly in front of punishments from the Scottish FA, UEFA and perhaps FIFA. The mainstream media only really began to report Rangers' financial woes in 2011, some 4 years before social media message boards had been discussing the eminent financial meltdown of one of Scotland's largest and oldest institutions. In this case, the

Scottish media had been tight-lipped on the matter and had gone as far to call these bloggers "internet bampots" – ridiculing their opinions and even evidence. It's no surprise that 5 years later, some of the key "internet bampots" who dared do some investigative journalism of their own are now respected news sources and even a winner of the prestigious Orwell Prize, and of course Rangers were liquidated proving them entirely correct. The point demonstrated here is that Social Media is powerful and it is influential. Social Media, particularly amongst football fans, has completely changed the way the game is reported about in the media.

The people who hold all the power are no longer the journalists or the club directors but the players, the bloggers and the fans.

In the past 10 months English Premiership clubs have seen an astonishing 172% growth in the number of people who follow their accounts on Twitter, on Facebook they have seen a collective 20.5 million new Facebook fans. Celtic in less than 6 months has accumulated 62,000 followers on Twitter – that's more than Celtic Park's capacity. On Facebook they have notched up nearly 3 times that number with a very respectable 176,000 Facebook fans.

Football fans are flocking to social media channels at an exponential rate and it will soon catch up to the number of those watching it on their TVs. Fans can talk directly with their favourite players on Twitter, transfer deadline day signings appear on social media before TV and bloggers are the new sources of journalism – whether it's a match report or an inside look at what exactly the clubs financial accounts really mean. Most of all, fans love this – they love to see other fans doing well and providing them with the content. Fans naturally trust other fans – more so than they would trust "the brand" of a commercial football club.

Social Media has unleashed a new type of football fan – one who is technologically savvy, a master networker and one who isn't scared to make their opinion heard and spread across cyberspace. Social Media football fans take all that passion and fanaticism and channel it into things like the Rangers Tax case blog which eventually won the prestigious Orwell Prize, and of course Rangers were liquidated proving them entirely correct. The point demonstrated here is that Social Media is powerful and it is influential. Social Media, particularly amongst football fans, has completely changed the way the game is reported about in the media.

The people who hold all the power are no longer the journalists or the club directors but the players, the bloggers and the fans.

In the past 10 months English Premiership clubs have seen an astonishing 172% growth in the number of people who follow their accounts on Twitter, on Facebook they have seen a collective 20.5 million new Facebook fans. Celtic in less than 6 months has accumulated 62,000 followers on Twitter – that's more than Celtic Park's capacity. On Facebook they have notched up nearly 3 times that number with a very respectable 176,000 Facebook fans.

Football fans are flocking to social media channels at an exponential rate and it will soon catch up to the number of those watching it on their TVs. Fans can talk directly with their favourite players on Twitter, transfer deadline day signings appear on social media before TV and bloggers are the new sources of journalism – whether it's a match report or an inside look at what exactly the clubs financial accounts really mean. Most of all, fans love this – they love to see other fans doing well and providing them with the content. Fans naturally trust other fans – more so than they would trust "the brand" of a commercial football club.

Social Media has unleashed a new type of football fan – one who is technologically savvy, a master networker and one who isn't scared to make their opinion heard and spread across cyberspace. Social Media football fans take all that passion and fanaticism and channel it into whatever digital crusade they are currently on – whether that's causing the destruction of your greatest ally or putting pressure on an underperforming manager or team. Fans are now political, so it's time clubs started to treat them a little less like a customer and more like an influencer.

Commercially: The future of Social Media in football will massively rely on the investment and level of interaction that comes from the clubs themselves. In order for clubs to unlock budget to allow them to do a half decent job on social – and by decent I mean engaging with their fans in a creative and innovative way, not just flogging jerseys and lunch boxes – they need to understand how to commercialise the brand on social media.

Manchester City are arguably the best major football club worldwide that succeed at understanding and deploying social media to their fan base. Whilst City don't have the same number of Likes or Twitter followers than the likes of Arsenal or Manchester United – they do have one of the fastest growing and most praised social media presences in the world. The secret to their success? Not selling products.

City excel because they treat their brand not as a marketing brand but as an entertainment brand. They see football as a piece of entertainment that everybody can go and enjoy; you don't need to be a fan to visit the Etihad Stadium. Whilst many clubs continue to use social as a way to market match day tickets, hospitality evenings or merchandise, City use social as a means to entertain and engage their fans. How do they do this? By giving the fans what they really want.

As already stated, fans need to know every possible insight about their club they can. City feed this need by using social media to provide them content that no other club would even think about giving away. For example, City place cameras in the tunnel at every home game and in the training ground. They collect, edit and sort through hours of footage to find the moments and insights that the fans want to experience – so City's dramatic winner to clinch the EPL championship was caught on camera. Fans got to experience so much more than the locker room content, but the emotions and events of all the background staff who are never seen, the opposition players reactions after the game, the pre-match rituals and even a very humorous video of a few of City's African-based players astonishment at the rain outside the tunnel. Similarly in the training ground they used social media to follow what happens to a player when they sign on by shadowing Owen Hargreaves on the day it was announced he would be a City player. They don't just interview the player, but they interview the doctor, the grounds man, the kit man and even the social media team themselves. This level of "inside access" appeals to a football fan and is more likely to be watched, shared and commented on than a bog standard 400 word press release.

So what are the commercially benefits? Why do all of this? Why spend the money on nice videos?

Difficult questions, but not unanswerable. Increased engagement with your fans creates loyalty, loyalty creates quality customers and quality customers produces revenue. As any football fan knows, loyalty is regularly tested – a run of a few bad games, a bad signing or a bad substitution can make you question whether you want to turn up on a December morning in the freezing cold rain and watch your team obliterated by Ross County. What usually starts as negative comments on a fans message board can very quickly become a mobilisation of a full scale protest outside the stadium on a match day. 200, 2000 or 20,000 fans protesting or criticising the club all makes for bad PR, and bad PR usually ends up with a drop in season tickets and merchandise sales. By creating wealth of loyalty and rewarding loyalty – even when clubs don't really need to, they can offset and slow this gradual transition when things turn sour. By using engaging content they can do more than sell match day sales; they can sell an experience and identity to the consumer. By using social media channels they can target and reach out to fans, old and new, across the globe.

This is where Celtic are moving towards and really need to be, more so than ever.

The future of football social media lies in understanding the fans psyche and tailoring content to meet their needs, not the clubs. Money can still be made and whilst it's a long term plan – it yields greater results in regards to international fan base, *crisis management and fan loyalty. Somewhere, many clubs have forgotten that football is meant to entertain and as such they've neglected the fans or dealt with them like a car salesman talks to his customers. Social Media is the perfect vehicle to promote an entertaining brand, it moves quickly and the fans are already there just waiting to be directed to the right place. If clubs ignore this then they risk finding themselves in the same position the Scottish journalists did – out of date, alienated and made to look like fools.*

One Night, Nine Hours and the Longest Hour

"We travel, some of us forever, to seek other states, other lives, other souls"

Anais Nin

Why Chicago?

Well, I have a very good friend there. More of him later. The main reason was "Getting in". You see, after all the shit I'd gone through, I wasn't sure how my Green Card stood. I spoke to the American Embassy in London, at £1 a minute, and they were helpful saying all was fine BUT reminded me that the guy, the border agent dude whoever it may be, could still say no. I knew that and wasn't overly keen in getting into a situation where I get a guy in NYC who raises a flag and suddenly I'm in an orange jump suit again. I was still in the land of the unknown and had no idea if people were still looking for me in New York so I decided that we wouldn't arrive in New York state. The second thing was, we needed a holiday before getting back to the grind. Let's not forget, as much as I had gone through in the last two years, Trisha had gone through it all as well and had a baby too. So after a few discussions and a few emails, Chicago was offered and gladly accepted.

The summer of 2010 was a mixed bag for us then. We spent a lot of time giving stuff away from the house, tying up loose ends, and spending as much time with James as possible. James was a rock then. He was four years older than the last time I left and he totally understood it this time.

That all said, it didn't stop his father crying buckets when he said goodbye.

So our plan was to fly to London, stay a night in an airport hotel, and then fly to Chicago the following day. We flew down and the flight went fine until Jake decided to be sick all over the plane just as we came into land. After we cleaned it up, we went to our hotel and actually had a relaxing evening. We were free of Edinburgh and all the nightmares we had, mostly my own personal ones, and for a brief moment we could be a normal family again.

The following day we made our way to the airport and I had a feeling of nerves and excitement. Nerves at the very real prospect that I may not get back in America and then what? I hadn't quite given my flat yet, I'm not that fucking stupid, but mentally I'd left Edinburgh, I'd said goodbye to all who mattered to me and most of all, I needed this. The excitement came from the fact that in nine hours, nine poxy hours, I could close this nightmare chapter of my life, that had gone on for two years, and start a new one.

As we queued at the gate, maybe behind 40 other people, the stewardess at the front of the queue motioned for us to come forward.

Oh fur fucks sake.

My heart was pumping as we walked forward, fully expecting to be told we were being stopped, arrested or whatever.

These kind of things were happening regularly and I won't bullshit you, they were taking their toll on my health, what hair I had was going grey and I perspired more than Big Mooney in a peep show.

Then the girl said "Please stay here, we will put you on the plane first" Then she played with Jake.

Wow.

So we got on the plane and thanks to Jake's horrific behaviour for nine hours, we basically ended up with our own section. After the usual long flight type shite of bad films and worse food, the hour was approaching. Trisha and I looked at each other in a "Here we go" type of way and I psyched myself up. Although the last 24 hours had been stressful, the real horror would start if the border patrol guy "Can you follow me?"

We got to immigration and there was a huge queue. It was hot, Jake, as usual, was cranky and we were scared shitless.

We had to crawl round for an hour, watching lots of people get pulled up and told to wait.

A sure sign that you're fucked.

We got called and, as a family, we went over. Carrying Jake, I handed over our passports. The guy scanned them, looked at the info and then asked me for a thumbprint and retina scan. I complied and as he looked at the info, Jake yelped, and the guy said "He just wants to go to sleep" and smiled.

My blood pressure lowered a bit.

After what seemed like an age, he calmly handed us our passports and said "enjoy your stay"

That was it. No questions, no "explain this", nothing.

I took the passports and motioned to Trisha to follow Jake and I. My arms were almost falling off carrying Jake but I had to hold it together.

We walked past a row of people who had been stopped. Poor bastards who will face an uncertain future. None of them were terrorists.

We though, had others things on our mind then.

Our new life had just begun.

Nigel's Yank, Chicago Mikey, Mick The Yank or Gunner Mike

"A desire arises in the mind. It is satisfied immediately another comes. In the interval which separates two desires a perfect calm reigns in the mind. It is at this moment freed from all thought, love or hate. Complete peace equally reigns between two mental waves."

Sivananda

One thing I can speak with total authority on is when you are at your lowest ebb, some people stand by you, others fly the nest. One guy who stood by me was Mike Boyd from Chicago.

I've known Mike since I first got on the internet regularly 13 years ago. I first met him in Las Vegas in 2005. I say met, after a mega session, I got to my bed, with newly acquired company it has to be said, around 7am when around 45 minutes later the phone in my room went and Mike was on the end of the lined and he commanded me, after being delegated by one Thomas Donnelly, to come down and collect my dinner dance tickets.

Bleary eyed and hungover to fuck, I made my way down and met Mike. I have to say that, out of the entire world population, there are very few people who could have kept me from going right back upstairs and Mike turned out to be one of them. Way back in July 2008, I got the following text from Mike:

"I'm not sure what your bail conditions are, but you are welcome to stay with me as long as you like"

I almost cried when I read that text.

You see the day I got it, it was an hour after reading an email from someone which said, summarising, *"I've had a great summer, can't help you, see you later"*

So when a low ebb came again and I explained to Mike that I had to come back and face my demons, he said *"You know my offer still stands"*

It felt great booking the tickets but nowhere close to walking through arrivals at O'Hare and seeing Mike there. See, because of the delay, he had been waiting well over an hour and was worried. So much so that he had started to thumb his phone for lawyers. That sums Mike up. A lot of guys I know, with great intentions it has to be said, would be wanting to steamroller in there, shouting the odds, Mike was staying cool. That's why he is the perfect ying as VP of the NAFCSC.

He looked genuinely elated to see us when we came through arrivals and in all the bullshit of life sometimes it's easy to forget how little moments like this can be enormous in life, just like someone being glad to see you. There is so much selfishness in the world now that you get that rarely, same with others putting you first or thinking about you unprompted.

It also dawned on me that although Mike could drive, he didn't own a car, yet had hired a huge people carrier to fit in the three of us and all our luggage too. That's thinking.

As we travelled through the Chicago streets, the sun set and a calmness overcame us. Jake crashed out and it was dark when we got to Mike's house.

He ordered Pizza and we put Jake to bed.

Than I called Gary and said "We're putting the band back together..."

The Game Changer - Part 2

I often wonder if Phil Mac Giolla Bhain had any inclination at all that the second Dougie MacDonald overturned that penalty at Tannadice, many lives would never be the same again, none more so than Phil's.

There are many things that can change your life. People say swimming with Dolphins does. being saved from near death, finding faith or even meeting the right partner. All of these require the same thing, at some point you need to hang your balls out there and go for it.

It is often called "Walking into the Volcano"

Immediately after that game at Tannadice, a cover up was taking place. Of course, we did not know this as supporters but then most of us suspected anyway. Hugh Dallas was amplified all over the media to tell everyone what had happened, that it was in fact Assistant Referee Steven Craven who had alerted Referee Dougie MacDonald that it wasn't a penalty. He alerted him by saying into his mic "Dougie, Dougie"

The press swallowed it and we were called paranoid again.

Then something happened that Hugh Dallas, the SFA and the media never thought would, someone broke ranks.

Steven Craven did an interview totally refuting Dallas claims and saying not only were they all nonsense, he was bullied into repeating these version of events AND they had lied to Neil Lennon.

As pressure grew on Dallas, he was busy organising a strike for all referees to save his own neck, of course we did not know that yet.

Then Paul Brennan from Celtic Quick News got hold of an email. It was sent by Hugh Dallas and it mocked both Pope Benedict and child abuse. It was sent from an SFA address.

Paul knew this was huge.

He knew he needed someone to manage this properly so maximum exposure was guaranteed. So he contacted Phil Mac Giolla Bhain.

And if you know Phil, you know Phil is running into that volcano.

All sorts of machinations were going on behind the scenes, all of which you can read about in *A Rebel Journalist* by Phil Mac Giolla Bhain.

My own take is when I look back on my youth, it's littered with sunny days. I had plenty hurdles to overcome, a low income household and having Perthes Disease were hard things to deal with looking back but then if it's all you know, you just get on with it. My football memories all through the 80's are pretty fantastic because Celtic won something almost every year and, if they didn't, they went down fighting.

Then things changed.

I was 16 in 1990, on the cusp of starting work for the first time, feeling comfortable in pubs and realising there were women other than the ones at school with me. Sadly the 90's were a disaster up until 1998. That's because no matter how many good bevvy sessions you have or good looking girls you meet, if you're like me, your memories come in seasons not years.

We won the league in 1998, ten long years after the previous one. Then, after a couple of seasons where it looked like we may slip back to mediocrity, Martin came and things were never the same again, save for eight months with Tony Mowbray. Yet even in the Martin era we still couldn't really enforce how good a team we were because we lost leagues and dropped silly cups. No one could figure out why.

A Rangers juggernaut spoiled most of my youth. From around the age of 16 I realised they were pretty much unstoppable. On and off the park. I remember one point, October 30th 1994, where Rangers thrashed us 3-1 at our adopted "home" of Hampden and their supporters absolutely reveled in it. This was six months after the Fergus McCann takeover and the feeling that day was one of hopelessness. No matter what we did, they always had an edge. It felt at these times that everything was against us, the refs, the media, everything.

Would we ever come back?

As I said, I first became aware of Phil Mac Giolla Bhain around 2008. He was writing about the so-called "famine" song and was writing stuff I agreed with. I followed his blog from there on in and was captivated by his articles, some great, some thought-provoking, some I never agreed with but none that were ever boring.

A couple of years later I was in The Celtic House in The Bronx watching Celtic thrash Aberdeen 9-0. It was one of those glorious days that happen every so often with Celtic and as I walked home that day I was on top of the world. Logging in to www.celticminded.com as I often do after games I was unprepared for what was about to unfold. Quite frankly, Phil was about to set the Internet on fire and start the process of vindication for The Celtic Family. As I sat glued to the screen the walls of bigotry at the SFA were tumbling down as Phil laid out the story on his blog, Hugh Dallas had been caught sending an anti-Catholic email. I took a long intake of breath. I'd never forgiven Dallas for his performance on May 2nd 1999, inventing penalties and flashing red cards at us with pleasure and here he was smearing The Pope, after years of us being told we were paranoid when we questioned his integrity. Soon he was fired, we were delighted.

If Phil's involvement in Scottish football ended then I think it's not a bad C.V. at all. However we now know, as one great man once said, it was just the beginning.

Phil was the first guy I ever saw write the phrase "Rangers Tax Case". As the story unfolded on his blog it was clear that something colossal was happening. Scotland's Watergate and Enron were being laid out in the same story and it's all about one club, Rangers, yeah, that team ruined my youth. With a ruthless streak that Charles Bronson would have been jealous of, Phil took a scalpel to Rangers and trumped the old media time and again and another phrase was born "New Media". He also was able to do that thing that means people are really taking notice of you: all you had to do was mention his first name and people knew who you meant.

I heard Phil around this time talking on The LostBhoys podcast and he said something that stuck with me:

"No more back of the bus"

I loved that.

You see the reference, of course, was to Rosa Louise Parks, a prim, bespectacled, 42 year old African American woman who refused to give up her seat to a white man on the Cleveland Avenue bus in Montgomery, Alabama. Her act started a 381 day boycott of the city's bus system led by Dr Martin Luther King and is widely considered to be birth of the Civil Rights movement in America.

In our world of Celtic and Scottish football, what Phil did by taking on Rangers in public was to inspire a wealth of Celtic supporters the world over to embrace a new way of thinking. Things could be different and that we could sit at the front of the bus any time we liked.

There were many bumps on the way but this battle ended with the death of Rangers, and as all their cheating and corruption of the last two decades was laid out, the vindication of people like you and me.

It also means that we will never again have to sit and listen to the triumphalism of that Rangers I mentioned from 1994, because they are gone. And Celtic came back and we shall not be moved.

Phil played a monumental part in the death of Rangers and for that I will always be grateful.

The Men On The Moon

"And then when I went to Chicago, that's when I had these outer space experiences and went to the other planets"

Sun Ra

I should explain that the chapter that referred to Mike Boyd previously got that title due to all the nicknames he has had. There is so much to Mike that you could write a book about him alone. For example, he was on the famous TV quiz show Jeopardy in the 90s. He won the small matter of $42,000. What did he do with his winnings? Spent most of it watching football around the UK. Celtic, of course, plus his other teams Arsenal and a soft spot for Wimbledon and then AFC Wimbledon. Watching Arsenal and Wimbledon was what got him the nicknames, this was the early 90s and there wasn't the football tourism you get now so folk weren't used to hearing Chicago accents at games. Not that Mike is a football tourist, he has a knowledge of football as good as anyone I have met and a football library that I would die for.

The welcome Mike gave us in his house was out of this world. Although, this is America, things never run smoothly. After less than 24 hours, we were complained about. A note came under Mike's door asking us to keep the noise down. That noise was Jake running about and us trying to keep him under control, nothing else. This cow downstairs was clearly enraged that some had infringed on her precious life with, God forbid, real life. Not only that, she emailed Mike, furious at her idyllic existence had been threatened by normal people. I put a note back under her door, this is America remember, apologising but fucking raging at the fact that some fucking cow had made us feel unwelcome already. I saw her not long after it and, to be polite, a fucking sniper wouldn't take her out. If you ever read this, have a fucking beer, get laid, listen to The Who, chill the fuck out and remember the world doesn't cunting revolve around you. Also, all your cats? a clear reference to the fact that no one touches your pussy.

Anyway.

I have to say at this point that we loved Chicago. We were five minutes from the beach, 20 minutes from downtown and a short walk to Wrigley Field. After the stress of getting there and the boot downstairs, Saturday came and Mike asked me if I would like to spend the day drinking and watching football at his pub.

Oh I didn't mention the fact he was a part owner in a bar?

Oh yes.

So at 7am, we walked down to The Globe on West Irving and, wait a sec, I'm wrong, we got a cab, we walked back after it, and arrived on a beautiful Chicago morning, so beautiful that on a pissing down day in Scotland as I write this, my mind wanders to it...

The Globe is a huge football bar and had fans of all EPL clubs in it for games. Apart from that, it was fine like.

We spent a good eight hours eating and drinking, whilst watching a series of games and left to stagger out into that bright sunshine/totally pished feeling that all US fans of football will know, having been drinking for eight hours and it's still only 3pm. As Mike often said "I'm an early morning alcoholic".

As we walked back to his apartment, Mike asked me what our plans were, I told him they were to stay in Chicago for a while, then go to NYC, find a place and settle down for a bit. Mike said "you know you're always welcome here, and I'd certainly see about getting you both hooked up for an income, you know that"

Did I tell you I love Mike Boyd?

In all honesty, although we knew we would be going to New York again, we did love Chicago. If you've never been, it has a Greenwich Village vibe with beaches all around it and that mid west friendly attitude that can make you go all gooey when a waitress talks to you. We had some great days in Chicago. From Kathy Osterman Beach, to the Magnificent Mile, I felt myself falling in love with America again. Mike has season tickets at Wrigley Field and it was just one of those nights when he took me there, a Monday, where nothing really eventful happened, it was just a great night where everything went well, we had great seats, the Cubs won, pretty girls sat in front of us, the beer and dogs at the game were great, it was a beautiful night and we had a great drink after it.

Male bliss.

Incidentally, American bars are the best in the world. Fuck all these morons you see on TV saying Obama is a muslim or screaming hate about stuff they have no fucking idea about, you want the real America? You want to meet real Americans? Go to a bar. The beer is cheap, mostly, the people are always friendly, every night is a party night and no one is uptight.

Think about that, you go out in Scotland now and half the cunts out are wanting to fight or make an arse of themselves. Throw in the prices and the fact you can't smoke anywhere, is it any wonder the pub game is dying here? I've walked through Harlem, South Bronx, areas of Queens and Brooklyn in the middle of the night and never had a single problem. In Scotland you can get hassle going to the fucking Ice Cream Van.

Trisha, Jake and I spent a lot of time at the beach and Jake touched sea water for the first time. The heat was incredible but we didn't care. We were relaxing eve though we were getting some amount of headcases due to our involvement with Craig's List. Steady. If you're not aware if it, it's basically a website that people sell stuff on. We were looking at houses in New York and anything that looked too good to be true, was. The first one we went for, an African sounding gentleman called me one day as we sat at a lake and said that house we had enquired about was ours. He rambled on and on about how happy he was to rent it to us and all I had to do was write a cheque for $1800, send it to him in Nigeria and the keys would be sent to me. Sure pal, why don't I send you $2000 cause I like you so much? Then there were properties that were advertised that when you put them onto Google Maps, they didn't exist. Many people were delighted to rent to us, just as long as we were able to send them cash up front and always to a bizarre bank account. Even when we thought we had finally secured a place, the day we eventually arrived in NYC, we met the guy, he showed us the place and then said "So if you just show me your credit reports from the last two years, we're good to go" Um, we haven't been here in the last two years, we don't have any "Oh, ok, you give me $1150 right now and I'll see what I can do" I'll tell you what you can do, you can let us out before I put my ever expanding forehead right on tae yer coupon ya cunt.

Still though, that was in the near future, for now we were happy to chill and re-charge our batteries which was very much needed.

It was also good to spend time as a family again, even though it was in Chicago that we got our first real signs of what a handful Jake would become. In all honesty, we didn't see much of Mike, he helped immensely when my bank froze my account as I hadn't told them where I'd be, but one memorable night with him was spent in his local bar where he really opened up and spoke of a few things that have happened to him that made him sad. I felt we really bonded that night and we talked a lot of shit out that I think helped both of us. Yeah, we were drunk, but talking over your problems is cathartic and as we staggered out that night, I felt comfortable enough to ask Mike a question that had been bothering me since I'd arrived

"Mike, is that moon up there closer to us than it would be in Scotland?"

We did what all men would do in that situation, rushed back to his house, broke out a couple of beers, looked it up, confirmed it was, then spent all night talking about it.

I'd found my Chicago Gary.

Dancing With Myself

"Catch me at the X with OG at a Yankee game, Shit, I made the Yankee hat more famous than a Yankee can,"

Jay Z

After a great time in Chicago, it was time to head to NYC. I was pretty scared. After being able to forget for a while, fear overcame me and not because of the bad turbulence we encountered on the plane. No one was coming to meet us, work commitments and other stuff was told to us, fine, we understood some but were disappointed in others. Cest La Vie. From my perspective, I was glad not to have been arrested on landing and even the traffic on the Major Deegan couldn't quell my delight at that. I called Gary and when I think of it now, I think he was a bit shellshocked that I was actually back. It was Wednesday and we would see him Friday, as he and his family were watching Jake whilst Trisha and I attended a family wedding. Straight from arrival, we had our "$1150" incident that meant, after the five days we had in a hotel in Tuckahoe, we were homeless. You will have read, in the postscript of Albert, Dougie and Wim, what happened next, we had nowhere to go and Gary put us up, then we got a place but had to make a five day pit stop in North Bergen, a hotel, before moving into our new place on October 1st 2010.

Who the fuck would be my wife, right?

Our new place was small, far too small for our needs, but it was a roof over our heads. Trisha got sorted with a job pretty quickly, thanks to our connections, and the plan was for me to watch Jake, and get my head together until I figured out what the fuck I was going to do with the rest of my life. As much as I hate going back to it, just over two years previous, I was loaded, had a great place, tons of work and had little to worry about. Then I spent two years ill and skint, so my head wasn't exactly with it.

Trisha went out to work, I paid a month rent and a month security, and we tried to settle into a normal life again. It wasn't easy. We had no furniture for a week, I had to buy a cot for Jake the day we moved in and we slept on a blow up mattress for a good few weeks. Until I found the Walmart website anyway. You see I did spend one day, on foot, trawling round furniture stores fruitlessly and at that point I felt fucking off on the next plane home. Still, gradually we got furniture in, thanks to Walmart's excellent delivery service and Trisha being Trisha had the place looking pretty good in no time.

I joined the Bronx Bhoys CSC and my first game as a member, although I'd been in it a few times before, was that 2-0 defeat at Tynecastle where nothing went right. At this point, I should not have been too bothered, we had a home again, money coming in and Jake could settle. Still, despite all that, I was hurting bad after that game.

The old fire was coming back.

Some of you will know that I am a huge New York Yankees fan and it soon dawned on me that I was now living a mere 20 minutes from the stadium. I managed to secure a ticket for play off game against Texas and although Texas won, something happened that night that will stay with me forever.

In the seventh inning at Baseball games they stop selling alcohol. I had a few beers, just enough for a glow and pulled down my new Yankee cap when they announced that no more alcohol would be sold. As I did, sweat came from my brow and into may eyes so I pulled the cap back up to wipe my forehead. As I did, a voice behind me said "It is you, right?" and my heart sank. I slowly turned round and saw a guy looking right at me, where the fuck did I know him from? He put his hand out and said "You made it man" and it hit me, the guy was on my block in Rikers. In my nervous delirium I asked him what he meant by making it and he replied "Last time I saw you, you were sitting eating lumpy fucking bread in an orange jump suit, now you're here in Yankee blue, you made it"

I could have kissed him.

I did kiss him.

I got the train to Woodlawn that night and felt ten feet tall.

Like I used to feel in New York.

All I had to do now was figure out what I would do next.

Typically, Gary would provide the answer.

Hell Hath No Fury Like Gary Haley Scorned

"I never lie because I don't fear anyone. You only lie when you're afraid."

John Gotti

If you've read all my books, you'll know a lot about Gary Haley. Yet if you met him, you'd probably think it was a different guy than in the books. Gary has done so many things for me that I could never not love him. When I think back over the ten years I've known him, there are only three times he's ever pissed me off

1) He drove me 120mph up Queens Boulevard one night in a car that the fucking Griswalds would reject.

2) He was organising a night out for us once where he said he wouldn't work that day and then slipped in that he was working first.

3) He once borrowed a Spiderman comic book from a girl I was dating and never gave it back.

That's it.

Put that against the fact that he has put me up, bailed me out, got me drunk, got me laid, stepped in front people for me, got me a kick ass Lawyer, been a best man, and been my tour guide in the greatest city on the planet, he's got a lot in the bank with me. In fact, he could have a wild affair with my wife and I'd still ask him what he was wanting to drink.

So one night, in the House of Brews off 8th Avenue, we were talking and watching NFL and I was telling him I was feeling good again, having seen a lot of my fears and demons leave me, that I was now ready to take a bite out of the big apple again. He looked at me, in that typical Gary Haley way, and said:

"You know how you're always talking about how that day at St Mirren in 86 is you favourite game ever?"

Yeah?

"Why don't you write a book about it? You're always talking about it with so much passion, that's what you should do"

I'm sort of guy who often needs someone to say "Yeah that's a great movie" or "I love that song" for my brain to kick in. So when he said it it felt right. I hadn't written that way for years and was apprehensive but willing to give it a go. (The apprehensions about "coming back" to writing about Celtic were the only 100% true thing in *Channeling Charlie Mulgrew...*)

The next day I fired up the laptop and started to write. Then I emailed Albert Kidd who, as usual, was 100% supportive.

I gave myself a target of two months to have some form of stuff down that could be turned into a book.

The night Gary said I should start writing again, I told him of my apprehensions and he said the following thing "Listen, I've seen you go though a lot of fucking shit in these past two, two and a half years, and it's eaten away at me, so never forget, I'll always have your back, always"

Everything I've written since has been with those words ringing in my ears.

I had no designs on selling the book I was writing, I just wanted to finish it, so could I say I did it. I had done some writing in the last two years, a book that would become *Coasters,* but I hadn't put it out or anything at this stage, it was all about the cathartic process. I'd write during the week then talk to Gary on Sundays on the phone and discuss things. Sometimes I'd end the call sweating, now that only happens with Babestation.

My life in New York was now looking after Jake full time, taking care of the house, doing the odd bit of research work(which, during a good run, managed to furnish our whole house), watching Celtic in the Celtic House, writing what would become *From Albert, With Love* and going out drinking with Gary on a Sunday or a Friday. With routine, came happiness. Trisha was working her ass off and whilst that could lead to tension when we both needed a break, things were ok. Despite it being December, the weather was great. I'd take Jake into Trisha's work and have a meal and a couple of beers. We even once went out, with Jake, on Halloween, with a couple of friends who were over from Ireland and Jake fell asleep early in the night, With none of the ridiculous licensing laws you get in Scotland, we were able to relax that night and enjoy ourselves. Some of you may frown on taking a one year old into a bar, but listen, when you have a young child, and no babysitters that don't cost $10 a hour, what would you do? Jake was looked after night and day, fed, clothed and clean, and I can say from both us, fuck anyone who judges us that hasn't walked a mile in our shoes.

Anyway.

This was a good period in our lives, we had a house again, money coming in and we were among friends once more and I was writing again.

So if you hate me or my writing, blame the landlady who gave us the house, the bar that gave Trisha a job or Jake who fell asleep that night.

I just wouldn't blame Gary Haley if I were you.

The Blogger

Blogging, I love it. What's it all about though? Step forward Mark McClay...

The exact moment I was asked to contribute by Paul, I was intently glued to 'Poles 'n' Goals and Hesselink' but with one eye sneakily checking my phone for updates when I noticed the tiny envelope appear at the header bar. Unlike the default size type envelope which indicates you have a new spam e-mail, this was one of those direct messages which can usually be easily disregarded as being a viral follower who advises you - ironically enough - to click on a link as someone has "written a really bad blog about you". One day, I'll do the routine deletion and message to the follower advising of their newly hacked status, only to be told, that no seriously - someone thinks you are a complete and utter imbecile & has furiously chosen to pen the hatred which boils up inside them every time they see your ridiculous profile image.

So what was an exiled bampot from the Big Apple doing, asking a bampot like me to comment on blogging for? Of this, I am still unsure, but I was honoured that he did.

Rewinding first to March 2011, when the Rangers Tax case site first published its initial blog - Could Rangers fans reading this have saved their club? If they were at first aware at that early stage of the financial plight their club faced, and its impending demise - would they have been able to stage a fight back akin to Celts for Change? Matt McGlone and select others I suppose were my first introduction to non or pre-internet bampottery. But what this blog & its contributors achieved was nothing short of astounding - delivering the facts on a plate, unbiased and undiluted on what Scotland and it's media was failing to tell you about the grave financial state of one of its "greatest institutions" (copyright of The Big Hoose punter).

They made political writing into an art form - after being awarded the 2012 Orwell Prize for blogging, being a site detailing the tax affairs of a sporting team, they altered the landscape of the winning entry through their incisive and amazingly well documented content. Other than the RTC - out of hundreds of supposed journalists in this country, only two from major media outlets showed themselves to have any gumption & willing to research the troubles across the city - Alex Thomson & Mark Daly, the only ones to put their heads above the parapet.

I keep now referring to their deathly status as if they were "being brought down", instead of correctly noting it is justice or, their comeuppance - this is due, in the main to their own breed treating it like the end of an establishment, governing body or dictator - some of the excuses and drivel posted on Follow Follow would have Comical Ali squirming in his grave.

So, apart from that major development in the past year, what makes these web blogs such an important tool in the modern age? In reference to my own personal experience, if there is something I feel passionately about or enthused enough to comment on - why not put those thoughts into words? My hope of being an aspiring writer may be on the wane (I'm almost thirty you know!), but through my own site, the opportunity is greater than it was just dreaming about it. In the beginning, it was created as an output primarily for my *views on Celtic - but I now find myself delving into World Football, mental health and social commentary - the diversity and the sheer uncertainty is what I enjoy the most.*

The ability to give every person with a view or a voice, a platform to be heard, considered and heralded, is truly a great and liberated ideal. The creativity & debate it can manifest is what makes it a wonderful stage for aspiring writers. It also harbors no prejudice or pre-conceptions about what the subject is, or most importantly, who delivers it. The fact they are published on the internet, only emphasises the depth of narrative and themes which can be explored - and only on the internet, would you find such people willing to acknowledge & indulge in some of them (my own one especially!).

Given the extensive reach which online blogging gives, the opportunity to reach a worldwide audience, harnesses a potentially life-changing and inspirational tool at your fingertips. Every inhabited continent, & every person with access to a technological device, has the chance to stumble access, search for and read your articles and viewpoints - all of which will be thought-provoking - even if your rambling away like Bomber Brown at one of his zombified rallies!

Paper journalists, columnists, news anchors and celebrities have taken to penning their thoughts and news on their own webpages, not only because of the developed worlds ongoing transition into the cyber medium, but because it can also enhance their own prospective line of media. Prior to Channel four news hitting our screens at seven pm, even a potentially explosive blog from Alex Thomson during the day would have the same audience and more tuning in to watch it detailed again on television that evening. So even though words can be hard-hitting - the shock factor of the same prose being delivered by mouth, direct in your living room, still packs a punch which is not quite as brutal as online.

Some of the more well-known media outlets & publications, have also deduced that in the everyday fan or untapped writer, there is a new depth and freshness to be explored through online blogging, which may have been lost through years of tedious note-taking, stop press' & editorial restraints. The honesty and human connection this can bring to a story, can open up a platform of new online readers and help to bridge the gap between the media and supporter.

There are some gaps though which may never be filled, as within them lies deep wounds, amassed through years of mistruths, misinformation & pandering to lavish dinner tickets from supposed untouchable figures. This in turn led to a period of bias from what was, one of Scotland's top news publications but is now dwindling in revenue, staff, readership & quality output - if there ever was any! What you are left with is an angry, bitter & poorly produced comic book orgy of Z-list tales and shockingly misguided and tired columns from one-time savvy journalists, who now run scared, intimidated by the new breed of up and coming bloggers & writers. These new visionary authors show no fear, and many have shown up their supposedly "qualified" counterparts in the main stream media by doing some of their own investigative work.

Scottish tabloids seem to think their duty is just to give you the story in the bluntest, most banal version they can pen - what they ought to be doing is investigating and uncovering layers, giving new dimensions to existing news and engaging their readers so they come away feeling educated and able to *debate and comment further. They seem reluctant to explore, in case they find some skeletons lurking where they once dined themselves - in hindsight, 'Thugs & Thieves' should have been a headline reserved for future use.*

What a Marvelous Substitution This Has Been...

"I had a good record against Hearts so I asked the boss, Archie Knox, if I could play. Thankfully, he agreed"

Albert Kidd

It's exciting writing a book. It gets more exciting if you know at least some folk will read what you're writing. Of course, when I started writing *From Albert, With Love* I didn't know if anyone would read it other than me but it was a labour of love for me to write and I was enjoying it. One of the first things I had to do was get in touch with people who were at the game or were old enough to remember it;. The book you're reading just now is probably me at my most confident in terms of writing. Back then though I wanted others on that paper with me. In all the books I've written, I'm not aware of anyone who has slagged off the stories, the material or any of the content. I normally get digs about grammar or a typo. One time this got to me a bit and I asked Irvine Welsh about it who said "If you care, you'll be the first schemie who gave a fuck about snobby pricks" I thought if he gets it, then I must expect it.

I'd had experience with two books, but these were years ago, I had no idea in December 2010 when I started writing then if anyone would like my stories. At this point I have to mention David Harper. Harper is one of my own, he looks at things like I do, calls a spade a spade and is always great with advice. Any time anyone puts a snidey dig in at me, he spots it. Like me, he may be dumb, but he ain't no dumb ass. I definitely have a much thicker skin now than I used to but back then you're always going to be apprehensive. I've been a bit of a lad in my time, a lot of folk, men and women, hate me, and I am attempting to put myself in the spotlight. The there is the fact that I had no real platform for the book bar around 150 "friends" on Facebook and 30 in Twitter.

Still.

None of this mattered as I had to finish it first and foremost. One of the first people I contacted was Allan Hosey. I knew he would be up for writing a piece as he will take any opportunity to tear into Jambos. I spoke to folk like John Paul Taylor, Jason Higgins and Jamie O'Neil constantly, Tims of that era for any snippets that could jog my memory. I pestered Albert Kidd of course but anyone in that situation knows you can't go too far or you become an actual pest.

What I've realised is that you can get better at writing the more you do it but it has nothing to do with practice. It is really important to have a clear mind when about to write. When you're on the piss in your 20s and 30s all time, it's very hard to be any good at writing. You can put down the odd good story and things like that but you need to learn about structure, which I think is the most important thing in a book, and be sure that the reader has some idea about what you are blabbering on about. Also, fuck all the safe football books out there and fuck everyone who writes them. Waterstones are full of autobiographies of cunts like Gerrard and Neville who live boring, non anecdotal lives because they don't associate with real people. Their existence is peppered with arse lickers who would faint if they had to say no to them just once. Boring people who bring in boring ghost writers who are brought in to throw in a few lines that will look good in the tabloids. If you're a cunt like me, you are in competition with those type of pricks the same way the SPL is in competition with the EPL. The reason these fuckers are littered with PR people is they are incapable of keeping it real. I knew then and I know now that no matter how many folk bought my books, 1, 100, 1000, I had to keep it real, I didn't want any sanitised bollocks that would see me chatting with Gregor Kyle, I wanted folk to see the real stuff, the stuff the supporters talk about, think about. Supporters swear, they talk about shagging, they drink, they take drugs and they do things that are morally and criminally wrong. Not all of them of course, just some, yet we never see that recognised do we? What we get is a game awash with middle class wankers who pontificate about balance sheets, or wannabe intellectuals who swan about Celtic Park, turning their nose up at people who have put more into Celtic in one day than they will ever put in, in their lives.

Similarly, I wanted stuff in the book that was authentic, even if I looked like a bigger idiot than normal or worse pervert than I actually am.

I read the brilliant *Downfall:The story of Tommy Sheridan* by Alan McCombes and was captivated by it. It must have really hurt Alan to have had to write that book but he didn't hold back and was self critical throughout but also explained all decisions as he thought them out at the time. I really admire that, hang your balls out there. That's not a reference to Tommy by the way.

That's what I wanted from *From Albert, With Love* and anything else I wrote as well.

The story of Albert Kidd that day is brilliant because here was a wee guy from Lochee who changed the world. Did Hearts know that the guy who sunk their dreams earned £200 that week. £120 wages and £40 a goal. £40 a goal and we are still talking about them. How many of Les Ferdinand's goals are folk still talking about? When Albert walked off the park that day, he got to the dressing room, threw his shirt in the middle of the floor and never saw it again. Would any club allow that now? Christ almighty, eBay would explode if that baby ever came on the market.

Football was so different back then it feels like a different sport.

I wanted to write books about that sport, but books that were totally different.

Even if it meant being skint forever...hehehe.

We Need To Talk About Albert

"Fame is empowering. My mistake was that I thought I would instinctively know how to handle it. But there's no manual, no training course"

Charlie Sheen

The book was finished on February 20th 2011, inspired by a magical 3-0 gubbing of Rangers and came out two days later. I'd gone down the Lulu route after, and I have to be brutally honest here, not being arsed to find a publisher deal and being inspired by the movie The Social Network, I was going to bypass all the usual avenues and do it myself.

First day sales - 1

Eek.

I wasn't expecting that. I thought everyone I knew would buy one on the first day.

Naive.

Not that I thought it was going to be huge or anything, far from it, but plenty folk had been in touch with encouragement and so on. Still, I had a plan. See the night Gary convinced me to write the book, we agreed I wouldn't go into this half-assed and would give it a real go, so I tried to.

First week sales - 10

That made me feel great. Ten people had bought the book and I was pretty sure I didn't know any of them,

Round about the start of March. Chris McGuigan from the LostBhoys got in touch with me on Facebook and asked if I fancied coming on the show to talk about the book. I was absolutely flabbergasted. I'll let you into a secret, not only was I a huge LostBhoys fan but I often phoned in and left messages regarding games. To this day, I don't think they know that.

It was a big deal for me to be asked. I didn't know any of the guys on it at all before I was asked. I'd heard at that time another podcast had been asked why they weren't having me on and they said they never would. They've stuck to their words there anyway. That was ringing in my ears when Chris asked me so it meant a hell of a lot. It has to be said that whenever you raise your head above the parapet in the Celtic universe, there are plenty who will want to knock it off. As you stay above that parapet, you realise that you can deal with that pretty easily. You get verbals, you give them back and normally it's fine. It's the sneaky ones that are the worst. The ones who slither around trying to undermine all you do, they are the real snakes. I caught one in the midst of writing this book actually, some who did a 180 on me and it's good as you find out then that they aren't on your side.

Still hurts though.

The day of the podcast, Celtic won 2-1 at Inverness in the cup, Ledley scoring both. I'd left The Celtic House, picked up Jake from the babysitter and got home. I should have prepared, thought about what I wanted to say, who I wanted to mention and so on, but instead I spent all the time cajoling Jake to go to sleep. By now it was clear that Jake was a bit more hyper than most kids and needed a hell of a lot care and attention, This was now March 2011 and a lot of my time was either spent with Jake or recovering from spending time with Jake. Even as I write this, August 5th 2012, Jake is running about mad. if I make it past 50, I'll be amazed.

Jake did go down though and I sat on the couch, laptop ready and waiting for Chris to Skype. I was fannying about on the computer when disaster struck, the signal had gone. This was something that happened now and again, normally caused by snow, and it was going in and out. I cursed my luck. I text Chris and we quickly arranged to do it over the phone. I then had to charge the phone to make sure it had enough life in it as I was told the podcast would last at least an hour.

I did have some butterflies, I also had some Guinness though so was good to go. Chris called and we chatted away, and then more, and then some more and until Chris said "Christ, we better start doing this!" and so he started recording and we were away.

I can't remember much of what I said but I did enjoy it and felt good after it was done and a bit relieved also.

Chris said he would be uploading the podcast on the Friday night, this was the Wednesday, so I said goodbye and wished him well.

The next day was St Patrick's Day. Trisha was working all day, so I took Jake into Manhattan for the parade. It was a bit of a downer in all honesty. Pushing a buggy amongst drunk people enjoying themselves isn't my idea of fun and so after I'd stayed a few hours, it was back on the Metro North and homeward bound.

Jake was exhausted and went to sleep around 6pm, I opened the fridge and took a long swing of a Bud Light whilst firing up the laptop. I was a big Facebook guy then but for some reason I logged on to Twitter first. I had last logged on two days before to say I'd be on LostBhoys and had 31 followers then. Suddenly I had over 150.

Eh?

I also had a tweet from someone saying they loved the interview.

What the fuck?

I went onto Facebook and sure as shit, Chris had shared the interview after uploading it.

Gulp.

I wasn't ready for this but listened back and it did sound ok. Chris put a fantastic little montage together at the start all from season 85/86 and especially that last day. It actually made me well up a bit.

I thought I did ok, probably talked too much as usual but overall I was pretty pleased.

I have to say now that if it wasn't for that interview, that platform, that opportunity, I don't think you would be reading this right now.

Things changed for me after it. My followers on Twitter rose and kept on rising, the book started to sell ok and lots of people wanted to talk to me. It was really nice. A lot of the time I was "The guy who wrote that book" and that was ok by me. The support I got from The Bronx bhoys, and Chas Duffy in particular, was absolutely fantastic. It still remains as well.

All that would be enough and I would have been very happy

Then Albert said he was coming to The Bronx...

#Shambolic!

Podcasts were getting bigger and better, and coming from all angles. Step forward, Richard Swan...

In many ways the story of the Carluke Shamrock Celtic Supporters Club, and our Tic Talk podcast, mirrors the experience of Celtic and Celtic supporters the world over. Standing your ground as the underdog; being curious and always questioning; finding strength and support in a massive #CelticFamily; and being pleasantly surprised as to what can actually be achieved just from a simple love of a very special football club and family.

Like many other Celtic supporters clubs that have been forged in the dark mining towns of Lanarkshire, the Shamrock club first shone as a tiny lantern within Carluke's huge dark pit of an overwhelming majority of followers of the Forces of Darkness. Vastly outnumbered even to this day, with a recent very unscientific study amongst the members put the percentage of Celtic fans in our small town of 13,500 people at a lowly 5-8% at most.

The underdog status was so great in fact, that the club actually formed in 1987 by combining two towns together – Carluke and nearby Lanark – to simply get a bus to transport fans to the games. Those small buses would collect a ragtag bunch of hoops fans that had previously been using cars and trains to reach Paradise. The buses would depart from both small towns, driving through seemingly endlessly regular orange marches, and invariably returning to the town's market gardens to be greeted by union flag wearing enemies, gloating on their recent victory set against any one of our regular failures. Those SECOND nine-in-a-row years really were dark, dark times to be living in such an offset community. The turnaround in today's environment is truly remarkable; that tortuous period seems to have been a purgatory that had to be endured on the way to salvation.

Those dark times were epitomised by the club's first ever bus – heading up to Dundee for a 4-1 drubbing. That also happened to be my first ever away Celtic game, as I had previously just used the train with my mate Martin to take in games at Parkhead. I still remember standing on that open terracing as goal after goal went in against us – a truly harrowing time that reduced this Celtic teenager to tears.

However, the club continued on from this inglorious start, and has grown from strength to strength over the years. It now stands as a proud CSC in its own right, highly organised, well structured, and boasting a regular 70-seater coach heading to Paradise from this small town where we still lie outnumbered but unbroken. Like many other well run clubs, it has managed to raise tens of thousands of pounds for charity, and it has hosted many excellent functions with players and celebrities as guests, including our current boss Neil Lennon who collected a Player of the Year award from us, and even took time to take part in a video sketch that boasted comedic quality well beyond any "Only An Excuse" rubbish.

The members of the club form a spectrum of characters that would be recognised and smiled upon knowingly by any other supporters club. The kind of real life characters that we can all associate with fondly...

Mr C, Sandy and Hadds are those stereotypical elder statesmen that every club has, where they can mesmerise you with tales of bygone eras and games, but also infuriate and bore you with endless complaints about how "the 60s were better" and how "football's just no the same noo", and even try and spoil your Larsson enjoyment with argumentative references to Jinky.

Johnny and Kev are examples of those wild bhoys whose exuberance can attract the attention of Strathclyde's finest, and who can flawlessly quote you the unpublished 27th and 28th verses of some lesser known rebel song, but then at the same time slap the back of the head of any young Tim that might start to misbehave on the bus.

Michael is one of those Arthur Daley 'blagger' characters that can somehow manage to sneak you into the VIP area of an executive Celtic lounge, and magically produce tickets for a European final from thin air. Meanwhile The Connellys are the perfect example of those brothers you get that will bait, goad and argue with each other until the sun sets, but who would kill any stranger that dares to attack the other brother.

The Gardners are those brothers you get from even smaller outlying areas, where they're in your town yet still classed as "in-comers" – you know the type. Their exact geographical location for being born and bred (in this case, the mythical lands of The Forth) is trusted and constant ammunition for any banter and slaggings, but they're nonetheless considered part of the family.

Davie could quote word for word the label of a Buckie bottle, and teach the SAS a thousand different ways to smuggle and conceal a huge carry-out on a bus, while at the same time would go mental if he caught his son and his young pals even looking at a bottle of Blue Wicked.

BJMac, Kieran and Vinnie are those jovial characters you get on a bus who are the smiling assassins – they'll smile broadly at you, and look you right in the eye, while their razor sharp wit cuts you from underneath, and leaves you without an arse to sit on, much to the delight of any listening audience.

Those are just a smattering of characters "oan the bus", quickly chosen at random, that any reader will easily recognise within their own circles. There are dozens of other lads, quieter lads, and younger fans, who just get on with following Celtic, paying their dues to the club, and making their invaluable presence felt in the every growing success of the Carluke Shamrock. The perfect Molotov mixture that you could bottle up for an explosive podcast, wouldn't you say? J

The podcast – Tic Talk – arose as the answer to 2 personal questions I had in late 2011.

After years of shouting from the Jungle, later being a season ticket holder from the 1st day that Saint Fergus built the North Stand, quite a few years writing fans match reports on the infant internet's "#1 Lhist", and then singing and organising TIFO displays with The JungleBhoys, I eventually faced a personal impasse on the birth of my 2nd daughter.

After sleepless nights of deliberation I took the weighty decision to pass up on my season ticket for a while, to spend focussing on the early years of my two precious girls, knowing that I'd try and fill in the gap otherwise, and eventually return to full capacity when they were older. Buying an odd ticket here and there, or being kindly loaned some tickets for an odd game by pals on holiday, or being glued to radios and internet feeds while supposedly watching the girls in swing parks, and also using Carluke's infamous venue – Marshall's Summer Hoose – to watch games here and there on TV, all helped to ease the pain of that absence.

I then took on the management of the club's online systems at carlukeshamrock.com, using the launch of website, gallery, forum, Facebook and Twitter accounts to keep that umbilical cord of Celtic fascination stretched but intact.

Yet it still wasn't enough. No matter how hard I tried to balance the moral pull of family responsibilities against the lure of all things green, it never seemed enough. I craved more time to chat with the bhoys, get the 'craic, and feel that buzz. So the 1st question was born...how could I get more Celtic time with the lads, without impacting too much on my parenting demands?

The whimsical answer came – what about starting a podcast with the bhoys?

That immediately gave birth to the 2nd question – how the feck do you do a podcast?!?

Endless research, "how to" articles, YouTube videos, and countless emails and phone calls all gave the answers for how to get cracking. The Godfather of Celtic podcasts – Eddie Pearson of Celtic Underground – was part of that support from the Celtic Family. Tips and tricks on software and timings were gratefully received. The mover and shaker Tony Cassidy (@tonycassidy123) who seems to be the middle man between dozens of different Internet Bampot groups, provided contact after contact, including Eddie as mentioned above, and also some nefarious characters who were apparently doing their own shows called Beyond The Waves, The LostBhoys and HomeBhoys. Where on earth was all this clandestine networking leading this naive Carluke bhoy?

In typical Celtic Family style, these brief encounters led to some very welcome friendships, greater help and support, and some brilliant interactions and 'moments' in the virtual world and the real world alike.

I started lapping up all these other amazing podcasts that I didn't know about previously. Listening to The LostBhoys sparked ideas of creating some intro music to use; hearing the HomeBhoys run a phone-in style show led to thoughts of alternatives to the old media formats; and hearing "our American guy" Graham talk passionately from the States on Beyond The Waves gave birth to the simple thought of "what would Celtic fans from anywhere in the world want to listen to?"

So the thought of a talk show panel came to mind. I actually selfishly wanted to just get the 'craic with the Carluke Shamrock bhoys, I missed the general fun and banter of regularly "just talking Celtic", and I witnessed the old media competition with rotating panels of tiresome journalists on the likes of Clyde, Real Radio and Radio Scotland.

That was that then – "Tic Talk" – a panel talk show format that would provide "real opinion from real fans". The knowledge, the opinions, the arguments, the banter, the 'craic from my mates in the club would be perfect. It's the exact same mixture, collisions, agreements, laughs and memories that any group of Celtic mates could relate to.

The first show was set up – a group of us were squeezed into a cupboard-sized room in the St. Athanasius chapel hall – the iPhone was set on the table, an initial printed agenda and format was laid out, the record button was pushed – and boom: we were off. Tic Talk was born.

Chaos quickly ensued.

The tiny room was very reflective and led to hassles with the sound levels, and guys who started off in nervous silence just because a simple "record" button was pressed (try it yourself; the pressure is quite surprising) eventually forgot where they were, and belly laughs and arguments soon broke out all around the table. It was manic and yet perfect in equal measure.

I edited the 1st show and published it through our new iTunes channel, and then spread the word through our online systems, and amongst the new Celtic podcaster friends that had been made. Loads of very helpful criticism came back about sound levels and people talking over each other, while a greater level of warm feedback, praise and encouragement also bounced back. We were onto something here.

Over the next few shows I would try and keep a professional detached view for trialling new software, microphone attachments, format changes, intro jingles etc. but above everything else....we just ensured we were having fun. In a word...it was Shambolic!

That term "Shambolic" had long been the unofficial tagline of our supporters club. Flat tyres on buses, confiscated carry-outs, members going missing on organised trips to Moville and Seville, have all been incidents easily awarded with the play-on-words turning 'shamrock' into 'shambolic' – the perfect self deprecating humour that every Celtic fan is blessed with, and which makes the bumps in life easier to deal with. Remember how the ditty "always look on the bright side of life" got us through the dark times, and also confused and enraged our blue detractors in equal measure? Yeah...that kind of banter. You can't beat it.

The more we had fun, the more responses and interaction we got. Our internet bandwidth was getting hammered with downloads and we had to quickly upgrade, then emails and tweets from around the world starting coming in with questions and topics for the next panel to discuss. It was mental, and it showed the power of new media and the vast spread of the Celtic support at its best.

Each new day would bring a pile of emails: ex-pats in Canada and the States that would highlight what a great connection it was for them; a new friend called Dubravko that spoke of his new love of Celtic from his home in Livno in Bosnia would contact us regularly (I had to triple check his IP address before I believed it wasn't a wind-up!); a guy called John whose initial emailed question carried with it a long explanation of how he would download Celtic podcasts before flying out for extended shifts on oil rigs in the North Sea; and even contact from far flung places like Bothwell and Uddingston! J

With a month under our belt there were a few things that became apparent...

• This #Shambolic train was careering ahead fast, and we were simply along for the ride as happy passengers.

• *Humorous feedback ensured the death of a funky rap-style jingle (test #1) to be replaced by a more newsroom-style jingle that would repeat the phrase "Tic Talk" to the sound of a ticking clock (test #2).*

• *The format was bedding into place, and the guys on the panel were getting better and better at stating their points, and also finally giving the other guys a chance to speak too! J*

• *The "Shambolic" section at the end of each show, which was like the funny "..and finally" piece at the end of the news, was also proving to be a winner. Once all the very common chat about a recent match, viewpoints on goals, and thoughts about upcoming games were taken care of, this section allowed the panel a free run at a keyword or phrase that would spark different memories from being a Celtic fan. Matters like most memorable Glasgow Derby, best European night, or daftest piece of merchandise purchased, allowed the guys to head off in tangents that would bring interest and laughs flooding forward for panels and listeners alike. One particular panelist Stephen (@bhoypapa) has become legendary at picking out the most surprising and fascinating angles from his memory bank of all things Celtic.*

• *And the other thing that was becoming evident....the innocent promise to my wife of "it's just a wee hobby thing I'll be doing with the guys now and then" was turning into a weekly broadcast with all sorts of daily tasks to prepare for each show, and keep up with listener contact. Tic Talk now had a grip of my life in that typical nature of the Celtic infection.*

That infection was contagious and would appear with different symptoms in different shows. There was the manic depressive nature of the "catharsis" show that met head on with a set of incidents we knew would eventually appear sometime – Celtic defeats – and the whole panel tried to console and cajole each other out of our shared pain. Many listeners got in touch immediately on the night of that show to say how we had helped heal some of their anguish.

Another night found us mimicking The Green Brigade by singing an intro to the show across the hall to each other, in an amateurish 'come on you boys in green' fashion. Then there was the night where Kev became ever more frustrated with the panel guests Murdo MacLeod and Peter Martin trotting out the "blue side are too big to die" mainstream mantra; I was convinced he was going to have an embolism live on air (what a finale that would have made!).

And one of my favourites, probably because of the time I spent in the kitchen preparing for it, was our "jelly and ice cream show", where we celebrated our corrupt foes lapsing into administration on St. Valentine's Day. I had laboured the whole previous night, creating hand-made deluxe ice creams, and specially sculpted jelly glasses, for the panel to tuck into live on air, in amongst a cargo of alcohol that they had brought along for the party. Between the schadenfreude hilarity, the relentlessly flowing beers, the jelly and ice cream buffet, and even playing a game of 'pin the tail on the donkey'...that was one shambolic night!

Alongside the shows themselves, regular contact was now being made with our new Celtic Family friends too. Some great chat and personal connections were made with who is now "our American guy" pal Graham Wilson of the Beyond The Waves show. In typical Celtic fashion, two total strangers were now conversing in very personal terms, sharing a laugh, and opening our souls about the infection of Celtic.

Fellow newbie podcasters The Temporary Stand also hit the airwaves at the same time as us, and it was great to have these new hooped babies grow up together. Eventually it led to the empire builder Harper (@Harper1888) having the brainwave of bringing lots of Celtic podcasts into the Spreaker world that he already inhabited under the banner of Hail Hail Media. It was an outstanding idea and has created a 1-stop-shop for Celtic podcasts that at the time of writing has already broken through the 200,000 listen/download barrier, and will easily more than double that in this 2012/2013 season. This momentum also included the pleasure of working with Scotty from The Temporary Stand in creating our new family home – hailhailmedia.com

While we simply kept having fun in Carluke with the rotating panels, the charge was on to find out how else we could serve and entertain these listeners around the world that would ask for more and more content in their insatiable desire for all things Celtic. It was while listening to a Celtic Underground podcast that I came across Krys Kujawa (@Krys1888). Here was a guy that was taking the time and effort to go out and record during Celtic matches, and also driving out to and recording the admirable events of the Celtic Graves Society around the country. What an outstanding idea – off his own back he was attending and recording Celtic events that were impossible for every Celtic fan to be present at. That immediately led me to the challenge of trying to record outside broadcasts at any event we were fortunate enough to be at.

Over the piece we have had the absolute privilege and delight to be at some outstanding events, and talk to some truly notable people in the Celtic world. In amongst our standard panel shows, we ended up having special broadcasts that included Chic Charnley, Murdo MacLeod, and Peter Martin. Other events that exemplified the breathtaking generosity of the Celtic support were the Kano Foundation bash, where we interviewed the likes of Paul Brennan (@cqn) of Celtic Quick News, Tony Hamilton of Celtic, and the highly impressive Kano Foundation organisers themselves.

Our intrepid reporter Brian was at a CSA rally and recorded the likes of Neil Lennon and Charlie Mulgrew, and we recorded ordinary fans live before and after important matches. This passion to capture and share content and moments with the wider Celtic Family was infectious, and that bond of Celtic fans doing whatever little bit they can to help each other and help others around them, is of course a special quality we all share.

Just asking, is another common trait amongst the hooped brethren. Reams of text and blogs have been produced that rightly highlight the cultural differences between a questioning, militant, curious, and often cynical Celtic support that was able to group and save the club in its darkest hour without any internet communication lines to depend on, compared to the subservient, ignorant, entitled, expectant, and silent majority of blue hordes who witnessed their Glasgow club die before their very eyes when they had the full power and influence of new media at their beck and call.

That power of new media was colossal in the battle to ensure honesty, transparency, and the simple matter of sport was brought to the fore in each segment of battle that raised its head during the war between the blue cheats, with their compliant old media hacks and entrenched football governors, against the rest of the football fraternity that chased the simple consequences of rules without fear or favour. This war was discussed heavily on many Tic Talk shows and all of the other podcasts in the Celtic Family.

Aside from that more important and weighty use of the 'just asking' trait, another softer, nice and generous consequence became apparent. Whenever we 'just asked' an important and influential member of the Celtic Family to help out, or perform an interview, they more than gladly accepted. The eloquent Paul Brennan of CQN mentioned above, is a man with a very stressful calendar and the weighty daily duties of carrying one of the most influential football blog sites in Europe, and yet he never even blinked when accepting an invitation to be hastily interviewed in a draughty stairwell outside the Kerrydale Suite after he was spotted by us at the Kano bash inside Celtic Park.

That support, that willingness to help and encourage, that desire to talk and spread the word of Celtic has been a virtue that has shone through in all our Tic Talk travels thus far. This matter really came to light when a small group of us attended the Paul Larkin (@paullarkin74) book launch in Glasgow, which turned out to be the very night that Celtic clinched the league in Kilmarnock. Carluke Shamrock might have great timing in picking the perfect season of off-field sensationalism to start a podcast, but that author has perfect timing to celebrate a Celtic book launch!

Anyway, I digress. At that party in The Admiral Bar in Glasgow, a collection of merry bands of friends, clubs, and

Internet Bampots (the tag that would be worn with pride when cast over to us from the old media as a mocking term) all grouped together sharing championship hugs, raising title glasses, and meeting and greeting many stranger-friends that had previously only formed as textual exchanges or tweeted connections.

Rather than just the warmth of a title win, or the inner glow of a sunken beverage, there was a bursting desire to share the infection of all things Celtic. And again, simple requests for time and input were warmly welcomed. The author himself was gracious with his time and answered all manner of questions regarding the book, his own time in America, the Celtic team, and the shocking travails of our manager throughout the season. Jason Higgins (@aupaceltic) who had used twitter to rekindle old school friend connections with Kev and Johnny from our own club, also spoke. In the first instance he spoke warmly and coherently on stage as he presented the evening's host to everyone. Then later on, having been far too busy organising things, he finally had time for an interview where his victorious excitement and liquid consumption got the upper hand when trying to recall moments of the season. We've promised a future interview under more sobering circumstances to properly present his opinions and well formed thoughts. We'll see what happens there.

The curse of the tired hack world, and an NUJ card-carrying example of how journalism can actually function was also there that night – none other than Phil Mac Giolla Bhain. After months of putting old media to shame, and carrying the torch of truth in parallel with the likes of the phenomenal

@RangersTaxCase, Phil had made the trip over from Ireland for the event, spoke at length in Paul's favour, and was relentlessly shaking hands with everyone that wanted to meet and thank him for his work within the family. And yet he somehow also managed to show that supportive, generous trait by accepting an interview with us.

If you've ever conducted an interview, you'll know that you balance your mind between 2 worlds of forming the next question within your head, but more importantly, also listening intently to the current answer, as it more than likely can lead to a much better line of questioning altogether (this listening trait doesn't seem to be covered too well by most of our old media personnel who routinely miss the chance to pin someone down on an incredibly important point). It was due to this commitment of focus during the interaction, that a 3rd sphere of that interview did not strike me until much later at home when I was editing all the audio of the day...

That interviewee who had kindly given up some time to chat; that man that now stood in the less than salubrious surroundings of a wheely-bin area on Waterloo Street to record outside the noisy bar, was a man that because of his decision to strive for truth, to investigate and corroborate hugely important matters of corruption and treachery in our national game, was a man that had personally suffered endless months of abuse, threats, and very real challenges upon his personal and family life. His very journey to the country that day had been carried out in secrecy, into a city that different security officers had already warned him could carry the end to his life after several very real threats from very serious and very angry people, who were and are, none too happy about their corrupt Glasgow club being so publicly exposed and dealt with. This was a very stark counterbalance to the more jovial fun and banter that we ordinary fans have enjoyed in the safe online world as the incredible saga has unfolded.

And so Tic Talk and the Carluke Shamrock Club have entered a new season as champions. We take forward hope and excitement in a cheat free league. We take with us brand new friends in the virtual and the real worlds. New shows are already underway, Celtic games have been witnessed with many more lying ahead, and who knows what more surprises and fun lie in wait. We carry with us hopes and dreams of all things hooped; we acknowledge the many virtues and blessings of the Celtic Family; we celebrate what has been achieved, and we brace ourselves for the exciting challenges ahead.

Richard Swan

@CarlukeShamrock

Simon Says Go On Facebook.

"One love, we don't need another love"
The Stone Roses

One of the other spin offs of *From Albert, With Love* was my blog started to get a lot of hits. From that people started to take notice of what I was saying and from that I got to know Simon Donnelly.

The blog had started in the aftermath of the "Dougie, Dougie" incident and had primarily been just me ranting a lot and trying point out various wrongs in Scottish football. After around six months I tried to expand it a little with interviews. I interviewed Dominik Diamond, Tam Donnelly and John Paul Taylor and the JPT interview went world wide. At the time I was getting, on a good day, 200 hits on a blog, that interview got 10,000 and is still rising. A lot of that is down to the type of guy JPT is. Out of all the Celtic employees I've met in my life, I can honestly say that he is by far the biggest Tim. You meet some employees who get the bug after they join, you get plenty "badge kissers" who swan around like the biggest Tim on the planet yet have never paid into a game in their life and you meet plenty who couldn't care less about Celtic. JPT is a guy who worked there for 15 years and would bleed green and white. It was an absolute disgrace when he was forced out the door by Celtic. That's what happened. A guy who was universally popular with the supporters and people in the Celtic hierarchy undermined him, plotted against him and finally left him with no opportunity but to resign. This angers me. Particularly when I see some of these halfwits who are still there at the club now.

Anyway.

Through JPT, I was able to ask Simon Donnelly for an interview. At first I tried to "friend" him on Facebook with no success. Then I sent him a message and explained I knew JPT etc and about three hours later he replied saying it was no problem. Being in NYC and him in Scotland, the best way to do it was to simply send him the questions. Not ideal but it worked as Simon is a good writer and understands interviews so it went on the blog and got a lot of hits also. Then about 25 minutes later, he accepted my friend request.

That felt fantastic!

Then what happened was I was sitting in the house, after another stressful day with Jake, and was sinking a cool one, laptop on the legs, Facebook open, and a chat window popped up. Normally it would be someone half cut from back home so I didn't look right away. Another swig and I spotted it was Simon. Obviously I opened it up right away and he just started chatting about stuff, normal stuff, "How you doing, what you been up to?" and so on. I was in a bit of panic in these discussions, anxious not to make an embarrassing prick of myself or say the wrong thing. We used to chat a lot on Facebook and I loved it, it was really exciting for me. Then in May, Simon went to Ecuador to do a walk for the British Heart Foundation and our Butterfly Effect moment was approaching.

It was the day of the Scottish Cup Final in May 2011. It had been a hard month for Trisha, Jake and I as, right out of the blue, we had to move house. This was something that started back in February. What happened was the radiator in the living room started releasing steam at a ferocious pace, very loudly, every hour or so. I phoned the landlady who did sod all for three days then finally got a plumber who fixed it. The effect of the steam had chipped the paint off the wall above the the radiator this exposed us all to lead. We didn't know this until March when Jake had a routine blood test and it showed very high levels of lead in his blood stream. We had to radically change his diet and find the source, so to both flush it out and stop any more getting in. About three weeks later a guy appeared at the door to check the lead and found the source above the radiator.

That was that until about 10 days later, once Friday night, I was lying in bed watching Baseball. I was in a good mood as we were playing at Ibrox on the Sunday and Gary was coming in for it. Trisha had text to say she would be on the 9.30pm train, Jake was fast asleep and I felt content.

Like always, I should have fucking known.

I heard Trisha come up the stairs of the apartment and come in the door. I was waiting on her poking her head round the door when I heard her say "Paul, you better get up"

I got up and walked through and she handed me a letter. My cheeks clenched as I opened it up and saw it was from a lawyer instructing us that we had to leave the apartment as soon as possible. Work had to be done on the apartment and it could not be done whilst we were there.

Let's get this one straight then.

Our landlady, after ignoring our pleas for three days to fix the radiator and not content with almost killing our son, gets a letter from the state of NY saying she has to fix the lead problem in our apartment. Does she offer to put us up in a hotel? Does she compensate us? Does come round and apologise?

No.

She goes to a lawyer and pays him to write a letter telling us to leave as soon as possible.

I think the phrase rhymes with "Clucking Hunt"

One sleepless night later, Trisha went to the places that had apartments for rent and arranged a few viewings. She found a place not far from where we were which was a lot more expensive but far, far bigger, better yet we could move in at the end of the week.

We were delighted.

That's because we didn't know then we had just made the biggest mistake of our lives.

In May 2011 though, we were just delighted have a roof over our heads.

It was that roof over my head the night everything changed with me in terms of Simon and it almost never happened.

I'd gone to watch the Cup Final in The Parlour on 86th and Broadway and met up with Gary before it. The plan was to watch the game and go on the lash. We met Jim McGinn in there and were delighted to see the Bhoys left the cup. Problem was the AC wasn't working properly and I started to feel really unwell. I went after the game to a pharmacy to get some really cold water and stood outside trying to feel better. We left soon after and chilled for a bit until I felt ok. I felt a little better and we hit our reserved table at The Perfect Pint for some good, cold beers when and were sinking the first when disaster struck. Gary got a call from work saying he had to go in. FUCK. By this time it was 6pm, and I gave him an hour before calling it quits. I was fucking mad. I rarely got the chance to get out and it was a great day ruined. I was on the Metro North home when Gary called saying he was good to go. FUCK. I could have got off in Harlem and got a train back but I was fucking raging so just left it. Worse yet, someone had panicked in Gary's work and he didn't even need to be back. Worse than that, I was going to the Yankees the next day and had to print out my tickets, had no paper and Gary was giving me some. FUCK FUCK FUCK! So I got home, relieved the babysitter, steady, and stewed for a bit. I fired up the computer and when I logged into Facebook, Simon came on. He then told me a story. He had been doing the walk in Ecuador, got altitude sickness, had to go back, felt like a failure for Phil O'Donnell and the British Heart Foundation, got back to the hotel, the TV was showing the Scottish Cup Final, and the first song he heard was "THERE'S ONLY ONE PHIL O'DONNELL"

He fell off his seat.

I fell of my seat when he told me.

I knew then that I had to write a book about Simon and Phil, and the 98 team.

As I sat pondering this, I got a call from Gary, he said "Come outside" and hung up.

I walked outside and he handed me a huge stack of paper.

I was going to The Yankees tomorrow again.

Plus life wasn't that bad.

When Albert Came To The Bronx

"Ice Cube, is not for the pop chart"
Express Yourself-NWA

When Albert Kidd said he was stopping off in New York in May 2011, I had a mixture of feelings. My life was structured in a way where I based everything around being in my house all the time. This allowed me to be there to watch Jake always, unquestionably the hardest job in the world, but be on the computer all the time as well. It worked up to a point but the stress of looking after a young child full time, mostly on my own as Trisha would be working, often made my life unbearable and by extension very hard to create anything. The stress was killing me. An average day would run like this, up at 6am with Jake, make his breakfast, keep him entertained for a bit, make his lunch, take him out to the park for a bit, come back, keep him entertained, give him his dinner and then try to get him down for around 7pm. Thrown into that mix were having to change him, pick him up when he falls, cope with the incredible heat/cold and deal with all his moods and emotions. There was also the fact that he was obsessed with milk then and would often be sick in the most inappropriate places. He's not a child that can watch TV for any length of time or ever took afternoon naps. So when you finally did get him down, roughly between 7-8.30pm, you had to pray that the folk downstairs wouldn't wake him up with their noise, but they often did. Because of the intense heat in the summer and us having limited AC, we had to get the balance between keeping him cool and keeping the noise at a level he could sleep. When he finally dropped off, you'd go and sit down and kind of de-stress for an hour, normally with a cool one, often being held at your forehead for a long time first. By this time it would be 9-930pm and if there was no research work or writing for money type stuff on the go, you'd try and write a few thousand words of a book, trying to stay awake long enough to see your wife but knowing you need to sleep again soon because you're going to be getting up and doing it all again in a few hours.

No one outside Trisha and I could understand this and we barely did ourselves. When family and friends baby sat for us, which was rare, no one could handle him and we would often get calls saying he was out of control and so on. The only people who did cope with him were the Haleys, but they have their own kids to deal with, far less ours. Then when we got a babysitter in that we paid, we caught her, at nights, taking Jake out of his bed, sound asleep, waking him up, and taking him to her house until around 1am then bringing him back and just before we were due to get in. I'm surprised the poor kid didn't die of exhaustion. The other thing was it got to the stage where we needed to get out but we were so tired and grouchy, causing lots of irritable type arguments, we ended up not wanting to go out or when we did go out, being utterly exhausted within two hours.

So.

When Albert said he was coming to New York and wanted to take me out for the night, my first reaction wasn't delight, glee or excitement, it was "Who the fuck is going to baby sit?" See,

New York is a wonderful place but if ever lines in a song summed it up, it's In The City by Joe Walsh

"I was born here in the city

With my back against the wall

Nothing grows and life ain't very pretty

No one's there to catch you when you fall"

Unless you're absolutely minted, that's the reality of it and so, for example, if Trisha loses a day of work to watch Jake as I go out for a day of eating and drinking, she's losing $250 and I'm spending $250. That's us $500 down.

In one day.

When you're paying $1500 a month rent, $200 a month cable and have a young kid, you can't afford to drop that every day.

So with lots of fucking around, she went out late to work, I went out to meet Albert and we paid a babysitter $12 an hour.

Oh, things were later complicated by an old friend being in NYC earlier that day so I had to go meet him too as you can't say no and that's more midtown bars at $7-8 a pint.

Safe to say that by the time I got the train in, I was, as usual, stressed out of my mind.

Stress is a huge factor in my life. About four months after being back in the US, I started to get incredible headaches, put down to stress. Then one night I lay my head on the pillow and thought I heard a huge wind outside, I looked out and there were no signs there and it soon dawned on me that noise, a sort of swishing noise that sounded like symbols in a shell, was coming form inside my ear. All because of stress.

Things like this never used to happen to me. Pretty soon though I realised that it was effects of the PTSD. It was never going to leave me, I just had to control it better.

That wasn't easy.

So I met the old friend and then made my way round to Faces and Names, on 54th between 6th and 7th, and waited for Albert. It had been eight and a half years since I'd seen him in he flesh and as I sat there for a little bit, the stress left me and I relaxed. Faces and Names was a love-hate thing for me. I'd met some great people and had some great lays from it but I also had an incident in there one night around September 2007 where I was with a girl and this drunken cunt was annoying the fuck out of everyone in there by pushing them, laughing and generally being a prick. Not only that, the barman thought it was hilarious. It was embarrassing and I said to my companion that if the cunt comes near us, I was going to knock him out as my blood was already boiling at this drunken fool. Temper was another thing that I was having to control a lot more than normal after 2008 but in 2007 I was really going to lose it. Eventually, as this guy grabbed a woman from behind and intimated that he was having sex with her, whilst her husband sat terrified, I snapped. Now, I can be a brash, sexist cunt at times, a total deviant, but this was a fucking joke so I pulled the barman and said "Are you going to so anything about that cunt?" he looked at me, smiled and said "It's just a laugh" I could feel the red mist descending and my girlfriend then grabbed my arm. I sensed that the barman was mates with this cunt and later had that confirmed. I looked over and the scene was pathetic, 3am and a terrified woman being molested by this prick and her husband sitting there not having a clue what to do as this cunt took liberties. I snapped, walked behind him and grabbed his neck, causing him to fall right on his back. He was out the game completely so could offer little resistance and I left him to it. The couple left sharpish. The barman looked at me, raging, as I walked back to my seat and said "Who the fuck are you?". Now I should say at this point, if you don't know me, I'm 6 ft 1 and 240 pounds, he was about 5 ft 4 and 160 pounds. I stopped dead and grabbed him, pulling him right over the bar and saying to him "That's who I fucking am" and he just started at me. In all honestly I would never encourage violence but I fucking hate bullies.

Anyway.

So I'm sat there nursing a Heineken and watching the door, when in walked Albert and his wife Maureen. The last time I met him he looked exactly like he did on May 3rd 1986. Now he had aged a bit and the trademark moustache was gone. That said though it was still the same old Albert. As nice and as humble a guy you could meet, with stories flying at you like mosquitoes on a hot day. It is incredibly surreal for me to be standing with the man who had the greatest impact on my youth and, arguably, my life.

Gary was supposed to come in too but ended up three hours late, a combination of traffic and tiaras.

In the meantime Albert took me for a very expensive meal and dazzled me with his wine and wine knowledge. It was documented in his foreword for *Albert, Dougie and Wim* but Gary ended up coming in just in time to drop Albert's wife Maureen off at their hotel and take Albert and I up to The Bronx. We arranged to meet a few of The Bronx Bhoys. This, along with something that was to come in December 2011, was a small token of the appreciation I had for the welcome that Chas Duffy and The Bronx Bhoys had given me. Also Rod Stewart and Billy Connolly had been in The Parlour, it was time to bring a real superstar to The Celtic House.

We spent a great night of drinking and telling stories, the ones Albert could tell now certain ears were out of shot(not involving women, just drunken escapades) and suddenly everything seemed great in the world again.

I'm aware enough to know that if you'd told me in, say, 1991, that 20 years later I'd be sitting having a meal with Albert Kidd in New York, it would be akin to telling me now that in twenty years time I'll be living on Mars.

What I do know is, such was his impact, in twenty years time they'll be talking about the night Albert came to The Bronx.

1989, Another Summer

"Most of my heroes don't appear on no stamp"
Public Enemy

After *From Albert, With Love* I had no real plans to write
another book. Then I had a thought, one of the things that
inspired me whilst writing was watching and listening to The
Thai Tims videos. I won't patronise you, you know who The
Thai Tims are, but I thought I could do something to maybe
get a bit money for them. Of course, what would that be? I
had no clue, it was the summer and I sought inspiration, fuck
it, I put the blogs together and released them as a book,
Dougie Dougie, and charged a fiver for them and all proceeds
would go to The Thai Tims. This meant around $3 a book so I
was quite chuffed to be able to hand over just under $500 for
a book of stuff that folk could read for nothing if they really
put their mind to it. It should have been $700 though. I added
bits of course but it was generally just previously published
blogs. It came out and sales were steady then disaster struck.
As books started falling through doors, folk were getting in
touch to say there was Thai writing all over them, scrawled,
but printed. I had no fucking idea what was going on. After
contacting the publisher, the full story had came out and it
was very sad. Basically the PDF of the book was hacked and
the people who did it put stuff about child abuse in Thai
writing all over it. I've no idea to this day how it happened and
have never had any bother since, but it meant the replacing of
about 50 books, and times were very tight at that time for me

with the new house and all, so apologies to The Thai Tims, it should have been more.

I was actually asked to write the story of The Thai Tims not long after that, and got a good 10,000 words down but, as you'll have noticed since, Celtic got involved and there was no way they were even going to entertain a cunt like me doing the book when they have a series of fabulous writers on the pay roll anyway.

I don't think any book is going to be published at all now, which is a real shame, but if it does or it doesn't, I wish Paul Lennon and all The Thai Tims the very best for now and the future.

Dougie Dougie was never going to outsell The Da Vinci Code and if I'm honest, it's my least favourite book, but people still ask me about it a lot and I know a lot of the anger I poured into those blogs really resonates with people til this day.

At the same time all this was going on, Frankie Fraser asked me to play football at Sunnyside Park in Queens one July Saturday. I say one July Saturday, it was the one in the movie *Do The Right Thing* judging by the heat.

Now, those of you who have seen Frankie and I will know, Bolt and Blake we ain't. We felt that too when we lined up, me sweating before the game had started and Frankie wearing knee pads for protection for his aging knees, the opposition were looking at us like circus freaks. Game kicks off, ball breaks to Frankie the centre half position, he looks up, I run, he floats an inch perfect pass right over the head of the opposing centre half, it comes down, I volley it first time, in off the post, BOOM, 1-0.

I could say now that Brazil 1970 sprang to mind but this play was a quality way above that. In fact, when I back heeled the winning goal, let me repeat that, when I back heeled the winning goal that day, some people say they had seen nothing like it since Pele was at the Cosmos.

Being the shy, retiring types, Frankie and I made little of it, Frankie politely commenting "Think this is good, you should have seen us play Basketball last week, we were like the Boston Fucking Celtics!!!"

After the game, a few spliffs and a burgers, and all was well with the world.

So something had to go wrong, right?

HomeBhoys, HomeBhoys, HomeBhoys

"Three feet high and rising"

De La Soul

Things would go wrong but not yet.

With *Dougie Dougie* out, a clear path for what would become *Wim's* Tims was ahead of me. Round about this time I was first asked to go on Beyond the Waves Celtic Show. I've always been able to talk better than I write, how the fuck do you think a cunt like me always had a bird?, and I seemed to be well received on these shows. Graham and the guys put a hell of a lot of work into their show and if you think they just pitch up and talk, you're wrong. Ok Rev does. What will happen is he will ask you to go on the show a week in advance, then he will start sending you the sort of stuff he would like to talk about before a proper outline for the show will actually appear in your inbox around 24 hours before you go live. Then you'll call in about 15 minutes before it starts and have a sort of pre show chat before going live. It's a very good set up.

The first time I went on was in August 2011, right after Anthony Stokes scored to give us a 1-0 at Pittodrie, and I was looking forward to it. As usual, I talked and talked and talked but it seemed to go over well and I got a lot of new twitter followers that day. More so though, a real friendship was growing between myself and Graham, as well as the other guys of course, and we quickly arranged a weekend in Philly for the upcoming Rangers game. it's also an honour for me to have Graham write the foreword for this book. If he has one flaw, it's that he's too self critical and he shouldn't be, he's a fucking great guy.

About a week after that show, I was asked to go on the HomeBhoys show. I was an avid podcast listener by then and had recently discovered the HomeBhoys so I was delighted to be asked on. I was asked to participate in their oft quiz "One, True, Three" where you tell three stories and only one of them is 100% true. I had a great laugh doing it and again, it went over well. Also, people were buying my books after I would go on these shows. It was maybe a month later when Harper got in touch with me and asked if I'd like to come on the show as a full panel member every week? In my life I have made many terrible decisions, but saying yes was one of the best decisions I've ever made. If it was all to end tomorrow, I'd never regret at second of it. The laughs I've had on each and every show keep me going sometimes and certainly did in NYC then. The first night I went on, there was a fantastic reaction and a big audience spike. Right away you could tell there was great chemistry between Harper, Joe and I. Joe, of course, is Joe McKenna. I really like Joe. I can't ever recall him being in a bad mood and he always makes me laugh. He's a very talented singer/songwriter and songs like *Worldwide Tim Parade* and *A Bhoy* are absolutely brilliant. More than that though, I love listening to how Joe creates his songs and he has a keen eye on most things.

What can you say about Harper? Probably nothing as he keeps a low profile. I can say plenty though. Harper is a unique guy, he's the only Celtic supporter I know that can't really be bothered with any other type of football. He also doesn't care what people think, not in a bad way, so it makes him a really focused guy. He's helpful, down to earth and has all the qualities most people look for in a friend.

He also drinks like fuck.

Whatever it was with the three of us, it worked. Ratings started soaring and the feedback was immense. More callers were phoning in, Twitter was alight when we were on and the buzz was incredible. You have to remember, whilst Joe and Harper were cracking cans in Ireland at night, it was 2.30pm on a Monday afternoon in NYC for me yet I was drunk on the vibe. Even when I came back to Scotland, it was still as good. Ah, coming back to Scotland, when things started to go wrong in NYC.

Not really. Just, kind of.

In October 2011, my eldest son James came over to see Jake on his 2nd birthday. The brothers were inseparable and something started to stir in me. Then when James left, always horrible, My Ma, who was also there, told me that James broke down in tears as they pulled away.

Hmmmm...

Then there was the fact that Trisha and I were not really enjoying it any more in NYC.

Then it was becoming obvious that My Ma wasn't getting any younger and a decision had to be made.

Then there was the fact that our landlady, who lived beneath us with her family, was about as welcoming as a fly in the ointment and had made our lives a misery pretty much from the week we moved in.

We booked flights home and suddenly a weight was off. On St Stephen's Day, we were coming.

Not before a Celtic wave came over The Bronx though...

Wim's Tims, Beyond The Waves and One Day In The Bronx

"Ladies and Gentleman, The Bronx is burning"

Howard Cosell

Wim's Tims came out at the end of October 2011. I'd gone on The LostBhoys again to promote it amid a backdrop of a dreadful 0-0 draw against Hibs, an argument with Trisha because she had to stay in the bedroom with Jake whilst I did it, and a feelings of sadness because of James recent visit.

As usual, it was a great time with Chris and we talked and talked and talked. Ok, I did.

Even scarier though, and something that had been eating away at me the whole time I was writing Wim's Tims, was that I knew Simon Donnelly, Jackie McNamara and, much more importantly, Phil's wife Eileen O'Donnell, would be reading it. That scared the shit out of me. What if one of them read it and was appalled at my language or thought the stories were inappropriate? This haunted me throughout the process. The other thing that was happening to me was I was becoming aware of a few snide comments by certain individuals. Anyone who has ever raised their head above the parapet in the Celtic world knows this was par for the course. I'd seen a change for the better in some folk, one in particular who seemed to badmouth any time possible despite not knowing me at all suddenly was being nice all the time. Others though revealed things to people they thought didn't know me. The recurring theme was that I was an uneducated, guttural, loud mouth who was not liked by folk at Celtic or folk close to folk at

Celtic. Funny thing is, all this is true. I did some stuff for Celtic way back in 1999 and 2000 and the opinions expressed did not go down well with some people. Particularly a certain employee who remains at Celtic Park to this day. This individual would routinely tell anyone who would listen at Celtic that they were going to batter me the first chance he got. This went on for years until he said to the wrong person who said "I wouldn't bother trying if I was you" and it ended there and then (to my knowledge). In terms of the other stuff, yeah I didn't get any qualifications at school (I did much later) and yes my writing is guttural because the folk around me pretty much all my life have all been pretty much one step from the gutter. It's how we talked and how I write it. I know it absolutely infuriates people but I can't write like Stephen Fry because I'm not Stephen Fry. Perhaps I should have had a pretend name and liked an obscure band and tried to be Pat Nevin? Ah, well. It can eat away at you this type of thing, right up until you have things like a book launch and folk come up to you and want to cuddle you, shake your hand, kiss you and, most importantly, say that they felt like you were writing about them. Those are the people I try to write for, people like me and almost certainly you.

The thing is though, whilst I did fuck around at school which makes me dumb, I ain't no dumb ass. I read all the time, mostly factual stuff but the odd fiction now and again. I'm a news and politics junkie and if you've ever heard me on a show, you'll know I have an opinion on everything. Fuck, that's where they get the loud mouth stuff from. It's hard being me (cry ya bastard!)

So the book launch was fast approaching and I was delighted to hear that Graham, The Coach and Rev were booked in for The Bronx. There was a backdrop, of course, there is always fucking is with me, is that I knew by then I was coming home. A combination of things had built up to the point where I knew it was time. I didn't say anything to the Beyond The Waves guys or The Bronx Bhoys as I just wanted it all to go well.

Some days in life make all the shit we all put up with worthwhile. Dec 10th 2011 was one of those days.

Everyone who said they were coming on the day, did.

All the books were sold.

The Beyond The Waves Show was fantastic.

Pretty much everyone who means something to me, and could be there, was there.

You know the scene in Goodfellas where the camera goes round everyone in the restaurant and Henry introduces them? This is what it was like.

You had Chas Duffy, who ensured everyone got a great welcome and was fed with traditional rolls, bacon and sausage. Moreover he exemplified, again, what a truly great friend he has been to me.

Then there was Frankie Fraser and Nicky Laveglia from Queens, who brought a lovely authentic New York feel to proceedings as well as the knowledge that if anyone here fucks around, they're dead.

You had Kevin Devine who ensured The British Heart Foundation made a fortune from the day.

You had the Beyond The Waves guys who gave it an American vibe in what felt like a relay of Celtic.

You had Marti Crampshee who took over the "Scottish guy moaning about the buffet" role (Kidding!)

You had Kevin Logan the barman who ensured nothing was too much trouble.

Then you had Gary Haley. A year on from a conversation in House of Brews in Hell's Kitchen, here we were three books in and having a book launch. Gary and I, as you've read here, have been through a lot of shit together. This is why these moments are so special. Just like Gary.

The rest of the day was spent in drunken bliss as we all sunk cold ones and I looked around and knew I'd miss the place.

Just nowhere near as much as I would miss the people.

An Empire State of Drunk and Disorderly

"I might get drunk one day and fall in love or fall over a hooker outside, and I would have consummated a relationship that I couldn't necessarily believe in."

Oliver Reed

Despite all the bad shit that ever happened to me, New York was very good to me when all is said and done. For example, I did get married there in June 2011. Trisha and I tied the knot in the shadow of Yankee Stadium and took a honeymoon in my favourite place on the planet, Montauk. Oh, I tell you a story about Montauk, from way back in May 2007...

"Listen, if you're going down there, you gotta go to see Captain Ron", I'd mentioned to Gary that I was going to Montauk for the weekend and he got really excited. "Why?" I had to ask. "Don't you fucking remember anything these days? Captain Ron is the guy Glenn is always fucking talking about, his "big buddy in Montauk", Glenn and him ran Montauk for years and all that other bullshit, you gotta go on one of his fishing trips and find out what he really thinks of Glenn, you gotta! YOU GOTTA!!!!!!!!!!!!! I GOTTA KNOW!" Ok Gary, breathe.

We took the Long Island Expressway. The "We" being myself and a girl I was with at the time who Gary christened "Tracy Turnblad". Ok that wasn't her real name like but he called her that on account she was carrying a few extra pounds, hey aren't we all, but she had strong arms and could carry more than most, so she was ideal for trips like this and a lot of luggage. I'm kidding! Added to that, she could drive and I can't and I'm not getting the Long Island Rail Road to Montauk, who the fuck am I, Jim Carrey? We bombed down there, Wu Tang Clan pumping on the stereo, me on the Blackberry emailing all the way and we arrived at the Montauk Yacht Club around four. No, 4.30 it was. We had a beautiful room, right on the private beach and a balcony that enabled you to walk right onto the sand from your room in seconds. We dumped the stuff and I gave her a quick length on the bed, she did drive remember, and we went out to dinner that night.

Montauk is a phenomenal place. As well as being home to people like De Niro and Pacino at times, Andy Warhol had had a place down there and Mick Jagger wrote a song about the Memory Motel here, that a lot of people say was about Carly Simon but a local guy here told me it was about the receptionist who worked there and gave Mick the old "Spanish archer" one night. Mick still has house here too. It's right on the tip of Long Island and is great for fishing, Sea and River, walking, surfing and golf. I loved it. It was a relaxing place and it was kind of like my Lourdes. Any time I went, and I went loads, I felt great again. In a funny way it reminded me of home, the green grass mixed with the weeds, the Ocean and the relaxed nature of it all really made me feel at home. To get all new age on you, I've always felt great when near an Ocean, kind of settles me, makes me feel at peace. I've no idea why, I'll think about it more and get back to you.

We had a nice meal, chilled out, and went to sleep. I got up, showered and Tracy, as normal, was out cold. I went out for a look about and the peacefulness enraptured me, I could die right here and now and be happy. The tranquillity of it all was something that I had not yet experienced in America and for once, I felt totally content. Not chasing anything, no pursuit, it was right here, happiness. It didn't last long. A motor was getting louder and louder in the distance. I cursed it and went to walk away when I saw it was heading for the bay next to us and that it had writing on the side of it, I waited so I could get a good bead on it and there it was in big bold letters "The Capt. Ron". Motherfucker! I'd clean forgotten about it and now here he was, in the bay next to us. I shook Tracy, apologised to the neighbours about the pictures falling off the wall, and we went to get a charter. On approaching the office where the boat was next to I immediately knew who Ron was, the moustache and stoned 70's drawl gave it away. "Hey there folks, what can I do you for?", Fucking hell. I asked if we could hire the boat for the day and could come with us? "No" he says, that is out of the question, Tracy and I look at each other before he says "I'm kidding, of course you can". It was easy to see why he and Allen got on. So we jumped on board, Tracy slowly, and he took us out into the ocean and it was great I have to say. The guy was clearly eccentric but knew more about fish than Captain Birdseye and it was pretty fascinating. Essentially it was relaxing in the spring sun and drinking beers, sounds good to me and I felt really great again. Another tick for Montauk.

After about three hours and a little urge to get back onto dry land and tickle Tracy's wobbly bits, thankfully no one had harpooned her, it's a joke! I hit Ron with it; "By the way, I know a guy who knows you, Glenn from East Meadow, he work..." Ron leapt up "Glenn, you know Glenn, how do you know Glenn?" Before I could say, he said "Me and Glenn used to run this fucking town, we were like Butch and Sundance, we owned this fucking town!"

Gryy would be raging, what he thought would be an ideal touchdown on Glenn had turned into a fumble. On the other hand, I could make Gary's life a misery now about Glenn being the King of Montauk.

I've thought about the Ocean thing again and I still am none the wiser about it. I even asked Gary about it, after breaking the Glenn news but he fucker used it to hit back, "I've no fucking idea but you did take your own whale with you Ahab!"

So when it came to a honeymoon venue, there was only once place for me.

Drinking and taking a lot of drugs in New York, got me into a hell of a lot of bizarre situations, mostly great it has to be said. That combination of Guinness and Coke was always a winner. I've thought about what story would sum up my life then and I think one weekend in Atlantic City, right after I came back from Montauk, would be the best monument to it.

Like most times I take a trip, as soon as I get home, I want another one. So I was hardly in the door when I booked a weekend in Atlantic City with Anita. Anita was a 45 year old danish woman who was working in NYC and I had met her in a bar one night and we stayed in touch and touched a lot. I could say the ocean was calling me again but I'd be lying, it was the thought of fucking Anita all weekend and the Class A drugs she was going to bring. Cards on the table here, Anita was fucking loaded and I was making a mint from the bars and various other things going on with the gambling and other shit, so we could have taken the Penthouse Suite at The

Borgata, Atlantic City and not batted an eyelid but Anita had a naughty look in her eye when she picked me up, "Let's stay somewhere seedy", at first I wasn't sure why but then she explained it; "Look, we're going to be doing a lot of coke and lot of naughty things darling and I don't want some fucking nosey night-porter interrupting us every five minutes". You got it. So we ended up in a little place called The Ascot Motel, jut up from the boardwalk, at $100 a night, non-inquisitive guy who ran it and a huge big bed and table in the room. Perfect for our sick needs. It made me relax more too as well. On the way down I got a little paranoid about things. Anita and I were two months into a full on affair by now, her husband was away a lot and I had been doing his wife pretty much any time she felt like it. I know that doesn't put me in a great light but then a fucking lighthouse wouldn't. It was maybe my constant chalked-up state, at almost three grams a day by now when I could get it and with the connections I had now that was any time, that was fueling this paranoia but it was still there and I was still a bit concerned about getting caught as the concept of America being so fucking huge had not really entered me yet and that the chances of being seen by anyone we knew down here were minimal to say the least.

The reassurance came quickly though, I'd gone to the bathroom in the hotel, lost at least seven pounds, and by the time I got out Anita had laid out eight lines on the table, lit me a cigar and was wearing something that could be best described as a belt with shoulder grips. That buzzing feeling again. The paranoia gripped a little again, what the fuck do I go for first, it freaked me a little so I snorted a line right off the table and then jumped in bed with her as we had very rough, very physical sex. Just the way she liked it. I got the feeling that her husband, whilst a high-roller in the business world, had forgotten to taste the real honey in life and I had no qualms about taking his pot from him at this fucking time. We did more coke, including her doing a line right off my cock and me doing one up the crack of her ass and I sucked a on a fat cigar whilst she sucked on a fatter one.

Sex with an older woman is an experience any man 35 and under should try. At first, you don't think it will be all that, the woman is starting to lose her looks, her skin is getting more like chewing gum and her tits are dropping faster than the water at Niagara Falls. So as you get closer to her, you do feel a bit like you're about to fuck your Auntie, as scary as that seems. She will kiss you first because this woman has been round the block a few times, she ain't going to fuck around waiting for you to make the first move, she will go for it and within seconds you will realise that you've gone from wondering if the ride is still open right to the front of the line. She will take control immediately and she will suck your cock like a fucking hoover not because she wants to necessarily please you but because she wants you as rock hard as possible so you can fuck her with all you've got. Because you'll need to. See if you have a woman 45 or over, she will have been fucked quite a lot, probably have dropped a few kids and therefore will have a cunt deeper than Atlantis, so you'll need your guy solid, reliable and with stamina at Olympic standard.

Thankfully, I seemed to work for Anita, she loved it. She could not get enough of it. She really got off on being a bad girl, drugs, illicit affairs, dingy hotel rooms, she got off on all that. Well that and my big Patrick Duffy down there.

We spent the rest of that weekend fucking, snorting and fucking. I think we stopped to eat once but I can't swear to it. It wasn't really the weather walking hand in hand on the boardwalk, come to think of it wasn't really the relationship for it either. Anita and I lasted another couple of months, she started working away again, my needs were such that I couldn't wait on her and we agreed that we would end it one night after a few drinks and a state of the union address. That's not strictly true actually, she said I could come back to her house for one final fling as her husband was away and she had bought some new silk sheets. Bingo. We took a taxi up there, they had big place on the Upper East Side and, thinking about it now, I should have been more wary, but the coke made me feel invincible at times and this was one of them. We got out the taxi and went into her place, it was stunning. According to her Al Pacino once lived in it, way back in the 80's and it was regal enough but I couldn't imagine Al in it if truth be told. We did fuck on her silk sheets, I took her doggy style because I knew she hated it when I was in control but it was a final act for me to show her who the boss was I guess, pathetic as it seems most men do do that, and I came all over her ass and sheets for the same reason, something that really pissed her off. I admit now that I got off on the danger of it but in all honesty, I fancied a dip back in the shallow end again by now.

That story pretty much sums up what kind of guy I was for most of my life and pretty much all of my first stay in New York. My rationale for NYC behaviour is that when I went, I never had as much money in my life. I'd had women before, enough, but when went to NYC I could get loads through my accent and bulge in my trousers, that's money by the way. I was living my dreams and fantasies out, I was young, free and single.

Incidentally, if you're judging me on Anita thing, you're right to. It doesn't make it any better but later that year she found out her husband had two kids to another woman whilst they were married.

I don't tell these stories to brag, I tell them because they are real and, in all seriousness, when you're in the depth of hell through poverty or mental illness, it's good to be able to look back now and again and remember it doesn't always have to be like this.

That all said, I fucking loved it.

Plus we took the Long Island Expressway to Montauk for the honeymoon.

Home James (Part 2)

"Never underestimate how little people can give a fuck"
Paul Larkin

The last two weeks we spent mainly packing and giving away stuff. I have to say, it was a horrible time. It's always at times like these where people reveal their true character. Some people went out their way to help us, whilst others continued to try and fuck us again and again. I'm not going to give oxygen to those who did that, but two things happened in the last two weeks that, in retrospect, made us know we made the right decision. As you know, we were flying out on St Stephen's Day but on Christmas Day, we spent the night in a hotel at JFK. We had no real need to in terms of the flight, but the landlord asked us if we could leave a day early, yeah, that's Christmas Day to you and I, so we had nowhere to go that day except a hotel. Which will, I know, have a few people reading this saying "But wait a minute, couldn't you have..." Yeah, you'd think that, right?

Anyway.

We spent the night in a hotel at JFK and by that time I was tired of it. We had moved around a lot and it was time to settle down. Fucking dreary hotels and hauling bags all over the place was getting boring and although I love New York and the people, most of them, I met, it was time to act like a grown up and be near family. My family. James. You can kid yourself on as much as you like in New York, and especially in Woodlawn, but to pretend everything is cool living there is just nonsense. You see a lot of people cannot leave. Well, they can, but if they do, chances are, they ain't getting back in. So they are all living in fear of getting "That phone call" from back home. I know guys like Chas agonised this for ages but then guys like Chas have heart and soul. Others couldn't give a toss so it suits them.

You do meet a lot of folk in Woodlawn who excel at being arseholes. So much so, you'd think they were training for the Arsehole Olympics, such as the folk who tell you they left home to "Get away from all the immigrants" or the ones who make a couple of bob for the first time in their lives and start to behave like Paris Hilton. It's not all like that though, you meet people who have an understanding that there was sod all good going on in their lives back home and are just delighted for the opportunity to try and have some cash in their pocket and the dignity that comes with knowing they have earned it. They are humble people who help you because they have experienced what you are going through when you just arrive and you realise, the longer you stay there, how invaluable they were.

One guy I met like that was Graham Maher. When I first went to New York to stay in 2006, Graham was the first friend I made over there. He was a barman in Connollys on West 54th St and we just clicked. The first conversation we had was about John Gotti because I had bought a Mafia book and Graham asked if he was in it. We quickly found out from each other that we both supported Celtic, had the same sense of humour and loved the ladies. Graham, at this time, was staying in Long Island and I was in Queens and we both shared a loathing of Woodlawn. It tickles me now that we both ended up staying there. Most of the stuff Graham and I got up to in those days could never be printed here (which may give an indication of how bad it was given the stuff you do read here) but one of the big regrets in my life is that, after I came back to Scotland the first time, we drifted apart, then he got hooked up and had kids and when I went back we only had one night out, which was nowhere near enough. No matter, Graham, if you ever read this, I still love you man and will never forget the nights in Connollys, the party in Chelsea we never quite made it to or the times we had every women in the joint clocked. Slainte, pal.

Our trip home was going to via Dublin and Newcastle, primarily because of all these wankers who had booked flights to go to Edinburgh for Hogmanay.

The flight from JFK to Dublin was fine. Jake slept most of the way and there were no real issues.

The flight from Dublin to Newcastle was an absolute fucking nightmare.

Jake suddenly became aware of what was happening as we took off and went into a mass of hysteria. The whole flight we tried to comfort him but nothing worked. As we began our descent a stroppy stewardess said that Jake must have a seat belt on. Trisha explained she was trying to calm him down and and the stewardess put her hand up, in that cunty way, and said "Not my problem". This caused a scene as other passengers told the stewardess she was out of order and the rest of the plane instantly assumed we were members of Al Qaeda.

By the time we got out of Newcastle Airport we were exhausted and stressed out of our minds. We had planned to be in Newcastle around six hours and then get a pre booked Megabus home. In reality we got a Metro to Newcastle Central and jumped onto the first Edinburgh bound train. To hell with the cost although we did pay a fortune and didn't even get cunting seats. By that time though, I didn't care. I just wanted to get home. The plan was to stay at my ma's for a week, go over to Limerick for a week and see Trisha's family then come back to Edinburgh and get a flat. All seems simple and it did turn out to be that way but it was against the constant backdrop of parents making constant judgement calls about us and for the first time in ages I started to get symptoms of Post Traumatic Stress Disorder. I was pissing a lot, nerves, getting flashbacks and anxiety attacks, and it probably took six weeks to get back on an even keel.

Aren't old people supposed to be wise?

Still, back on December 27th, when we got back to Edinburgh, to an empty house that was locked, I had two things on my mind, see James and the small matter of a Glasgow derby the next day. We stood outside my ma's and wondered what to do, I took a walk round to James house but no one was in. We ended up going to Lauriston Farm and eating, again, and then traipsed back to my ma's who had finally decided to show up. Protestations were made about times and so on, but we were completely fucked off by now. We'd been awake around 30 hours and just wanted to relax.

Thankfully things got a lot better as James appeared and at last someone seemed glad to see us.

I woke the next day after a mega sleep, in a bit of daze. When you wake up a in a new place, it's always like that but times it by 10 if you're jet-lagged to fuck.

There was also a huge argument with Trisha about me going to the game. Can I take this one opportunity in a book to not have to explain myself to you, the reader?

I got the bus through and met up with my old friend John Paul Taylor. John and I have been friends for so long he's like a brother to me. I can't tell you how great it was to be back then and meet up with a man like him, right back in the old routine and sharing loads of laughs at his house before heading to the game. John got me the ticket for the game, didn't charge me and it was only when I looked it at properly did I realise that I would be in with The Green Brigade.

This was magical.

Having played no part in any mass huddle or organised singing, to spend 90 minutes doing it was just fantastic. Although, of course, not as good as Joe Ledley planting that header in the net and putting The Bhoys top of the league and hammering another nail in that blue coffin.

Anyone reading this who has had long gaps away from seeing Celtic playing competitive matches will appreciate how much means when you see them again. It was inspiring and very emotional.

When I'm in that mood, there is only one thing for it.

Write another book.

Six Goals Up and Rising

"Glasgow's Green and White"

The Celtic Support

A week in Ireland had been done and we were back to the grim reality of Scotland once more.

The week in Ireland was spent in Limerick. Sometimes relaxing, often frustrating, none more so then when I tried to watch the Peterhead v Celtic game. Nowhere was showing it despite it being live on SKY Sports.

After we came back, we landed at my ma's again and set about getting a house which we acquired in six days but my ma will tell you it was actually 6000 years. The house was in Dudley Ave South in Edinburgh, posh area, shite gaff and we couldn't wait to leave it. The ceilings were too high and it was a nightmare to heat. Also, you couldn't get cable there so there was no internet or phone and a very crappy freeview. I fucking hated it. The only thing that kept me sane then was writing what would become *Poles 'N' Goals and Hesselink*. I wrote the whole lot in an internet cafe in Leith Walk and that was my get out from the horrible, freezing house. I lost myself in that book and wrote the whole thing in one month, feeling good about not being in the house and having no screaming kids or horrible neighbours to contend with. I loved the freedom. All the while though I was trying to get us another house and duly did so within about two weeks that was temporary but far more suitable. It was just opposite the Royal Yacht Britannia but apart from that it was fine.

One thing that had happened then was that Jason Higgins joined the HomeBhoys. I've known Jason almost fifteen years but his memory is so pickled with drink he never remembers. I was chatting to him on Facebook one day and he was asking me about podcasts and so on as he had little, if any, knowledge about them but after I explained it we quickly agreed that it would be good to try and get his brother John on a LostBhoys podcast. I spoke to Chris McGuigan who naturally jumped at the opportunity and, before long, John was on a podcast to great acclaim. Shortly after, Jason started calling HomeBhoys and like that he was a regular member of the panel. The show was already going from strength to strength and adding another bow to it merely kept it evolving. The chemistry is great and although the four of us don't always agree, I've never seen a grudge held.

It was during one of the shows that I dropped in the fact that I was currently writing another book and Jason immediately insisted I should have a book launch in Glasgow. with the help of Liam Power, they quickly set up a night in The Admiral in Glasgow for April 7th, but this was in February and we had no idea just how significant that day would be...

Meantime I was churning away at the book and had it completed by Mid-March. I was seeing old friends again and had a great day with Evan Watson on February 19th at Easter Road. A 3pm kick off, a stomping 5-0 win and brilliant day on the beer were good enough, but the great day came from the news that on February 14th, Rangers had gone into administration.

More of that later.

Days like that are great as they hard to achieve in America, mainly due to kick off times. I was having a wonderful time catching up with folk and Celtic were flying on the park.

Great times.

Throughout March, we tried, as best we could, to prepare for the book launch. My own thoughts and calculations were that around 30 people would turn up. I'd never been to a book launch and had no idea what happened at them. I was pointed in the direction of a youtube video of a book launch where the author sang songs he had written himself.

If I tried that, I'd get murdered.

Then there was Ibrox and a possible league win. I had two tickets for the game but didn't go. First of all, at £42, the price was a disgrace. Secondly, I'd witnessed many great days at Ibrox and my eldest son James had never been. So I gave up my tickets to him and headed for the Gallowgate with Evan. You knew that day this was Rangers last hurrah. Anything and everything was done to stop Celtic winning the league that day. Penalties and sending offs aplenty, plus being 3-0 down, we still almost snatched a draw and when Rogne bulleted a header in to make it 3-2, for a minute, we dared to dream. It was never going to happen though but deep down we knew that although they had won that particular battle, we would win the war.

First though, the book launch.

I was up at 6.30am on the Saturday, with it being an early kick off at Rugby Park and the knowledge that Glasgow Central would be pandemonium, added to the fact that I was meeting

Mike Boyd from Chicago who was flying in, I didn't get much sleep the night before given the importance of not sleeping in.

I got up to the bus station in Edinburgh in plenty time but we almost didn't get away as a woman asked the driver if he had time to go to the toilet, she did, but still stood for five minutes berating the driver in case he did leave her. FFS. Still we got to Buchanan Street bang on time and not long after I got a text from Mike saying he was on a bus to Glasgow Central, which I had just arrived at and already there were about 1000 people waiting on the 10.12 to Kilmarnock. We all crammed on and the journey was uneventful save for a stop at Stewarton where a lone currant bun stood on the platform opposite and was treated to a huge rendition of "The huns are going bust"

Arriving in Kilmarnock we met up with Jason, Liam, Joe, Jim and crew. Arrangements were made for post match and the Book Launch and we all made for Rugby Park via the odd saloon. I was on my own at the game but it didn't matter. The Celtic Family was at it's very best as a spine-tingling atmosphere made for the performance of the season in a 6-0 win that saw a few tears shed as our manager, the wonderful Neil Lennon, got his hands on the trophy that bombs and bullets denied him last season.

A sharp exit from the Moffat stand saw me up the road and catching the 14.27 from Kilmarnock. Which no one else did. I only caught it by three seconds to be fair. Texts went around, meetings were arranged, and Mike and I were in the The Admiral for around 3.45, 5pm start for Launch, and were quickly joined my mate Paul and girlfriend Steph, then Evan appeared asking whose round it was. There was no sign of Jason and Liam who were the main organisers and I'd probably say at this point was the only point I had any doubt in my mind that day, I'd never been in the Admiral, there didn't seem to be anyone here for the Book Launch and whilst making small talk, I looked at the clock nervously.

In a flash, all that changed. The first beaming face through the door was Joe and the then the rest of the crew followed. As we all embraced Marc from the addy came up and introduced himself and asked me what my plans were? I said "When folk starting showing up, will head downstairs" upon which he informed me there were around 60 people downstairs already and the final scores weren't even in.

Holy shit.

As I went downstairs, the greeting was incredible, overwhelming in fact. More and more streamed in and as I turned there was Phil Mac Giolla Bhain standing there beaming. I only knew that morning he was going to be there and had told no one but as soon as folk were aware Phil was in the building, they were, obviously, all over him as well. A real honour for Phil to travel from Donegal I must say, very, very humbling.

The crowd kept coming, probably peaking at 150, which was about 100 more than I had predicted would be there. The Rebel MC Jason kicked things off with a very funny opening, poking plenty fun at me, which helped relax the crowd big time and then Phil took the stage. I must admit it was a bit of an out of body experience for me as when he talked it took me about five minutes to register that he was actually talking about me.

After that I took the stage to talk about the book and I am incredibly appreciative that folk listened.

As for the rest of the night, it was bliss. I met lots of the Twitterarti who included @fultybhoy @thesammcleod @shoegirl81 @celticnetwork11 @krys1888 @gaffney67 @nicolamcginley1 @hobbesghirl @machrie72 @maxibhoy @teammcguire_bob @celticparanoia and countless other wonderful people whose Twitter names I can't seem to locate on my phone the noo...;-)

By the end of the Launch folk were in full party mode, The Amadans band immense, with a huddle when rangers die and then a conga out the door. I'd say it went well.

Afterwards a few of us decanted to a bar with a karaoke. It was rough and ready but good fun and I ended up giving a few licks of Forever In Blue Jeans which, even though I say so myself, brought the house down...

Krys Kujawa then belted out Mack The Knife, fitting given that a recipient from the night was The Tommy Burns Skin Cancer Trust.

By about 10.30 Mike, Evan and I were done. It had been a long day, fueled by the black stuff but I honestly can say I could have floated back to the hotel such was the good vibe I had. Not just from the Launch but it was easily the best celebration I've had after a Celtic league win.

The next day I was up early, wished Mike farewell and headed home. The reaction online was great, and that made happy that folk enjoyed themselves.

All the bad shit you have read in this book, that night made it all worth it.

The Warrior

"You Warriors are good, real good"

A Gramercy Riff

What you've read in this book is my story. I didn't want to re-hash opinions or have you read things you've read a million times before.

However.

There are some things that have to be commented on and one of them is the treatment of Neil Lennon, in particular, the last two and a bit years.

There is something about Neil Lennon that a section of Scottish society simply cannot stomach. We've heard lots of reasons as to what that may be but "Successful Irish Catholic who loves Celtic" will outweigh them all. There is a man who played for Celtic who hated Rangers when they existed. He gave everything against them, scored lots against them and was even sent off three times against them. He loved rubbing it into them when he scored, often cupping his ear to ask them why they were silent and even noising up their players after he had smashed a ball in their net. His name is Alan Thompson. Yet, he never got sent bullets or had an attempt made on his life with a bomb. He was never attacked in the street or assaulted on the touchline. No one burnt effigies of him nor scrawled graffiti about him outside his house.

What's the difference?

You know what the difference is.

Yet Neil takes it all and, not only that, fights back.

Could you do that?

Why does he?

Jason Higgins has a theory:

To a complete outsider, the madhouse that is Scottish football, there is a question that cannot be answered by anyone other than the man himself, hence, I'm not going to give you the true answer although I might luck out and hit the nail on the head. I'm going to give you my opinion on what the answer would be and it is my opinion alone and nothing to do with the man himself. My answer would be different from the man and I'm sure 99% of you would answer the same as me.

"Hurry up and tell us the bloody question pal"

"Ok, say I"

"Neil, why do you stay at Celtic?"

I've been racking my brains on how to write this piece as requested from Mr Green and White writer. Being honest I've struggled terribly in even trying to guess the magnitude of what Neil Lennon has went through these last couple of years hence this probably won't do the horrid situation any justice whatsoever but here goes!!

A simple question in an ordinary society, with ordinary people, but no matter how much we dress it up there is no way we have an ordinary society when it comes down to a few things, namely, football, the 'lack of religion' and bigotry. I use the phrase 'lack of religion' for the reason that anyone who took the teachings of their religion seriously wouldn't act with the evil intentions of hurting a football manager.

Neil Lennon manages a football club whom he captained as a player and supported as a kid. He is from a normal working class family and he is living the dream that thousands of us could only fantasise about. Why in heavens name has this guy been demonised like no other before him in, not only football circles but in Scottish mainstream society? Simply put, in my own words, the cause is unadulterated bigotry on a grand scale and I include some mainstream journalists as part of the problem. Very often when photographed, Neil would be pictured snarling and with a permanent scorn and if he ever strayed out of line it would be back page or even front page news. A referee and his assistant at Tannadice concocted a story and lied to Neil post match and I don you wt need to go into the fallout and the resulting referees strike etc and yet Neil was made out as the guilty party. Incredible, but true.

The well documented abhorrent acts aimed at Neil were the work of maniacs. The media just helped stoke the fires with their portrayal of Neil as some form of devil figure. I've lived and worked in Scotland all my life and a Mr Neil Lennon brings out the bigots in greater numbers than any before him. The ironic thing here is ask these journalists what they think of Neil Lennon and 99% of them will say he's a very personable guy who has a lot of time for anyone who shows him respect and he's a great communicator about the game we all love. He's honest, shows great passion, and in his new profession as a manager of a major football club he's relatively inexperienced in the grand scheme of things. Let's cut him some slack, eh!!

It would have been great if they followed through on this!!

I'm eating lunch at work with various fans of other clubs and there are 2 words in the English language I have heard uttered more than any others when the chat turns to Neil Lennon. "But" and "However" have been slipped in often enough to get my blood boiling. "It's a disgrace what's happened to that Neil Lennon BUT (exchange BUT for HOWEVER at any time)". No, my learned bigot, there are no reasons any sane minded individual can even begin to try and justify what has happened to Neil and the use of they 2 words just tells me everything I need to know about how your devious subhuman mind operates. What has happened to Neil Lennon is an abomination and an even bigger embarrassment for this country is that outside the Celtic support there was no campaign to show our disgust at how the pond life in this country are behaving towards a young man trying to do his best at the Football Club he's loved for most of his life on this earth. A game of football isn't worth living or dying for.

Neil Lennon has a family and is a normal guy who likes a laugh and a pint the same as most of the 40ish age group who regularly attend football matches in Scotland. He represented Northern Ireland in International Football and has played at the highest level in both England and in Scotland enjoying most of his success playing and captaining the club he supported as a kid, Celtic. The question on most peoples lips who have no idea how this guy courts so much publicity and attention of some of the vile elements of society is "Why him?"

You'll need a mind greater than mine to try and rationalise the mindset of these bigots who would deny a kid from County Armagh, from a normal working class family who went on to live out his dream, the chance to live a normal life. These lunatics do not belong in a normal society and are a danger to all and sundry yet they save it for Neil. Take away the tribal rivalry of the football field and I'm sure the vast majority of people who didn't know Neil, and got to know him would think he is a lovely guy and would begrudge him of nothing. I'm rambling now and I've no clue where I'm going here as I've no answers to these issues in our society.

Live and let live could be an idea?

Fast forward to season 2012-2013 and, believe it or not I'd say Neil isn't on the front pages of the rags any longer. He's not in front of disciplinary committees. He's not being whispered about in works canteens and offices. He is leading Celtic, his Celtic, and our Celtic into the Champions League against the mighty Barcelona, Benfica and Spartak Moscow. He's blooding a plethora of young talent into the Celtic 1st team and he's looking a million dollars with a weight off his shoulder. In my opinion life is sweet in the world of Neil Lennon at present.

Back to the initial question, why Neil choose to not walk away from Celtic? I'm not ashamed to say that if I was in a similar position I feel I would have walked away as I'm not sure I could have handled the heat but again I'm not Neil Lennon.

So why did he not walk away?

Because, simply put, he is that man.

He is Neil Lennon

My theory expands on what Jason has said. I think Neil has a version of monoamine oxidase A. This is better summed up as

"The Warrior Gene". To simplify it as much as possible, this where people have a shorter fuse than others. Now, some people may never even know they have this, the conditions around them will dictate it, nurture over nature, but then this can also mean, given the environment, they are prone to extremely aggressive behaviour in many forms. So if someone was to carry it and, say, they were a soldier in a war, they would happily shoot the enemy and not be affected at all. Some American soldiers came back from Vietnam completely unaffected by what they had seen and and what they had done. Others came back badly damaged mentally, why? Because they could be.

I think, given the fact that Neil is financially set for life and has great things all around him, his Warrior Gene means he can't back down. He actually does not have it in him to turn the other cheek in the face of hatred and intolerance towards him. He will not stand for it and will, happily, fight back with everything he has got. That's why they hate him.

And that's why we love him.

Free At Last, Free At Last, Thank God Almighty, We're Free At Last

Well that's the book done then, hope you enjoyed it and...wait a sec, there's something, uh, what is it again, I meant to talk about something else, oh yeah, first of all, here is Brogan Rogan Trevino...

Good Morning,

Imagine the scene. You are six years old, sitting at your desk in the Primary Two class at St Peter's Primary School, White Street in Partick, when you are suddenly faced with the steely gaze of the then headmistress. She is a small diminutive, be-spectacled nun by the name of Sister Magdalene. She wears wee flat shoes, a skirt or dress and a kind of short grey nun's headdress.

She does not teach Primary Two and she has only entered the class to make some sort of announcement or other, but as she is the "Heidy" her arrival causes a stir. Having made her announcement and addressed the class, her gaze falls on one six year old............ Me!

The date is the 23rd of February 1968, and for the first time in my life I am about to be asked a question to which I just don't have an answer. It is not a question which will result in me getting into any trouble no matter how I answer, nor is it a question being asked by an angry or an authoritative woman. It is a question being asked by an adult who wishes to engage with a child, about something that the child has shown an interest in and for which he has a degree of personal knowledge and enthusiasm. It also shows the human side of the "heid nun".

The following day, Saturday 24th February, The Scotland National Football team would play England at Hampden Park, with the winners going on to meet Spain in the European Championships. Anything less than a Scotland win, would see Alf Ramsay's England progress whilst condemning Scotland's role in the championships to that of spectator.

In the corresponding fixture at Wembley the previous April, Scotland had beaten the new World Champions 3-2 to become the unofficial World Champions. Some 4 weeks after the victory at Wembley, Celtic had beaten Inter Milan to become the official European Champions and Cup Winners.

For my part, I had made a wee bit of local news the previous November when I had been taken out of school during term time so that I could travel all the way to Buenos Aries Argentina to watch Celtic Play in the infamous World Club finals against Racing Club. I was the youngest fan there, and my return was delayed when I also travelled to Uruguay for the replay in Montevideo.

Accordingly, I was perhaps known as the class football fan-maybe the school football fan --as I had even been interviewed on TV by Archie McPherson, and so when it came to asking a football question, Wee Sister Magdalene had no hesitation in stopping at me and giving me her stare and her question:

" Tell me this" she said " Everyone knows that Scotland will play England tomorrow in a very VERY important football match—and we all hope Scotland will win. But if Glasgow

Celtic are THE best team in Europe, and if all of their players are Scottish, why doesn't the Scotland Manager simply pick the whole Celtic team and play them against England—as surely they represent the very best chance of ensuring Scotland win?"

I sat there. Sister Magdalene looked at me. My teacher, Mrs Welch, looked at me. I felt the whole of the class look at me. I felt my face grow red and eventually I answered with the only truthful answer I could think of to such a logical and persuasive question.

" I don't know!" I said—almost apologetically.

Well, Sister Magdalene smiled, nodded, and more or less turned on her diminutive heel and headed for the door. However before making her exit she parted with the words "No. Me neither—maybe you are just not allowed to do that?"..... and with those words off she went, out the door and down the corridor to the next class with her announcement.

Between 1967 and 1971 the manager of the Scottish National team was Bobby Brown. Brown is accredited with being the very first full time manager of Scotland.

He was also the last Amateur Player to be capped by Scotland. This occurred in 1946 when he was still a goal keeper with Queens Park, although in his last season with the Spiders he was only between the Hampden sticks in 50% of games, because he shared the goal keeping duties with young keeper who was emerging through the Queens Park Amateur ranks. His name was Ronald Campbell Simpson.

When he left the Hampden amateurs, Brown turned professional and went on to keep goal for Rangers for the next ten years under the management of the legendary Bill Struth. He was the final line in the famous Iron Curtain defence.

In 1956, Brown left Ibrox and played for a further two years for Falkirk before eventually retiring in 1958.

Throughout his time at Ibrox, Brown was a part time player earning just £20 per week which he added to his main job which was that of P.E. teacher. He did get a signing on fee however, and Rangers twice paid him a lump sum of £750 in return for 5 years continuous service.

When he retired from playing, he went back to teaching for a living, although he became manager of St Johnstone before getting the Scotland job in 1967, where his first match in charge was that famous victory at Wembley.

For that game he chose to give a first cap to Ronnie Simpson— the young lad he had shared goal keeping duties with at Queens Park some 21 years before. Despite Simpson having a very successful career at Newcastle, he had never represented his country until that time.

The full team at Wembley was:

Simpson (Celtic), Gemmell (Celtic), McCreadie (Chelsea), Greig (Rangers), McKinnon (Rangers), McCalliog (Sheffield Wednesday), Bremner (Leeds), Baxter (Nottingham Forrest), Law (Manchester Utd), Wallace (Celtic) and Lennox (Celtic).

Now it should be noted that Jimmy Johnstone and Bobby Murdoch were injured and both were seen as a loss to the team with the implication being that they would have played if fit.

However, it should also be noted that Billy McNeil had held the centre half's jersey until he suffered an injury and so Rangers' Ronnie McKinnon took his place.

Take particular notice of Jim McCalliog, because this was also his debut in a blue shirt (a scoring debut at that), and he would go on to amass---- 5 caps--- 4 in 1967-68 and a single further appearance in 1971 by which time he played with Wolves.

The captain on the day was John Greig, a player who would feature for Scotland more or less constantly during this era— whether at fullback, centre half, midfield or even forward, and this despite who was injured or otherwise available.

Brown would later say that he chose McKinnon ahead of McNeil because he wanted to maintain the club pairing of Greig and Mckinnon in central defence, although in later games he would play any combination of players McKinnon and McNeil, Stanton and McLintock, McKinnon and Moncur --- any combination of centre halves you could name—but a place always had to be found for the Rangers Captain.........somewhere.

By the time we get to the match at Hampden in February 1968 we have a different looking team.

Simpson (Celtic), Gemmell (Celtic), McCreadie (Chelsea), McNeill (Celtic), McKinnon (Rangers), Greig (Rangers), Cooke (Chelsea), Bremner (Leeds), Hughes (Celtic), Johnstone (Rangers) and Lennox (Celtic).

Between these two matches, the only members of the Lisbon Lions side not chosen by Brown were Stevie Chalmers and Bertie Auld. Every other single member of the Lions team had *started for their country in the space of the previous ten months. Chalmers and Joe McBride had played for Scotland in 1966 immediately prior to the arrival of Brown. Auld played 3 times for his country............ in 1959!!!!*

Celtic would be the dominant Scottish team throughout Bobby Brown's stint as International manager, reaching the later stages of European Competition and indeed the final of the European Cup in 1967 and once again in 1970, obviously losing to Feyenoord.

Yet despite this, the clubs representation within the national team in this era would never again be as strong as it was in that first year or so of Bobby Brown's tenure, despite the fact that they were matching the best in Europe with an all Scottish Team.

So, more or less repeating the wee nun's question of all those years ago—why should that be so?

Now, with the benefit of grey hair and a bit of experience in the world, I can answer the question—and I believe that my answer is an honest and a fair one.

The answer can be summed up in one word.

Politics.

Maybe that is not the word that some were expecting. Maybe some would have said bigotry or prejudice or bias or favouritism. Maybe there is an argument for all of those words but I prefer politics... and I do so for a reason.

Brown damn nearly picked all of the Lions to represent Scotland—just not at the same time.

Imagine what would have happened to Bobby Brown if he had fielded all 11 of the Lions for Scotland and they had lost? He would have been flayed alive by some as would the players with the accusation that they only played for Stein or in the Green and White of Celtic. Equally, the big man would have been none too happy at someone else taking his charges, his team, and playing them in a fashion or a style that lead to defeat and so undermined and damaged their reputation and confidence.

Equally, imagine Brown had played the Lions and won? He would have received no credit at all, and it might even be said that Stein would have been undermined with the notion that this group of players could in fact play under anyone's management.

So—Politics and self-preservation played a part in determining who would wear the blue of Scotland in those early Brown years. There is an argument to say that such politics was even more important than actually fielding the best team for Scotland and doing what was best for Scottish Football.

Now let me make one thing very VERY plain. I have it on good authority, that Bobby Brown was always a gentleman, a good man, a kind man, with not a bad bone in his body. I do not believe him to be any sort of bigot, or from a prejudiced background or anything of that ilk whatsoever.

So why, as Stein's team progressed both domestically and in Europe, would fewer of his players be selected for their country under Bobby Brown?

To be fair, Brown had other great players to pick from. Denis law, Alan Gilzean, Frank McLintock, Willie Morgan, Bobby

Hope, Eddie Gray, Billy Bremner, Peter Lorimar, Pat Stanton, Bob Moncur, John O'Hare, Peter Cormack, Eddie McCreadie, Ian Ure, Jim Baxter, Jim Forrest, Charlie Cooke --- not to mention the Rangers contingent who regularly featured— Greig , McKinnon, Colin Stein, Willie Johnston and even Davie Smith.

In his last 4 matches, between May and June 1971, Brown used Davie Hay, Jim Brogan and Jimmy Johnstone at some point—but by this time was picking players such as Tony Green, Davie Robb, Drew Jarvie, Frank Munro, Billy Dickson, Bobby Watson, Jocky Scott and Hugh Curran as well as any number from the list above in preference to those who played for Stein all across Europe.

Apparently, the Celtic players of the time were simply not considered good enough against the galaxy of stars that are listed above.

Now, does that in any way strike you as........ odd? Because with the greatest respect to many of those mentioned above, Stein would not have tried to recruit them for his Celtic side.

Well, let me sprint forward a couple of decades, to the afternoon when Dougie McDonald infamously reversed his decision to award a penalty at Tannadice.

Forget altogether whether the decision was right or wrong , let's go to the events that occurred immediately the bold Dougie blew the final whistle.

I think it is accepted now that Stephen Craven ran towards McDonald and asked him in a panic "What are we going to tell Jim McBurnie?" who was the match supervisor on the day.

McDonald replies " Tell him whatever you want. Tell him that you shouted Dougie Dougie-and pointed out I had made a mistake......." And so on.

Let's pause there:

Should a grade one official not be astounded that he was even being asked by his linesman about what should be said to the match supervisor --- wIth the implication at least that they would have to come up with.... A story? Should Steven Craven not have been afraid—even bloody terrified--- to pose that question, or make any such suggestion, to a superior official and should he not have been utterly astonished that by the time the game had come to an end McDonald had already thought of the same question, had posed the same problem to himself, and had come up with a ready made false answer?

How astonishing is that?

What about Charlie Smith—the other linesman who was party to all of this and who said precisely nothing? And who continued to say nothing even when the pre rehearsed lie was repeated to not only Neil Lennon, but in front of and to the SPL delegate- because remember, the Celtic Manager could not have entered the Referees room to get any explanation unless he went through the SPL delegate who must be present and must organise any such meeting and discussion. Whatever happened to Charlie Smith? Whatever happened to the SPL delegate?

Does the fact that the lie happened at all, or the whole Dougiegate scandal, the notion of such a conspiracy and cover up about the awarding of a penalty at a football match—not just strike you as odd?

Why would any of that actually happen?

McDonald was and still is a professional man- working in a responsible job which takes no small amount of professionalism and professional reputation, earned over a number of years. Why on earth would he and others lie about such a thing given that background?

Further, having admitted that he had lied, having declared that he made up an answer to cover a mistake and that he had deceived the Celtic manager and the SPL delegate, why would a panel of ex referees only censure him for a minor misconduct and think that such a sanction would simply be swallowed and accepted as an end of the matter? Surely they could see that these actions would have far reaching repercussions for his standing and the referees standing in Scotland as a whole?

The whole thing is most odd and the answer can only be found in............politics and self-preservation...............and perhaps the long held notion that such behaviour is the accepted order of things and that this is simply the way that such things have always been dealt with........ when the need has arisen to deal with this type of thing.

Then there was the referees strike and the shipping in of foreign officials to take the place of striking referees. These foreign guys were brought in, but it was only after they arrived here that they discovered the true reason that they were needed---- because the SFA didn't tell them the whole background as to why they were needed in the first place. Some of the visiting referees said that had they been told of the reason behind the SFA invitation to come and referee here, they would have politely refused to come.

They say that they were deceived by SFA officials at the time.

Now, does anyone think that the occurrence of a clutch of foreign referees stating that they had been deceived by officials of the Scottish Football Association is........odd or strange? Is it something that merits further investigation and comment?

Then again, who has heard the story that Hugh Dallas allegedly offered to have the referees strike called off if the SFA would drop the disciplinary hearing against Dallas in connection with the so called bigotry e-mail scandal?

I am not sure that anyone in Scottish Football—or beyond-- has actually been told the whole story about what actually happened there, and it is very easily forgotten given the story that lay around the corner.

The whole episode can only be explained by.............. politics and self-preservation on the part of the SFA and those within the SFA.

The point I am getting at here is that if anyone thinks that football is not affected by"football politics" and the self-preservation of those in an official position in this country then they are deluded, deranged and to be frank .....stupid.

Politics has played a considerable part in various Scottish football matters going back decades, and so no one should be surprised that there is a full political storm blowing in the face of "The Rangers Saga".

Except that where we stand today is very different to the simple notion that certain players, or players from one particular team, are preferred over others when it comes to national selection. When you are the manager of Scotland at a time when there are numerous class players to pick from, you can more or less justify each and every decision with a reasoned argument without necessarily making it obvious that you are following any type of policy.

However, when there are a whole series of events that just don't sit right and appear to have no logical explanation, then that is a different matter altogether.

Today, football is very different in its make up compared to the 1960's and early 70's. Gone are the ex part time players and ex P.E. Instructors in management positions. Gone is the plethora of stars that were brought along on a seemingly never ending Scottish conveyor belt of talent. Gone are the slightly quaint ways of 40 plus years ago and more, where honour and duty were all too readily portrayed on the Pathe newsclips.

Now there are very professional managers and players, with professional egos and multimillions taking the place of what was perceived as honour and duty. They appear as celebrities on our TV's in running newsreels that spin round all day every day. Gone are the part time semi amateur administrators- replaced by so called professionals who are especially equipped for the job ---allegedly? Today clubs are businesses, with financial directors and goals, with targets and shareholders , with debts and bank managers to satisfy, with wages to meet from seemingly ever decreasing revenues that spell trouble ahead if not watched carefully....... And amidst all this somewhere and somehow room has to be found for football and the football fan who simply wants to watch his or her team play at the highest level they can.

No today, we are well into a new and far more dangerous era for football. Where businessmen can come along and deal in your club. They can come along and buy it, sell it, lease it, hawk it, bankroll it, bankrupt it, sell the assets, pawn the assets, hide the assets, steal the assets and tell you all of that never happened at all.

It is for that very reason that we need a strong but simple approach to football governance—both from the clubs and from those who govern our leagues and football associations, because along with the introduction of hard "business" into football comes the very real possibility—indeed reality--- of the professional chancer. The Spiv. The Conman, The Money Man, The Trader and the business guru who can dress a business up so that its customers and shareholders, its partners, creditors and sponsors are lead to believe that it is moving in one direction or another when all the time they are moving along a completely different path.

These are the guys who are not really interested in football at all. They are not interested in the clubs they claim to own or represent. They are not interested in the national team or developing Scottish talent. They are interested in themselves, their egos and the ability to make a few quid on the back of the mugs who will pay for a season ticket when told the right thing at the right time using the right buzz words.

The SFA, as the overall governing body, MUST be alert to such people and their practices, and they must be the watchdog on behalf of football as a whole. They cannot and should not be swayed towards or by any one particular team or individual In carrying out this role. Alas, thus far they and the other governing bodies have failed miserably in that regard for the very reason that has underlined and underpinned much of Scottish Football for decades --- and that is the underlying notion that despite all the rules of Football, Scottish Football must protect Rangers Football Club and those who purport to represent that particular club... and that protection comes by any means necessary!

Again, let me be clear. I am not saying that every other club in Scotland wants Rangers to win this or that. I am not saying that there are fans or players from various clubs who do or do not prefer Rangers over any other club if push comes to shove. I am not saying that there is an inbuilt bias here or there which favours or has deliberately favoured Rangers in specific matches--- although there are those who will argue that this is too is prevalent within our game. What I am saying is that there is an argument for suggesting that there is and has been an institutional prejudice within the officialdom of Scottish Football towards a belief that there must be a strong Rangers at the very heart of Scottish football and that anything that might just damage that situation or perception should be swept under the carpet and hidden away.

Accordingly when Bobby Brown took the helm with Scotland, it was not foreseen that Stein would make Celtic so dominant and stake a place among the elite of Europe with a team of Scots. In those days it was more or less accepted dogma that someone from Rangers FC must be in any Scottish team—no matter who else was available for consideration. Accordingly, with absolutely no disrespect to John Greig and Ronnie McKinnon, room was always made for them whilst nearly every other area of the team was chopped and changed—

despite there being many who could be said to be better players or at least as worthy of inclusion.

That is just the way it was..... and everyone knew it.

The recent attempts to cajole and bully other clubs in Scotland into allowing The Rangers Football Club into membership of the SFA under circumstances which would never apply to any other club is a modern example of the special "Rangers" status. The very fact that there seems to have been a TV agreement which virtually guarantees coverage of both Rangers and Celtic - no matter what - in return for maximum financial benefit, strikes me as the antithesis of proper sports administration. It doesn't matter that the agreement applies to both Celtic and Rangers... what matters is that somehow it has become accepted practice that there will be one status granted to some which will not be bestowed on others. Of course, if we are talking about commercial rights then all of this could be dealt with another way, with each team negotiating their own commercial rights and broadcasts and agreeing to pay a proportion into a communal pot. That would do away with any club having a status that is different to any other club in the league..... but that solution may well not suit some folk who would perhaps lose a degree of control of such matters.

However, it is the events leading up to the demise of Rangers PLC which show the true maladministration of Scottish Football in light of this seemingly unspoken need to protect Rangers.

If you want to chart the day when it became clear—or perhaps should have become clear ---- to everyone in the

Scottish game that Rangers FC were about to face calamity of an unprecedented nature, then that date is 31st August 2005.

That was the day when Rangers PLC released their financial accounts to the year ended 30thJune 2005 for the world to see, and from that moment on Rangers FC, Rangers PLC, and any combination of "Rangers" you care to use, was a dead institution walking!

In the previous 4 years the Rangers accounts showed losses of:

£17.531M --2001

£35.328M --2002

£29.605M --2003

£ 5.939M --2004

All before tax.

However, in 2005, in his Chairman's statement, David Murray proudly boasted that Rangers PLC had at long last made a profit even although turnover had dropped by a couple of Million pounds!

Yes, despite having less money coming through the gate, Rangers had made a profit of........£12.410M

Now given what has been said above about losses in previous years... does this newly found profit seem..... odd?

Now remember, in May 2005 Rangers had secured the league title on the last day of the season when Motherwell beat Celtic and Rangers played pitty patty with Hibs at Easter Road for the duration of the 90 minutes. By the time the accounts were released, Rangers had gained entry into the group stages for the Champions' league. So—champions, improved *financial figures, and Champions' League Group stages secured—so why do I suggest that this was the time of their downfall?*

The reason is simple, and it is this.

Amidst all of this good news, Rangers released their accounts and any small amount of close scrutiny was able to show you that what was being released by way of the accounts and the releases to the press was the most undiluted crock of shit to come this way in a long time.

Here are some direct quotes from those accounts. This is from David Murray's statement to his shareholders and the Rangers fans:

"Success on the field was accompanied by further improvements off the park. Our basic business strategy was laid out in the Rights Issue documentation of 9 November 2004. I would like to take this opportunity to thank those of you who joined me in contributing to a successful placing. You have played a great part in maintaining the Club's financial stability with £51,430,995 being raised. I was delighted at the response, with over 3000 shareholders subscribing to the Issue and in many cases applying for additional shares. This Issue underpinned the Club's financial structure and the results for the year to 30 June 2005 demonstrate the positive direction that your Board has taken the Club in the implementation of our confirmed business strategy."

In short, Murray had gone with a rights issue, guaranteed by him with the assistance of the Bank of Scotland, and had raised precisely £1,430,995 from the Rangers fans. He was now carrying Rangers debt in his MIH company—and that debt had been------ over £78Million!

He continued:

"Our operating loss for the year has reduced to £7.8m (2004 - £10.5m). The operating loss includes an amortisation charge of £5.6m against our player pool, but does not include the gain on player sales of £8.4m. The gain on player sales was due in the main to the sale of Jean-Alain Boumsong. All of the proceeds of this transfer were however reinvested in the playing squad and the efforts of players acquired at that time played a huge part in our eventual title success."

In other words, Rangers ran at an operating loss of £7.8M and would only scrape into the profit bracket because of the sale of Boumsong. By the way the players who came in were I believe Barry Ferguson who returned--Brahim Hemdani, Jose-Karl Pierre-Fanfan, Julien Rodriguez and Frederico Nieto.

Back to Murray:

"The profit on ordinary activities before tax of £12.4m (2004 - loss £5.9m) does include the gain on player sales, and an exceptional gain on the purchase of shares in our subsidiary company Rangers Media Investments Ltd. These shares had been issued for £15.0m on 12 June 2000 and were acquired back by the Club for £1 on 30 June 2005 creating an exceptional gain in the accounts of £15.0M"

In other words, to get into profit, Rangers had taken the gain on Boumsong AND this so called exceptional gain of £15M which arose as a result of buying something for£1 which had previously been sold for £15M!

In short, there appears to be no profit at all without these extraordinary items.

Here is new chief Executive Martin Bain on the same day in the same accounts:

"Integral to Rangers strategy has been the belief that success on the football field will drive turnover and improvements in all other areas of the company. We must obviously continue to bring our costs into line with our income and will focus on controlling overheads and improving revenue streams. However, our priority remains to field a successful team, supported by a successful business operation, and this will require sound financial planning and careful management."

Now remember that emphasis on fielding a successful team "supported" by a successful business operation- and remember that this was Bain's first year as Chief executive though he had previously sat as a board member so knew the strategy that had been followed over the course of years.

He continued:

"Advanced planning and the extremely close working relationship between the Club's football and business divisions has kept us one step ahead in the transfer market and has allowed us to do some excellent business, particularly in the Bosman market. For example, the sale of Jean-Alain Boumsong in December 2004 allowed us to pursue our targets ahead of the summer transfer window. As a result, we stayed in front of the competition in the pursuit of some players' signatures and gave the team more time to gel as a unit.

Ticketing income increased again this season on the previous year despite the loss of Champions League revenue. Demand for tickets continues to grow year on year and the number of season ticket holders again reached over 42,000 last season to continue to provide our largest source of income. We are set to break this record again with sales well up on this time last year. Indeed, demand for tickets is such that we are currently exploring opportunities to expand the Stadium's capacity, perhaps in conjunction with the introduction of a new product in our corporate hospitality portfolio.

It has been another extremely successful season for corporate hospitality with an increase in seasonal and package sales and the majority of games operating at or near full capacity. Despite a number of fixture changes, team performances and the close race for the title drove increased sales and in some cases we were unable to meet demand. On these occasions, external venues were used to supplement our own facilities, subject to ticket availability. Our events programme provided a valuable additional source of income we had previously not exploited to the full and an even wider programme is planned for the season ahead.

Sales of £20.7m this season increased the retail and wholesale division's turnover 10% from the previous year, making 2004/05 our most successful season to date. This was a significant achievement for the Club driven largely by our strong 'Buy Direct' message, our extremely loyal fan base and our continued policy of manufacturing and distributing our own replica kit. This season's new kit is currently outstripping all previous years' sales figures over a similar period and we are expecting to increase that figure for the coming year.

Our complement of shops has also increased, with new stores opening in Braehead and at the Glasgow Fort. We have also *opened a number of temporary stores outwith Glasgow and the Central Belt. Dundee, Dumfries and particularly Irvine have been well received and some of these temporary units may translate into permanent sites.*

We have also exploited opportunities in franchising and have opened a store in Hamilton via this business model, which we are confident will provide a sound basis for further expansion.

Sales from our Internet store have seen a staggering 143% increase in the last year and continued development in this area is one of the key features of our business plan going forward.

Rangers media portfolio continued to grow last season with the addition of Rangers TV. For the coming year new partners CRE8 have further expanded the Club's income from media sources thanks to a three-year, £1 million publishing deal to produce the Rangers News and matchday programme.

Rangers official website and exclusive content zone, Rangers World, continue to attract high numbers of users, with rangers.co.uk achieving on average almost 200,000 unique users per month.

Developments in this sphere over the last year include the live broadband broadcast of SPL matches to overseas supporters and increased revenue from on-line ticketing and Rangers Direct. Our partnership with T-Mobile also offers supporters up-to-date match news and exclusive breaking stories on our SMS service, including video goal clips, games, graphics and ringtones.

Rangers TV has now been integrated into a bundled Setanta Sports package. This will protect the long-term future of the

Rangers TV channel, ensure production standards are maintained and allow the Club to access a wider audience of over 130,000 subscribers.

Our sponsorship portfolio continues to feature some of the UK's leading brands such as T-Mobile, National Car Rental, Honda (via Hyndland Honda), MBNA, Adidas, Coca-Cola, and of course our Official Club Sponsor Carling.

The partnership between Carling and the Old Firm continues to perform exceptionally well and was recently recognised with a prestigious Scottish Sports Sponsorship Award. We are therefore delighted to announce the extension of Scottish football's largest ever commercial sponsorship deal, which will see Carling appear on our jersey through to 2010.

We have also extended our long-standing relationship with Coca-Cola for a further three seasons, demonstrating the long-term commitment we have to our partners and the success we enjoy together."

Could anything be any clearer? Rangers had turned a profit, were champions, had record sales for the retail division, were opening shops, were looking at expanding the stadium yet again.....could it get any better?

Oh yes it could because here comes the finance directors report courtesy of David Joliffe. Let's see what he had to say in full—without interruption as it were:

"The results for the year represent a continuation of the progress made over the past two years. Combined with the successful Rights Issue during the year this has helped to strengthen the Clubs balance sheet.

Turnover was marginally down from the previous year to £55.1m (2004- £57.1m). The reduction in turnover was due to lower revenue from European competition, which totaled £4.6m compared to £9.9m in 2004. All of our other major sources of revenue such as Season ticket sales, Sponsorship, Hospitality and Retail increased from the previous year.

Net operating expenses were £57.4m an increase of only £0.5m from the prior year. The increase in net operating expenses is principally attributable to a higher retail turnover, with a higher associated cost of goods sold. Player bonuses were higher than prior year, however overall our wage costs decreased during the year.

Cost control and a pursuit of value for money continue to receive appropriate focus in all areas of the Club. Our ratio of total wages to turnover has been brought down to 49.5% and we will continue to pursue cost reductions where these can be achieved without adversely affecting levels of service and value for money.

The player amortisation charge for 2005 was £5.6m (2004 - £10.6m). Gain on the disposal of player registrations was £8.4m (2004 - £8.6m) and principally relates to the transfers of Jean-Alain Boumsong and Mikel Arteta.

The profit before interest and tax was £15.6m (2004 - loss £1.9m) and was due in the main to an exceptional gain on the acquisition of preference shares in Rangers Media Investments Ltd. of £15.0m. The Club acquired these shares for £1, the shares having been originally issued for £15.0m by Rangers Media Investments Ltd. on 12 June 2000.

The retained profit for the year was £12.7m an improvement of £18.6m from the prior year (2004 - loss £5.9m)

Funding

The success of our Rights Issue in December 2004 was assured by the underwriting of the issue by Murray MHL Ltd. It was though greatly encouraging that the issue was backed by so many shareholders. Over 4500 individuals subscribed to the issue, which raised a total of £51.4m before expenses.

The receipt of these funds, together with the restructuring of our bank debt has given the Club a strong financial structure to build upon.

Our total net debt at the year-end was £23.1m (2004 - £73.9m) and it is our intention to continue to drive the level of debt down while at the same time ensuring that sufficient funds are made available to put a strong playing squad on the park.

Accounting Policies

The Group's accounting policies, set out in Note 1 to the Financial Statements, remain unchanged from the previous year.

Tangible Fixed Assets

No significant investments were made during the year.

Intangible Fixed Assets

The net book value of the playing squad, which does not include a valuation for players joining under freedom of contract or through the youth system was £6.6m at the year end (2004 - £1.5m). It is a key objective of your Board to manage the player pool to protect long-term financial value.

The transition of players through the youth system to the first team squad is integral to this strategy.

External development

The Club announced on 23 March 2004 its plans for redevelopment of the land opposite Ibrox stadium and the Albion car park. The planning application for the Hinshelwood Estate and Albion car park sites was lodged during September 2004 and is due to be put forward for planning approval by Glasgow City Council imminently.

DAVID JOLLIFFE

So, If I pause there—lets see if I get this straight.

The turnover was down but the operating expenses were up.

The share issue attracted a grand total of 4500 investors (although Murray said 3,000) out of the worldwide Rangers family.

The profit was made from the sale of Boumsong and Arteta together with a clever switcheroo of shares between Rangers Media Ltd and Rangers PLC which added £15M onto the profit and loss account—which is what effectively brought about the declared profit?

All other revenue streams are higher than before and at breaking point, yet there was still an operational loss and (following the share issue) over £23M of debt compared with the previous years £78M?

But hey-there is always the planning application for the creation of the Govan village?

By the way, did you notice his reference to the "club's" balance sheet?

Then, there are the notes:

"5. EXCEPTIONAL ITEM - NEGATIVE GOODWILL RELEASE

During the year the company acquired 15 million, £1 preference shares in its subsidiary company, Rangers Media Investments Limited, from a third party for a cash consideration of £1. These preference shares were shown as a minority interest in the 2004 consolidated Balance Sheet. As the fair value of the liabilities acquired was £15m and the fair value of the consideration paid was £1, negative goodwill of £14,999,999 arose on the transaction. The negative goodwill arising on the transaction has been credited immediately to this year's profit and loss account.

and

"The Rangers Employee Benefit Trust and Murray Group Management Ltd. Remuneration Trust were established to provide incentives to certain employees and other service providers. Payments to these Trusts are charged to the Group Profit and Loss Account in the year incurred."

It will be interesting to learn who these "other service providers" turn out to be? Who was in the know about what was happening at Ibrox in 2005? Who had connections there and with the rest of Scottish football, the world of banks and finance, the world of players and agents and so on?

The accounts go on to reveal many other interesting snippets of information but rather than bore you to death with these let me just point out the following.

Within two years Joliffe would be gone, all the shops and the retail income would be gone and Murray would have put the entire enterprise up for sale—with the result that not a single buyer would emerge over a period of 4 years while the club was officially and freely on the market.

Why would there be no buyers?

Because Rangers could not make any kind of sustainable profit and had not made any kind of sustainable profit over at least a 5 years period and it was getting further and further into debt despite the rubbish printed in the accounts. Any business person any professional finance advisers worth their salt, looking at those accounts could tear them to shreds and see that these wear the financials of a company that was getting into ever increasing trouble. There was clearly no desire from Rangers fans to buy into the club—only 3000-4500 had even bothered to buy shares in the placement. Revenues were stated as being as high as they could be , the Govan village was pie in the sky and the expansion of Ibrox a fairytale. It would cost Millions to expand the stadium—Millions the club just did not have and didn't seem capable of raising on its own.

In short, there and then—Rangers were bust. Bust as bust could be without clever accounting, and an underwritten share investment used only to reduce debt and for no other purpose. The EBT scandal wasn't even on the horizon and didn't need to be for there to be real concern about Rangers Football Club.

Now that was there for all to see—including the SFA and their financial auditors, the press (financial and sporting) ,the banks, the fans, the shareholders and the potential purchasers.

Yet, did anyone really pay any attention?

No- because this was Rangers—too big to fold and too big to die.

Surely, however, those who had the job of monitoring Rangers finances for the SFA and the SPL could see the potential writing on the wall? Surely the professional administrators— with their experience and professional qualifications—could see that Rangers were at severe risk at the very least? Surely, such administrators would not govern and preside over such a situation within the largest and most successful club without making enquiries and considering the worst case scenario and the impact that might have on the whole of the Scottish game? Surely, they would not carry on in a fashion whereby every other club would be left exposed if the worst came to the worst at Ibrox?

To govern in such a way would make no sense at all. That really would be.......odd!!

Yet any examination of the Rangers board at the time shows that a number of people may have seen the writing on the wall. Joliffe left and went to a national Cement company. Campbell Ogilvie went to Hearts.

D. P. Levy resigned as a Director on 27 August 2004 and N. Peel resigned as a Director on 21 March 2005 and at the time this left:

D. E. Murray (Chairman)

J. F. McClelland CBE (Vice Chairman)

M. Bain

D. Jolliffe

R. C. Ogilvie

J. Greig MBE

A. J. Johnston

D. C. King - -

J. D. G. Wilson

Now always remember that Dave King had supposedly invested £20M in 2000—so where had that gone? Where had the money from Joe Lewis and ENIC gone?

One recent report seemed to disclose that by 2001 King had in fact received about £15M in income from Rangers! How could that be? Where did that money come from and just how did it get to King for him to declare in his tax return?

Remember too, that this same Dave King fairly recently said that he had been deceived by Murray in relation to the Rangers finances. In fact he threatened and promised to sue Murray. What did he mean by that and where is his action? Has the SFA or the SPL chosen to make any enquiry of Dave King as to what he meant?....... or as Wee Sister Magdalene would put it.... "Are you not allowed to do that?"

Yet, despite these accounts, despite the fact that no one was prepared to buy Rangers other than Craig Whyte for the princely sum of £1, despite the fact that within twelve months of the Motherwell born Billionaire taking the reins at Ibrox the company was in Administration and will ultimately go into Liquidation, despite the fact that the Administrators could only muster £5.5M for all the assets and alleged potential of a company that was praised so highly, and valued at over £120 Million in the accounts referred to above....... We , the footballing public, are expected to believe the powers that be within the SFA and the SPL when they say that this is an institution which is vital to Scottish Football and should be saved by any means necessary?.

When asked the reason why it is so vital, the response is that without the commercial pull of Rangers every other club will suffer....... Let me get that straight then for a moment. For Business A to be successful, You need business B—a wholly separate company with completely different owners and which operates in direct competition to business A--- to be even more successful?

Does that whole concept not just strike you as....... Odd?

Does it sit comfortably with you at all?

Further, for whatever reason, the Scottish Football Press are reluctant to look at Rangers and see what has really happened. Not for them the enquiring mind of a wee Sister Magdalene! Oh No. The frequency with which the Scottish Press do not ask any questions when it comes to certain matters is........ well.....Odd.

It was only when the fans and an assortment of so called "internet bampots" started to ask some questions that it became plain that the ordinary Joe football fan would not stand for the administrators behind closed doors solutions.

The SFA and the SPL executives took the view that the "concept" of Rangers was so vital that rules had to be changed, deals done behind closed doors, shareholders kept secret and so on just to preserve the notion of "Rangers" for some to hold on to and in some way protect.

That protection comes with the stigma that nobody from the body of Rangers supporters—and here I refer to those who may be supporters of the business of Rangers as opposed to the fans who buy the tickets and part with their money to watch football—no one in business- not a single person- was prepared to come along and offer any realistic money to the creditors left trailing by Messrs Whyte and crew. Of those who did appear, the leading candidates were American, or from Singapore, or an Edinburgh Rugby man and not from Govan or Newton Mearns, or Bearsden or Bothwell etc.

Did that strike you as odd? Why would people with no real connection to Rangers, or even Football, or Scotland for that matter want to buy a club with such a huge mountain of debt and a trading history such as those brought out in successive Murray prepared accounts?

What was that all about?

In any event they all eventually backed away for different reasons.

Accordingly, by running Rangers clean into the ground over a period of at least a Decade, David Murray ensured that the club—a once proud club despite its distasteful and undefendable signing policy and social stance—is left at the mercy of carpet baggers such as Craig Whyte and yes Charlie Green—who makes no secret that he is here to make a few quid and then beat it!

Green is not interested in Scottish Football. He is not interested in the SFA or SPL structure or their reputation. He openly calls them micky mouse organisations and panders to those who will turn a blind eye to the last two decades of catastrophic maladministration so long as there is a "Rangers" to support—and that may well be a Rangers that many Rangers fans don't like and which leans towards an element which no one wants to see or hear in Scottish Football anymore.

Yet the irony is that there is a place for Rangers or a Rangers in Scottish Football in the 21st century—of course there is. However that place comes when everyone starts to recognise that David Murray's Rangers did not truly exist. It was a mountain of straw which was set to crumble as far back as 2005 and which served only his ego and his desire to be a leading financial light in Scotland and the UK. It was based on a platform that was never sustainable and which was clearly heading for the rocks.

That ambition, in itself nothing to be ashamed of if that is your goal, drove Murray to ignore the reality and the truth which was that Rangers could never sustain their lauded position at the pinnacle of Scottish Football without some form of creative accounting and /or massive never ending financial support. That became absolutely plain once Celtic had gotten their house in order with regard to their own finances and began to compete with the Ibrox club who enjoyed an almost a decade long period where everyone else in Scottish Football was cash strapped and having to live within their means. However, as soon as Fergus McCann's action plan began to bear fruit, Murray had to rethink and re-plan to maintain a status both he and his Rangers had become accustomed to.

However, Murray's ambition and ego, when taken together with the ridiculous sums of money he spent and lost, the ludicrous and inaccurate status bestowed on Craig Whyte by a press who would not willingly look into his background, the inactivity of the SFA and SPL when Whyte's real situation was *revealed on the internet and the overall desire not to upset the Rangers applecart has let the fans of Rangers FC down very badly—with the rest of Scottish Football not far behind.*

Once again, the seeming reluctance of the games authorities to do anything other than accord Rangers a special status, or to question the wisdom of Ibrox governance, has left Scottish Football as an also ran—far from the top table of European Football. Whilst there can be no pretending that other countries have stronger leagues and greater financial pull for a whole variety of reasons which the SFA cannot control, it has to be said that there is an argument which suggests that the SFA and the SPL simply allowed Rangers to get stronger and stronger in a footballing sense and on a basis that was to the potential prejudice of other clubs.

The recent statement by Alastair Johnston where he revealed that a UEFA licence arrived at Ibrox in 2011 without much ado following an initial enquiry which according to him must have revealed that players were being paid by salary and EBT is a case in point and an example of how Scottish Football deals with Rangers.

What to do? There appears to be a regulation breach which would prevent Rangers from playing in Europe? OK well say nothing and issue the licence anyway! We can't have Rangers not playing in Europe—unless we are forced to. Hopefully, it will all go away.

There appears to be no consideration of whether such an action is right or wrong, or whether another Scottish club would have benefitted from a properly won European place? Further, since Johnston's statement I have not seen any evidence of this line of enquiry being taken up with the SFA or the clubs.

Maybe, it will all go away?

Alas it won't go away. The SPL is due to have an enquiry start on 13th November and the FTT is about to rule—a ruling that will raise far more questions than it will provide answers. That ruling will further damage the reputation of Rangers Football Club and some of those who have been responsible for running it over the last twenty years or so. It is very possible that those tribunals and their findings will make for some uncomfortable reading for those at both the SFA and the SPL.

The finances of any Rangers club in the future have to be very different to those painted by Murray and company as ultimately they were neither realistic nor sustainable.

Perhaps, however, the biggest change is in the politics. Where once the footballing public were almost suppliant to the SFA, their club chairmen and the press—that is no longer the case. The press corps has been played and used far too often for the public liking when it comes to Rangers, and the more the old attitude of protecting Rangers at all costs and by any means necessary seems to be utilised by the SFA, The SPL or the press, the greater the chance of more and more people relying on the internet for a genuine and meaningful discussion on football matters.

Oh yes—the internet. That place which is inhabited solely by Bampots and nutters, where-as Craig Whyte would say—they talk 99% crap.

Except that it is on the internet where you will find people who are interested in football and the experience that football brings, and who are perfectly capable of pointing out something that you might not have hitherto considered ... odd. Yet when those odd moments are studied and analysed, compared and contrasted with other decisions and then looked at from a different angle.... Maybe they reveal an answer or two to a previously unanswered question--- perhaps posed by a wee nun to a six year old who simply could not provide an answer.

Q. Why did the SFA not apply the rules and act quicker and with proper purpose over the Rangers debacle?

A. eh......Politics?

Sadly, the very same politics which drove Bobby Brown to ensure that he did not risk playing many more of the Lisbon Lions together in a Scotland Jersey, has contrived to ensure that the Scottish Football Association, The Press and many others did nothing about the impending demise of Rangers Football Club until it was far too late to save it and the reputation of many currently employed in Scottish Football. Stewart Regan used to Tweet—"Nothing proven yet.. it is all just accusation".

The Problem is Stewart,you should have made your own enquiries, and when your organisation did make enquiries, they never followed them up, never acted upon what info you had and were all set to declare everyone on the internet as a "bampot" not worthy of listening to whether they had relevant information or not !

Lying referees, lying club executives, lying financial managers and the like do not bode well for Scottish Football. Lack of transparency, failure to actually work together with fans and to take note of what they have to say is a recipe for failure. And you should avoid failure at all costs.

On 23rdFebruary 1968 Scotland drew one each with England before a crowd of 134,000 spectators at Hampden with John Hughes of Celtic scoring Scotland's goal. With that result, Scotland missed out on yet another major championship, while England progressed.

With that disappointment, there was some speculation that Brown may well lose his job. His next match in charge was a friendly and it may have been important for the manager to restore the faith of some in his abilities. Scotland played The Netherlands in Amsterdam on 30th May and secured a scoreless draw.

The team that night was:

Clark (Aberdeen), Fraser (West Brom), McCreadie (Chelsea), Moncur (Newcastle), McKinnon (Rangers), Smith (Rangers), Henderson (Rangers), Hope (West Brom), "Dandy" McLean (Dundee), Cooke (Chelsea)and........... Greig (Rangers) who was also Captain.

On 16thOctober Scotland played another friendly against Denmark in Copenhagen, securing a one nil victory featuring:

Herriot (Birmingham), Gemmell (Celtic), McCreadie (Chelsea), Bremner (Leeds), McKinnon (Rangers), Greig (Rangers),Tommy McLean (Kilmarnock), McCalliog (Sheffield Wednesday),Stein (Rangers), Hope (West Brom) and Lennox (Celtic).

Just over a fortnight later Scotland played their first serious competitive match since the draw at Hampden—a vital world cup qualifier against Austria at Hampden. Lining up for Scotland were:

Simpson (Celtic), Gemmell (Celtic), McCreadie (Chelsea), Bremner (Leeds), McKinnon (Rangers), Greig (Rangers), Johnstone (Celtic), Cooke (Chelsea), Hughes (Celtic),Law (Manchester Utd) Lennox (Celtic)

Over the next year there would be a further 9 competitive internationals between world cup qualifiers and home internationals. In addition to the Celts mentioned above, Billy McNeil, Bobby Murdoch, and Willie Wallace all featured, though the 8 Celtic players never featured together in the one team ....unless it was for Celtic.

Scotland did not go to the World cup in 1970 and instead watched on as a brilliant Brazil side defeated Italy in the final with a brilliant final goal from an attacking fullback.

Some six weeks before, Celtic lost out in the European Cup Final in extra time.

Celtic had reached a final defeating the champions of England and a host of other clubs who all fielded international class players.

They reached the final playing 11 Scottish born players for the second time in 4 years.

Jock stein never tried to sign John Greig or Ronnie Mckinnon.

Sister Magdalene died about a year or so ago, but never asked me about the Scotland Football team again.

Had she had a computer in 1968, then she would have been...... the original internet bampot!

Ooh I just went all tingly

So let's now take a walk with one of the most consistent and articulate Celtic writers on the downfall of the Murray Empire. Step forward and take the hand of James Forrest as we walk through wonderland...

Glasgow Rangers: My Part In Their Downfall

1. I remember where I was when I heard it had happened. I was here, sitting in the same seat I'm writing this piece. Where else was I going to be? I was surfing for rumours, sniffing, like a tracker dog, for information on how close the event itself might be. We all knew it was coming, those of us who could be bothered to look, and to read, with open minds. We all had access to the vast research being conducted by ordinary guys like ourselves. We had seen, over a month before the Sunday Mail put it on their front page, the sensational picture of Craig Whyte's "overseas base", from which he owned Rangers; a portacabin in a field of cows. We had seen the pictures of the "offices" in Bath Street, Glasgow, where another of his globe-spanning companies was based; a grated window, looking in on an empty room.

We had pored over the lists of companies in which he'd been a director, and which had gone to the wall. We had read Paul McConville's detailed account of the "many Craig Whyte's (or was it White's?)", and been tantalised by RTC's hints about "boiler rooms" and other dastardly deeds. We had been riveted by Mark Daley and his investigative brilliance, which tumbled onto Whyte's directorship ban, and we'd been thrilled at rumours of unpaid taxes, of bills being shoved in a drawer, of sheriff officers arriving at the stadium and a dozen other little gems, all building a picture of an "institution" badly out of whack, and about to come crashing down.
The media either didn't know, or maybe they just didn't want to know. We knew. For months we'd waited for this, like a kid at Xmas, except that instead of looking at a faraway date which we'd already ringed on the calendar, we were all

looking at the calendar and wondering which date it was
going to be.

When the announcement came, on Sky Sports News – and
thank the Gods for delivering it to us on a day when Jim White
was in work – it was both something we'd been expecting and
pleasingly out of the blue. It was February 14, 2012. Happy
Valentine's Day, Rangers fans. Craig Whyte just sent a love-
letter to everyone in the Gallowgate.
Later that night, Whyte walked out the front door at the
ground and read his prepared statement to a cacophony of
boos. He had decided to place the club in administration to
save it.

We knew better.

They were in the early stages of an unfolding financial
calamity. He didn't tell us what part he'd played in it, but
some of us knew the broad strokes. Some of us had made it
our business to be as informed as possible, the better to write
about it, as many of us were doing on our blogs, our pages,
and in the various Celtic fan forums, sharing what we'd
learned, speculating on what the future might hold and
generally gloating about how bad it all looked for "Scotland's
biggest institution after the Church", as David Murray had
once ludicrously referred to it.
At the time, I considered myself a small cog in a big wheel, as
part of an insurgency, devoting much of its time to uncovering
as much information as possible about Whyte, and putting it
in the public domain so that others could read it, and perhaps
be inspired to do their own digging.

Like any insurgency, we saw ourselves as operating outside
the normal lines – those of so-called serious journalism – and,

really, flying by the seat of our pants. Little by little we knew Rangers fans were starting to read a lot of what we were writing – with great interest, as much of it was never going to see the light of day in the mainstream press – even if they didn't want to believe it. Some of us made it our business to harass journalists into investigating our claims properly, others wanted to put our theories where the public could hear them by getting onto the radio. There, an early name was coined for us. It still makes me smile. We were tagged "the fundamentalists". It was meant to be a disparaging label. Like others, it became a badge of honour.

I had been writing about Rangers' woes for four years in the lead up to that day. I had penned an article for E-Tim's called "The End of Rangers?" in 2008, after the publication of Murray International Holding's accounts for that year revealed a devastating hole in their balance sheet. The club was so dependent on MIH for its financial security I knew it was in deep trouble the second the umbilical cord between them was cut. From that day, I began to pay close attention to their financial affairs, and got an early sniff of trouble when I heard a trouble-shooter from Lloyds had been placed on their board of directors. Then the story of the Big Tax Case hit, like an atom bomb, and from that moment on, I considered Rangers on death row.

On the day the administration announcement was made I realised the impact it would have on Scottish football, and that as the full horror of what it meant became clear for Rangers fans there would be a concerted effort by people at the club, and their allies, to limit the scale of the devastation. It also took the club to the edge of liquidation itself – which *the evidence I'd seen, and things I'd heard, suggested was more and more likely – and that this too, when it was fully realised, would spark an enormous public, and media, reaction.*

I didn't know it then, but myself and the rest of the "fundamentalists" were about to morph into the "Internet Bampots." Our guerrilla campaign ended that day. We weren't insurgents anymore. What happened in the next few months made us revolutionaries instead.

2. Throughout my life, I've had two twin loves, which have held my attention, at times kept me sane, and at others driven me to despair. Those loves are football, Celtic in particular, and politics. I am a committed lefty, with this club in my blood, who grew up watching Rangers winning league titles and Tories winning general elections. For years I thought I was a jinx. Then 1997 changed everything, as Labour swept to power and shortly thereafter wee Fergus unfurled a league flag at Paradise. All seemed right and good in the world again. Yet years of trial were to follow.

I left behind one of my great loves in 2002, when the party I had given as much of my life to as I'd given to Celtic betrayed everything it, and I, stood for by leading this country to war at the whim of a liar and on the basis of a fraud. I have never taken part in organised party political activity since, and probably never will again.

It was the Iraq debacle which came back to me, time and time again, in the months following Craig Whyte's Valentine's Day decision to place Rangers in administration. The campaign built around the notion of "saving Rangers for the good of Scottish football" had echoes in the one the governments of

Bush and Blair constructed around the paper thin premise of "saving the world from Saddam Hussein." Resistance to both was inevitable.

For myself and the other Internet Bampots, if we'd wanted a fight, the world around us had a thousand vastly more important battles in it to choose from. Another Tory government was in the process of dismantling large chunks of the state, in the name of "fiscal necessity". The Middle East was still shuddering from the aftershocks of the Iraqi invasion, almost ten years on. Scotland was gearing up for a showdown with London on the independence referendum question and life itself, in the age of austerity, was becoming tougher by the day.

The feeling, out in the country, across not only Scotland but the UK, was that people had become so removed from the centers of power they now had no way of influencing events at all. The media was being dragged through the gutter of Levinson. Yet they were still influential, because for many they were still the sole source of information about the world, and could therefore still frame the nature and tone of the debate. The political classes had, only two years before, been unveiled as routinely venal, corrupt and divorced from reality. Trust, faith and hope were in short supply all round. People felt helpless in the face of the juggernaut of "officialdom".
Yet this one was different. This was right on our door, and we had some expertise in the matter. We knew the principals involved, knew the politics and we could look the enemy squarely in the eye, and bet on who blinked first.

As the Rangers situation developed, and the attention I devoted to it grew in turn, more than once the people in my life asked what was worth so much time and effort. Those closest to me became increasingly frustrated at the way I scrutinised and dissected each new development. They didn't understand how events surrounding a football club, which wasn't even the one I supported, could have become so important. Some of them still don't. They view the whole thing as an extension of the game itself which some of them hated to begin with. Others, perhaps because they are still influenced by what the old media writes, thought to a certain extent that myself and others were motivated only by the tribal nature of life in the West of Scotland.

Others still, those who didn't know me well, accused me of being motivated by hate, of being a bigot, of seeing everything through green tinted glasses. To say they have me all wrong is to let them off the hook. Some of them see the world through their own prejudices and nothing more. My motives were much simpler – but in a sense more complex - than they will ever understand. There was a point – it was shortly after the liquidation of Rangers became certain, and just before Sevco was born - where, to me, it ceased being about football at all.

That's why I don't think the word "revolution" is the wrong one to use here.

3. At times like these, I find an ability to be detached helpful. I find it instructive to look at this from the outside. Let's try to place, in context, just what it is we are talking about here, stripped of all the flags and scarves, of all the emotive language and of all the tribal paraphernalia. Let's not even view this through the prism of sport. This more than a football story.

This is about a huge financial, social and cultural institution *which, for at least ten years, perhaps longer, was engaged in a scheme which Revenue and Customs say was nothing less than tax evasion writ large.*

During the same period of time, that company was also the beneficiary of an enormously generous bank, who were prepared to ignore high levels of indebtedness and extend them a line of credit far beyond what they should have been qualified to receive. The bank involved later teetered on the brink of total collapse, and was saved at the last minute by a business rival, after political intervention from the Prime Minister himself. Only when the deal was sealed did the new owners find out about the scale of the debts they'd bought.

The saga of the bank is currently the subject of one of the most complex criminal investigations in the history of this country – Operation Hornet.
The company at the centre of the tax scam, with its links to whatever was going on at the bank, was, during that ten year period, using the twin stratagems of its generous overdraft and credit facilities and its financial duplicity against the exchequer to gain advantages over its competitors which otherwise it would not have had. It was able to secure tens of millions of pounds by virtue of its "successes" in that timeframe without which even their high-wire financing would not have staved off a serious crisis in funding. Added to this was an ability to circumvent licensing regulations, especially those regarding financial disclosure, which was aided, in no small part, by a former senior director of said company being the head of the agency responsible for awarding the licenses. That meant the growing nature of their problems was kept concealed from all but a select few.

All of this was going on in full view of a media who's relationship with the company involved was clearly of the incestuous variety, and patently unhealthy.

The banking crisis of 2008, and the subsequent change in ownership at the bank, saw new people scrutinising the books and the breaks being applied to the expenditure which had created a huge black hole. The response of the company involved was to embark on a final spending spree, and to ramp up their tax evasion mechanisms, even after receiving notice from the exchequer that large sums were already due.

Their short-term splurge brought in short-term success, and the additional revenues were quickly seized by their new bankers to plug some of the holes, but it was all too little too late. The bank demanded swinging cuts, the kind of cuts that would have devastated the company in competitive terms – and this was the one thing they were never going to accept – and that's when the backlash began, led by the press.

And who was the backlash against? The company, who by virtue of fraud, friends in high places and creative accounting had accumulated tax authority debts of an estimated £50 million plus, as well as God knows how much due to the publicly owned banks?

Of course not. No, the media's angry guns were turned on the government which dared to insist that the company pay its share, and the bank which was, not unreasonably, asking them to pay back what they owed.

It was around the same time that takeover stories began to appear in the media, at regular intervals. Amongst the names involved in those early press stories included a man with overt links to Loyalist paramilitaries and another involving Russian gangsters, a tale which prompted a national newspaper (a paper which was later closed down after its own appalling proclivities became known to the public at large, including hacking the phone of a murdered school girl) to proclaim, with, as it turned out, startling foresight, that those connected to the company would not care where the money came from ... as long as the bank went on its merry way.

When a prospective owner finally emerged from the bizarre band of sociopaths and criminals who had wanted to boldly go where saner men feared to tread he seemed, on the surface, to be what a company in disgrace required; a man with money, with a close affinity with the company itself and roots right here in the West of Scotland, where the company was based. The press hailed him as a savior, vastly inflated his actual wealth and predicted an unlikely victory over the tax authority and the satisfying of the bank, followed by another spending spree. Yet even as they were writing what turned out to be blatant lies, others were doing their own due diligence. The man who had come to secure the company's future had his own colourful background; a history of dodgy dealings, failed businesses and alleged criminality. The media, with access to the same facts as those they later called "idiots with typewriters", and often much worse, were still not giving their readers the full picture when the company shocked this country by announcing its intent to enter administration, on February 14, 2012.

That came after months of legal wrangles, boardroom blood-letting and internal strife, very little of which was explored fully in the press until much, much later, when it was well and truly too late to matter.

The previous ten years of corporate malfeasance were only a prelude to the turbulent eight or so months in which their new owner, hidden behind a wall of silence, cowed staff, secretive strategies, and locked room meetings, managed to hive off assets, transfer money out of the company to his friends, mortgage off future revenue streams and finally, shockingly, decided not to honour any of their debts, great or small, including those to the tax authority the company itself had already cheated out of tens of millions of pounds – all the while telling a compliant, unquestioning press that HMRC were "open to a deal" on the original bill.

In the course of those eight months there was not a single board meeting, the company refused to publish its accounts and was finally thrown off the stock exchange on which it was listed, for a catalogue of un-fulfilled commitments under the rules. Most incredibly, because of the work of one BBC Scotland journalist, who's campaign for the truth was greeted in the rest of the press with a shrugged "there was little in there we didn't already know" (but had failed to report) the new owner was exposed as fly-by-night chancer who had been given a seven year ban from holding a UK directorship, for asset stripping two of his previous companies.

Despite all this, and during the same period, they were granted their annual operating licenses, as ever, despite mounting evidence, from a variety of sources, that those should have been refused.

When the company finally entered administration it appointing a firm with links to the takeover to oversee what itself, turned out to be nothing less than an enormous corporate debt dumping scam. Prospective buyers came forward, made offers, and vanished. Some later reported how their bids had been dismissed without proper scrutiny, as if the administration process itself was nothing more than an elaborate sham. Indeed, during the process only a handful of employees – out of over 130 – were actually paid off, and the company declared post-administration losses in the millions, even as the administrators were writing themselves cheques. When the huge scale of the amounts outstanding were finally made public, the estimates were in the region of £134 million – with £93 million of that potentially owing to Her Majesty's Revenue and Customs.

Everyone knew those debts would never be repaid, that even a CVA would end with creditors getting pennies in the pound, and the rest being written off.

As it was, the company was finally placed in liquidation, with the assets sold to another colourful character, who appeared out of a clear blue sky, for 1/20th the market value as set down in the administrators own report. For that he took over real estate, the corporate logo, the company colours, and even the old trading name. The whiff of scandal was, and remains, pungent. All the debts were erased. The tax payers were cheated. Small creditors were left with virtually nothing. This was, without a doubt, one of the largest financial scandals in the history of Scotland.

In any scenario one can conceive of, something of this magnitude should have ended with a full public enquiry, with a criminal investigation and the prosecutions of everyone involved. The media should have been hollering for heads to roll, for handcuffs to click and for prison doors to open, and then slam shut, with the sentences running in years.
It should have been seen for, called by, and treated like,

exactly what it was; an on-going criminal enterprise, finally brought to a juddering halt.

Despite the self-evident truth of that, an even greater scandal almost followed all this. The people responsible for corporate governance, in the field in which this company operated, fully intended to let the company die, throw its debt overboard, and assume the same position in the marketplace as before, as if nothing at all had happened.
The campaign to have it this way was spearheaded by the licensing authorities themselves, aided and abetted by the media, who early on prostituted their historical role as seekers of justice for that of cheerleaders.

To cap it, the political classes, who should have been as outraged as the public, were standing ready to give it their seal of approval. In order to make it all work, rules would have been broken, re-written or ignored; other companies in the same field would have been treated with callous disregard; and a new standard would have been set for corporate behaviour in the industry, with genuinely terrible repercussions for its future.
If it had gone just so, it would have piled one fraud on top of another, and it would have happened in just that way, had a small group of people – a number which later grew to cover the length and breadth of the Scottish game – refused to let it stand.

When people want to know what was worth so much of our time, I give them a condensed version of what you've just read. I offer that version now, in summation.
Our objective was to ensure that justice was done. Our campaign was about making sure the company responsible

for all of this was held to proper account, and to make sure the authorities were scrutinised at every turn, and their rules followed to the letter. We were engaged in a fight for the truth, in a battle against a campaign of official – and media – lies and smears, scare stories and innuendo unlike anything we'd ever seen before.

This was about a dogged bunch of ordinary people taking a stand against an enormous, well-funded, well organised and powerful group who were determined to excuse every despicable fraud, and every criminal act, to get the result they wanted. This was about people standing up to "those in power", campaigning to assure a rogue corporation was brought to book for its sins and punished in an appropriate way for a decade of corrupt behaviour.

It is a modern miracle, and a source of inspiration, that in this cynical age where corporations, even governments, can run roughshod over all that is right and just, that such a campaign was born, grew, soldiered on in the face of almost overwhelming opposition, and emerged on the other side with success, and the cup of victory in its hands.

On a personal note, speaking for myself, this is what should have happened over Iraq. That great engine of destruction should have been stopped in its tracks, or if that proved impossible, the people involved prosecuted to the fullest limit of the law. On those moments during the Sevco scandal, as first they seemed destined to play in the SPL and then, when that didn't work, they seemed to be headed for SFL 1, when I thought about Iraq, and how a similarly fought campaign had failed to prevent the war, I told myself "Not this time."

That failure is what spurred me to do my part in this

campaign. That's what was worth so much of my time, and effort, and trouble, and stress.

4. The revolution itself, in which I played a small part, will be remembered in times to come as one of the greatest victories for the ordinary fan that has ever been won in the Scottish game. This was the moment when the "customers", for too many years ignored and betrayed by the authorities, and even by their clubs, found their voices and made them heard. We put them on notice that we will not be taken for granted or treated with contempt any longer.

More than that, the media was humiliated at every turn and its role in the corruption held up to scrutiny. Reputations were tarnished beyond repair; some, like that of the man who wrote in his column about "diddy teams" and "muppets", destroyed.

The journalists who campaigned for a shameful sell out and said the smaller clubs would fold, that self-interest would win over sporting integrity, that finance was more important than fairness, were shown as out-of-touch fools, who might still hold positions and draw salaries, and inhabit their plateau of self-importance, but who have nevertheless been stripped of any relevance in the wider debate as to where the game goes next. They have neither the moral right, nor the intellectual dexterity, to contribute much more to that debate than background noise.

The Internet Bampots have seized the agenda, and demonstrated their talents for adapting and organising quickly, and to great effect. The books, like this one, which will come out of these events, are being penned by us because that's the way it's traditionally been done; history is written by *the winners. The corruption we helped to expose, the double-standards we revealed, the disgraces we fought to highlight, the outcome we battled to prevent and the one we worked hard to assure, all of it will be written about for the generations who follow us to study, and learn from, and revel in and enjoy, and they will be written by people in green scarves, who call Celtic Park their second home.*

Those books, not the chip wrappings of the tabloids, will be the standard texts by which this era will be judged, and these events explored.
Think on that for a moment, and how big a deal that is. Tell me that's not the stuff of which every successful revolution is made.
Scottish football will never be the same again, because of the work we did and the battles we won. Sevco, or perhaps some other company which has assumed the identity of the club we once called Rangers, will play again in the SPL, or whatever the top division in Scotland is called, but they will get there having started from the bottom and worked their way up. They will have started where all new clubs start, having lost years, and millions, to make up for the shameful way their predecessor club behaved. The corpse of the old club will – if things go as they should –be stripped of the trophies and titles they won in the ten years of tax evasion and concealment which future generations will know as "the era of the EBT's."

The present efforts of the press, and campaign by the Sevco fans, to present this period as nothing out of the ordinary will be forgotten, as will their current wailing over the "injustice of it all" because the rules have been applied as written. It is our version of this – the truth and nothing but – which will survive

for posterity.
Something else will spring from this, or so I hope, and it's a realisation beyond football.

This affair has reaffirmed my belief in the power of ordinary people to stand tall, to seek out facts and question the "official line", to come together and fight in a common cause.
When everything is said and done, that is the real victory which came out of this affair. This is why it means something to me above and beyond seeing Sevco beaten by Queen of the South in the Ramsden's Cup, about seeing them humbled in the lowest tier of the game. It's about more than the bragging rights, or years where Celtic will be on top. It is about more than just two football clubs and their respective places in the pantheon of the Scottish game.

As I have my heroes on the football pitch, those men I saw and those I wish I had, like Larsson, McStay, Moravcik, Johnstone, Auld, Lennox and Chalmers, I have my heroes in that other area where once I played a role. Too few of them got to fulfill their potential, too many of them were lost to us before their time had fully come. One of the greatest of them all was Robert F. Kennedy, and one of his quotes is a great inspiration, and comfort, to me, especially in these tough times where belief is difficult to maintain and hope is hard to sustain.

"Few will have the greatness to bend history itself, but each of us can work to change a small portion of events. It is from numberless diverse acts of courage and belief that human history is shaped. Each time a man stands up for an ideal, or acts to improve the lot of others, or strikes out against injustice, he sends forth a tiny ripple of hope, and crossing each other from a million different centres of energy and

daring, those ripples build a current which can sweep down the mightiest walls of oppression and resistance."

A terrible scandal was uncovered here. An equally great scandal almost came about. People like you, like me, like Paul Larkin, played a role in exposing the former and preventing the latter. There is nothing special about any of us; what counts is what we did. We found the facts, told the truth and drew a line in the sand. The result was exceptional; those who did the deeds were not. These things are possible if ordinary people believe, and have the strength to act.

I won't deny deriving real pleasure from it, aside from all that. Rangers, the club, had become a thoroughly bigoted, damaging, corrupt influence on our sport and our country. Their financial sleight of hand cost other clubs millions, robbed them of silverware and poisoned our memories of more days than I care to think of. Their hold over large swathes of the press has neutered proper journalism, blurred the lines between fact and fiction, and it prevented ordinary fans from knowing what was happening at their club.
The fans themselves were not immune from the corruption; some actively embraced the arrogance and ego, and made it their own. Large sections of their support had morphed into something truly evil and debased, from sectarian singing to flags of hatred, and even the occasional riot. Never was any football club so deserving of a disgraced and humiliating end.

I believe some version of them will emerge to challenge us in years to come. Perhaps this period in the wilderness will have a positive effect, and give them the self-awareness and respect for others they presently lack. Looking at the new makeup of the Sevco away support, I am not holding my

breath. Yet, perhaps those genuinely progressive elements in their support will get their chance to re-take the agenda, and stake their claim for the new club's soul.
That is their business, not ours. That is their battle to fight, their war to win. I wish them well in their struggle, but in that debate we will rightly play no role.

Our war is over, and in this little corner of Scotland some degree of justice has been done, some measure of sanity has been restored and a flame of hope now burns.
I can sleep at night knowing I played a small part in that. It makes me very proud.

Proud? I've went all gooey reading that.

Before I enlighten you with my thoughts, let's throw it out further than Paradise and take you to Leith, and Hibernian supporter Allan Hosey for his views on things like their downfall and our armageddon...

Hunbelievable

First of all, I will be using the word huns a lot during this. The ridiculous attempts to describe as sectarian a derogatory term for a football club and their fans can only be the product of minds ravaged by syphilis. Rangers are the huns. Rangers supporters are the huns. It's not a cipher for protestant and never has been. I have never even heard the term hun referring to anything other than the barbarian Germanic tribe or Rangers. So in the spirit of all things 2012, get it right up ye huns.

The floater in the bowl

The 80s were in retrospect (and at the time) a hideous decade. But not in Scottish football. Or at least not in all of it. The "Souness revolution" saw the bastard huns spending huge amounts of money on players mostly from England who were tempted to Scotland to play for the mighty (morphed lower) Rangers. This sort of "project" of slinging outlandish amounts of money has now became ubiquitous in football in France, Spain, and most of all England, but at the time this was genuinely novel. The tabloids declared the English clubs ban from playing in Europe as the pivotal reason for the northwards migration of several England internationals. But the real reason was the same as it has been for the vast majority of players for a long time now, it was down to money. Rangers would pay more than anyone else. To an extent this wasn't unreasonable. The huns were filling their ground and gate money was at thut point the main source of income for clubs, so anyone filling a 50,000 capacity stadium week in week out could have theoretically done this. But it was the bastard huns who did so. And it poisoned Scottish football.

It's not too difficult to draw a pretty straightforward conclusion about the correlation from the rise of the huns in the mid 80s to the decline in Scottish footballs standing in international football. A lot of people (myself included) really don't give much of a flying fuck about their international football side nowadays, but it's a pretty decent gauge of where countries lie in the general scheme of things. And Scotland are fucking terrible. There isn't a country bigger than Luxembourg in Europe who you would expect Scotland to beat 9 times out of 10. Yugoslavia eventually split into 7 states, the only one you'd fancy Scotland to beat would be Kosovo (and I'll admit to never having seen them, so this is possibly optimistic). Now what those countries have is a style of play, and a style of player they produce. Scotland has nothing like that. The genetic tanner baw saviour of Scottish fitba was deemed too wee, and a nation of midgets seemingly collectively decided that their football should consist of the biggest laddies who weren't necessarily very good at playing football. There is no DNA of Scottish football any longer. It's an amalgam of big strong boys (although not as big, nor as strong, as the countries with much bigger populations) and... well that's it really.

So how was this Rangers fault exactly? They were only one club when they existed. How could one club have turned everyones sides into ball lumping, skill free, big, useless bastards? Well it's the "Rangers Way" to start with. Across the land everyone else adored their lazy talented wee guys who entertained you. Rangers were the club of John Greig ('s a bastard). And there's a strain of football that Scotland has always had of big dirty bastards who were there to boot lumps out of the tricky wee players who folk paid to watch. It *just didn't used to be dominant in any way. There has always been a balance between destruction and construction in football, between being passive or active in the way you play the game. In Scotland it is the hunnish level of absolute destruction at the expense of all else which has left us where we are. And that was due to their success. Success which was bought on moonbeams.*

Financial doping

Rangers success in Scottish football from the late 80s to the mid 90s was built on nothing other than money. There wasn't a legendary manager making shite into cake, there was just money. There was no new style of football which forced others to adapt and build something to beat it, there was just money. There was no producing a conveyor belt of supremely talented youngsters, there was just money. And they spent it. And the hunnish hordes, and their headline hungry pet media, lapped it up. The message came through loud and clear that the only way to succeed in Scottish football was to spend as much as you possibly could. Preferably on better players than you could produce from woefully underfunded and ignored youth systems.

And there was only one club which could even remotely do this to the same extent as the huns had. Fortunately enough for Rangers, Celtic pretty much spent the first half of the 90s being awful. A club which was badly run from the top which permeated through the club. And it took Fergus McCann coming in and getting some professionalism in the club for them to come back. Rangers had had their time of dominating, and it became apparent pretty quickly that Celtic were a bigger club than them and that if they were run well should be the dominant force. So Rangers started cheating the taxman to be able to keep outspending Celtic. And everyone else tried to keep up. And re-build their grounds at the same time. At the point where grounds were having to be brought into the 20th century Rangers started a financial arms race by robbing from Her Majesties revenue. Clubs haven't recovered from this period. The only club who were in the top Scottish league in 1995 who have not been continuously in debt since 1995 are Motherwell, and that was only due to them having done a runner from their debts though entering (and coming out of) administration.

My club Hibs were relegated in 1998. My first reaction on hearing of the huns tax dodging inspired non disclosure of contracts revealed that they had been playing ineligible players that entire season was a bit of a geeky one. I checked to see if Hibs would have been relegated if every Rangers result was changed to a 3-0 defeat. And they wouldn't. Motherwell would have finished below Hibs I quickly figured out. So Hibs would not have been relegated. It genuinely took me a couple of minutes to realise that the side who should have been relegated that season was not Motherwell either. Rangers should have been. They started financially cheating the second there was a genuine challenge to them from Celtic. Despite having an absolutely enormous advantage over everyone else.

Their self proclaimed superiority could not be allowed to crumble. So they ramped up the cheating in future years. The only slight positive was that at least this eventually killed them.

It's not where you're from, it's where you're at

So what now? The huns are dead. But this isn't The Wizard Of Oz where Scottish football simply blooms in glorious technicolor after a transformative event. A couple of months in and so far crowds are holding up more than decently. It turns out that the ridiculous damaging scaremongering indulged in by the "leaders" of Scottish football like Doncaster& Regan was in actual fact just ridiculous damaging scaremongering. Much as predicted by pretty much anyone who was paying attention and who can treat editorial posing as comment in the media as opinion rather than fact.

But the game in Scotland is damaged. And so is every club in it. It's not due to the lack of huns, but by their actions when they existed. Vision is non-existent. And there is no-one at the top of the game who appears to have it.

We have a pitiful media who for the most part neither enlighten nor entertain. Their complicity in the cheating of Rangers is beyond all doubt. Their complicity helped to kill the club like a loving dog who steps on the trigger of a carelessly discarded shotgun and tries to lick the thousand bleeding holes in the body of the owner closed (before turning into a rabid devil dog with a taste for blood). But there has been no noticeable change in their practices, or indeed in their personnel. Journalistic standards are pitifully short of acceptable. Instead you have a mainstream media who would mostly rather take the crumbs off clubs tables to maintain "access" instead of simply writing intelligently about the game and showing some respect to the people who they should be writing for.

But it's not all doom and gloom. The brightest part of the situation is that the people who, despite everything, still love and respect the game are still there. Many fans throughout the country have been more clued up than the media reporting events. Many write with intelligence and wit (including the author of this book who is now due me a pint for being nice about him). And the media have been starting to be held to account. And most (yes Kilmarnock I am looking at you) clubs Directors finally realised that their fans are the ones who allow their clubs to exist and they will not be ignored. It's going to be a long road back from dismantling the damage done, but at least there may be a possibility of doing so.

And finally what of Sevco/ The Rangers/ Zombiehuns? Well for starters by the time of publishing they might have won an away game in the 3rdDivision. They appear to have picked up a lot of the people who supported the huns, and it appears as though they have come with skin which a stiff breeze would puncture. Maybe a few years in the lower leagues will teach them some humility and toughen them up. It appears as though they will not shed the despicable bigotry and sectarianism which they cling to as though it was something to be proud of, and which any sane person would have surely grasped with both hands the chance to discard. And it also appears as though they will trust someone who says that everyone is out to get them which suggests that they're pretty much proving Abraham Lincoln wrong because apparently you can fool all of "the people" all of the fucking time. So their best case scenario is that they fluke into an ownership who will not rip the pish out of them, despite the evident ease of doing so, and take them straight back down the same path they've just went down.

There you have it folks, they're gone, done, vamooshed from our lives. Or are they? Well, if you're taken in by the tribute act that are pretending to be them, more fool you. They are there as a freak show so that morons can be fleeced again, that's all. We're still here, in a hostile land, and we shall not be moved.

125 years and running

Revelations (Part 2)

Let's face it, there is something about me that doesn't seem to allow me to have a quiet life, despite the fact that is what I crave. I can't keep my mouth shut when I see something I disagree with, I can't turn down a drink when I've already had enough and I've only learned in the last four years how to keep my pants on when a girl smiles at me.

The burning question you probably have about this book is: was I guilty of the crimes I was accused of? In all honesty, yeah, a couple of them. I'm not going to lie to you, I did facilitate bets in bars occasionally. I also did know and socialise with made men. I'm not going to deny that and don't have any regrets at all. These people are my friends and I'm not ever going to turn my back on them because, when I was at my scariest point, they did not turn their back on me. Who are they? Well, that would be foolish to say but they have been mentioned here. As for the rest of the stuff, total bollocks. The whole thing came about because someone else got caught doing something somewhere and went through the New York phonebook naming people. I was lucky, I got out, some waited years in jail before they did. If this makes you feel any different towards me, I understand it but I'm apologising for it, that's just who I am.

That's not to say I spent all my time in New York consorting with gangsters, far from it. Bar none the best character I ever met in New York is a guy called Kenny Keegan. He is a serving US Marine and without doubt the funniest guy I've ever met in my life.

We'd sit in Donovans, now sadly gone, and he'd keep us on our toes with his stories and anecdotes, like

"Did you hear about my brother?"

"No?"

"He's dead"

"What the fuck?"

"Yeah, he goes for a routine check up at the Doctor? Suddenly it's an episode of House"

Or then there is this

"Hey, did I ever tell you about the time I saw Pele? My buddy, who is older than me, says to me he's taking me to Yankee Stadium. I'm over the moon, this is the 70's, I've never been to Yankee Stadium. So we drive over there, park the car and I'm feeling great, like I'm one of the gang now. We get in the stadium and it's only half full, now this is when the Yankees had a team again so I ask what is going on? Then I see, standing in front of me, the great Pele, it's a Cosmos game. I swear, no more than five yards from me, he made pass that God himself would be proud of. Anyway, after the game my buddy asks if I enjoyed the game, I tell him I loved it but I did think we were going to see The Yankees, he looks at me and says 'You think we would waste a Yankee ticket on you?'"

Plus there is this

"My father cost Brooklyn and Queens billions of dollars"

"Really? how?"

"He told the cable companies about the illegal cable we all had. Fucking moron. This is a guy who opens and closes the fridge door 50 times a night just to make sure the light went off. So Brooklyn and Queens were the last places in America to get cable, the mob already had it all sewn up. They go to my fathers house, the cable company, in the early 80s and tell him about all the great stuff they are going to have on it, my father goes 'I already got that' and that was that"

And that there is why I love New York, real people, real stories, they are my fucking Heroin. I've dabbled in all drugs, except Heroin funnily enough, and had one serious habit in my time, but nothing beats the company of people who are just like yourself, don't take life too seriously and know the rules.

My life went through huge changes in the last few years. Suffering from Post Traumatic Stress Disorder, I've realised that it never really goes away and you just have to learn to control it. Going back to New York extinguished a lot of my demons, facing up to my fears, talking and writing about them was very much a cathartic process. Mental health issues are still spoken about in hushed tones. It's time to shout about them.

The flip side of having incredible lows and fears is that you can recognise more the incredible highs that life will bring and with that being said, nothing will ever get close to the death of Rangers. I've documented many times the adverse affect they had on all Tims who watched Celtic in the 90s. I don't have any laughter in me about what happened to them, I am angry, downright furious if truth be told. The very fact they were able to spend other people's money for years and then oversee a scheme which gave them an unfair advantage over the rest of us sums up how far Scotland still has to come before we can even dream of talking about equality.

That said, anyone who knew me in the 90's, and shared my pain, you gotta love the fact that we outlived them!

Celtic supporters are fighting back though, I hope I have given you a taste of that in this book. When you listen to the great Housey and Davie on Over and Over on a Friday, broadcasting to the nation, let me tell you, in the 90s we used to have to pretend that Rebel dos were birthday parties just to get a venue. When you walk along the Gallowgate and see all the pubs bedecked in green and white, please remember it wasn't always like this. People had to fight every step of the way to make that possible. When you see thousands of people streaming to and from a game in their Hoops, remember, there was a time not too long ago where the vast majority were afraid to even wear colours in the street.

With the rise of the Internet Bampots, everything is changing. Sevco would be in the SPL right not were it not for the fans of other clubs.

I know this book hasn't covered everything, I'm just a minor character in my own story but this was my experience of the revolution that took place in Scottish football and in my own head.

Folk who really know me will know that I've never been backward at coming forward. Often to my own detriment. That's changed now. I've changed in that respect. I've added a filter. What I feel now, in light of everything that came out about Referees, Dual Contracts and EBT's, is vindicated. You knew and I knew that something wasn't right, you could feel it but you were called paranoid. You were ridiculed and hounded wherever you went, made to feel inadequate and unwelcome.

In 2008 they tried to make us feel unwelcome again and we got their song outlawed.

In 2010 they tried to cheat us and lie to our manager and we got them out.

In 2012 they tried to tell us it was armageddon and we showed them it was, but just for one club.

Whether it was a Cartuja jpg or a LostBhoys blog, Celtic supporters kept chipping away at the enemy and until it collapsed. If you said your piece on Celtic Minded or The Huddleboard, retweeted a link or quote, or gave an angry status on facebook, you were part of all that.

You helped change our world.

Things will never be the same again.

Thank you.

PS

To protect against our complacency, here's a story from this year

"I used to be a ref. When I was in the company of a few other refs one evening, one ref asked a category one ref, who had been promoted to category one and would be doing 4th official duties for an upcoming Celtic game, how he would

control Neil Lennon when he got him (I thought this was a ludicrous question at the time) and his reply was "hook the Fenian ginger bastard and send him to the stands!" to which a huge laughter erupted from other refs. I said to him that was out of order but they just classed it as a bit of banter but I said I was hurt by the Fenian comment. No one cared. Also, while I was in there I got ridiculed for having attended Catholic school. For example if I would do or say something silly or fucked something up it would be because I to went to a Catholic school. Funnily enough, this wasn't by the ref mentioned above but I would say at least three other refs said this to me"

Don't get careless, folks.

Projecting Paddy McCourt

I have a dream. Not like John Gordon Sinclair either. I'm standing on the steps of the Lincoln Memorial in Washington DC. Not just any steps, those that Martin Luther King stood on in 1963. That was August, this is November, 2012 and it's boiling. My dream, as I stood on those steps, was addressing a rally. Not just any rally, no no, this was a GRAHAM D. WILSON FOR PRESIDENT rally.

Anyway.

Wim's Tims has been out a month and I need to project being a successful writer so I've flown my Mum over. You've no idea what I had to do to get that money.

Until now.

In Philadelphia there is a hotel. It stands in Penrose Avenue. From the outset, it looks like a normal hotel, inside is a very different story. It is the world's most used snuff movie location. For those not familiar with this art, these are movies where people are murdered in them for real. No special effects, no Hollywood bullshit, all reality. Of course it's illegal, everything good is, but people pay a fortune to watch that shit. My role? I was a stunt double for the newly departed. In reverse. See, you don't want the actual people who are going to be murdered to actually appear on screen unless you can't see their face, so I was that face. You saw me killed on screen hundreds of times for $25 u pop. Well not you obviously, you'd never watch such depraved filth that sees real people executed for the sole purpose of getting others off. You'd never watch that.

Unless this is Jim McGuigan reading this.

I made $2500 in one week and given that it was tail end of the week that started off with me corn-dogging Graham Wilson repeatedly in the Sheraton in downtown Philly, all in all it was more fulfilling than most weeks. Plus Graham's only in the toilet twice a day now.

I stood on those steps in DC and had another dream. That dream was a book launch. A book launch for Wim's Tims. In The Bronx. On Dec 10th. All Tims Welcome. Not really of course, there's quite a few I didn't want there, let's face it, we all know ones like that.

I called Chas immediately, his answer to the call was strange "Cops been in touch?" and I replied in the negative.He's still paranoid about the bike, relax Duffster.

We were staying near Arlington, although In America "Near" means 20 minutes drive and I don't, so Graham, of course, picked my Mum and I up on Pennsylvania Avenue and in all honesty, I'm sure he drove right out of the White House.

Graham dropped us off at our hotel, motel or Holiday Inn, I don't fucking know, everything looks the fucking same in America.

Before he pulled away, in his car that is, I collared him about doing a show live in The Bronx at the book launch. After resuscitating him, he agreed.

So Chas was in and Graham was in, again, and we were off.

The next day I took myself to my favourite spot in America, the once place I can think, embrace, feel. The grave of JFK. I stand there and look across at the Lincoln Memorial, the

Washington Monument, Capitol Hill and all the millions of graves in Arlington, and I ponder, I muse, I think to myself: can you imagine fucking Jackie Kennedy? Man alive, she must have been the best five a side that ever lived. She got JFK to marry her fur fucks sake and he'd fucked everything of women born. Even Marilyn didn't get that ring on her finger, although I'm sure he got hers on his.

All this contemplation gave me an idea for a new book, but I had to get the Wim's Tims launch done first. I also was in a different frame of mind. I'd released a book in February, another in July and another in October, it was now almost thanksgiving and I wasn't dead yet. In fact, some people actually claimed to like me, although plenty didn't. Some people claimed I was capable of genius, others said I wasn't consistent enough, but the people who liked me, loved me. What was this phenomenon? What did people expect of me? I pondered. First Jackie's asshole, then what I had to do, there is only one thing for it, I needed to...

Project Paddy McCourt.

It was obvious to me that I've moved on from Charlie Mulgrew, I was three books in, he was only two medals in, I had to aim bigger. Go for the old "Flawed Genius" act that so many had pulled off before. I'm thinking of folk like George Best, Hunter Thompson, Jocky Wilson and Jason Higgins. I think it through and it's a great way to make folk buy books.

I head back to the hotel to get the Mother out but she's at breakfast, so I take the window of one handed opportunity and go for a wank. I would normally do it in the shower on occasions like this but with peace for once, I go for it on the bed. It's annoying because the more I get into it, the more the bed creaks and squeaks. I'm at the vinegar strokes part when the noise is deafening from the fucking bed. I'm like a wild animal now and climax just before cardiac arrest. It's at this point I realise that all the noise was my mum, tapping and scraping the window with her house key, trying to get my attention.

Let's move on.

Thanksgiving arrived and I was invited down to Queens by Frankie Fraser. I'd let Frankie know that I had invented the whole family thing, primarily because if you lie to him, he will kill you. It was also handy as I needed to be in Forest Hills the next day. Yeah, the ex wife was having her parents over and was probably spiking their food with laxative. Speaking of having parents, I had her mum. This old, flabby, chaffing body, slithering and sliding around. She looked terrible as well.

Dinner at Frankie's was great. It consisted of six blunts, 36 beers and a turkey that he got from the Cuban he fucks up the block. That's both a fact and a euphemism. He didn't invite her round though, instead he hired two broads from Nick Laveglia's set up, "Naughty Nick's Naked Lunch"

They couldn't cook for shit but they could rim for America.

That night we hit Roosevelt Avenue for a couple of beers, after telling the girls the way to the Subway station. We hit Donovans first and I hadn't had a sip of my Guinness when I got a call from Paul McCartney. I'd mentioned the cunt on HomeBhoys and Beyond The Waves Shows but I didn't tell them we had became terrific friends. I moved towards the quiet and discreet end of the bar and listened to what he said "Paul? Paul. Listen, I've been thinking about what you were saying last week and you're right, I'm all washed up, I need to do something new, can you help me?"

I'd told McCartney it had been a long time since Band On The Run and not long enough since The Frog Song and I would help him write new material. On visits back to Scotland in my role as Director of Football at Partick Thistle I was an avid Sky Arts fan and had watched a few shows so with that, and three books under my belt, I felt confident that i would be able to write songs better than The Beatles did.

I arranged to go over to McCartney's place in the morning to show him how it's done, but as I shut the cell phone, I walked over to the bar and saw I had bigger fish to fry, Frankie looked absolutely raging.

"Oh, what the fuck are you doing?"

I looked round, he was definitely talking to me.

"The cap, what the fuck you wearing that in here for?"

I looked in the mirror behind the bar and saw I was wearing a Yankee cap. Donovans, given it's location alone, is a big Mets bar.

"Um, sorry Frankie, didn't mean any disrespect, I know you're a big Met fan and this is a big Met bar, I'll take it off right away"

He looked me up and down. For a split second I thought he was going to pull his gun out and shoot me.

Then he said:

"Fuck you talking about?" He nodded at the screen "It's football season, baseball is done"

As I regained my heartbeat, Lisa walked in. Lovely Lisa. The love of my life Lisa. The only woman I ever loved. The woman who collapsed drunk on our first date. The woman who caused Kevin St. James and Scruffy Duffy's to be destroyed in my honour. I loved Lisa but we only had one night together, September 11th 2007. We kissed and fondled all evening, her beautiful skin bettered only by her breasts, the much sought after breasts of every red blooded male in Midtown Manhattan and I had them in my hands that night. If I could spend one day again for the rest of my life, it would be that day. Lovely Lisa.

"You, you bastard, standing there fucking drinking, your kid needs diapers, he's going to Kindergarten soon and you never see him you Muthafucka!!!!!"

I expected that.

As did Frankie who rolled his eyes and said "Oh here we go, fucking Aileen Wuornos is back"

Lisa shot him the paint stripper look

"Shut the fuck up Fat Man, no surprise your speciality is in hookers"

Oh Christ.

I settled her down with a Screwdriver whilst Frankie looked like he was going to take a hammer to her.

By the end of the evening, Lisa was in a coma but thankfully the kid slept through it. Whisky will do that to you. Frankie and I were well on, so much so that, on our new smart phones, we started sending messages to each other on Facebook rather than communicate by speaking.

"I love you, brother"

"Yeah, me too"

"We got the world by the balls"

"Yeah"

"Alright"

"Yep"

I woke up the next morning on Frankie's couch. The table in front of me had more tobacco on it than a French broad's ass.

I walked to 46th and Bliss to get the 7 Train to Grand Central, to then head up to McCartney's. Grabbing breakfast downstairs in Grand Central, I watched lots and lots of office workers get off trains from upstate and it reminds me that I must get up there more. Women from upstate's vaginas that is.

I walk out and towards 5th Avenue. Although I don't smoke now, I light up a cigarette. I think a "Flawed Genius" smokes. Paddy smokes, so Paul must smoke. I just get it lit, after three flicks of the Zippo (Can't you tell I've made it? A Zippo lighter for Christ sake!) and when I look up, I see a guy standing in front of me "Brother, can you help me out?" I look around, seeing if this is a set up. Although my confidence has risen, I'm still wary of being the target of a sniper's rifle but I soon realise this is actually a "Man of the people" moment and I give the guy $20. He looks stunned and says "Good looking out, man" and walks away to get drunk. I take a long drag of my fag and, head up, walk up 5th Avenue. It takes me about two minutes to realise that was the last cash I had on me. I'll need to tap McCartney.

I arrive at his apartment and press the bell which plays "Maxwell's Silver Hammer". Paul has this to warn off maniacs but, clearly, as I enter, it's not working.

I enter the apartment and, as usual, Paul is doobied up. "You know, I could walk to her house from here in less than 15 minutes" Oh christ we are onto Yoko Ono again. "I was watching John Lennon Live In New York last night, it was brilliant, John's vocals were inspiring, evocative, educating, then she appears, wailing more than Bob Marley's mob" I pull up a chair and say "Paul, we've been through this before, The Beatles were a long time ago. Besides, as I keep telling you, for all the bad Karma that Yoko gets for fucking up the band who changed America, she gets it all back for singing on 'Luck of The Irish' " At this point Paul stumbles up and, with a glazed expression, says "I wrote 'Give Ireland back To The Irish' !!!!"" I wait for him to sit down and say "I know Paul, but you also wrote 'The Girl is Mine' so let's move on"

I step out the room and pick up the guitar I leave here for occasions like this and walk back in the room. Paul is asleep but as i strum, he smiles and says "It's like being back in Abbey Road"

I tell him to pay attention and tell him that I've written the song for him already, in my head.

I make myself comfortable on his massive couch and start, Easter Bunnies Go Dancing At Easter, ok I'm ready

Long John Heather-Larkin/McCartney

"Her name was Heather,

She loved a blether.

Drinking pimms,

and prosthetic limbs

Chorus

My name is Paul

Not Living Doll

That was Cliff,

I like a spliff

Well I had Linda

She looked liked Cinders

She had both feet

but she didn't eat meat"

Repeat chorus

I put down the guitar and looked at Paul, he looked blown away.

"No need for words, Paul, you're back"

I made my excuses and asked him to spot me a $20 til Monday and he, still looking dumbstruck, told me to take it out the teapot on the mantle piece.

I made my way outside and slipped into Connollys.

Connollys is where I first met Paul and was a bar I used to pretend to read the paper in and look at women. My paper of choice was the Home and Away. Non drunks will not know that paper, it's effectively a propaganda sheet for Irish bars in New York. The sports coverage is good though and there is one highlight. Every week they have lots of pictures of girls who either work in Irish bars or go to Irish bars. As I finger the pages, my mind wanders back to a month ago. Just before my mum flew over, my new found confidence took me to a place. I was in my huge house when a package came to the door. Not by itself like, a guy brought it. In it was a very small camcorder/camera. I'd been needing a knew one as my previous two had succumbed to a mixture of semen, Jello and peanut butter. Fucking peanut butter on a camera, disgusting. I brought it into the apartment and started thinking, thinking, thinking, see, always thinking. I hatched my plan, splashed on the Old Spice and off I went. You see, it was prestige to be in the Home and Away, a badge of honour for all who worked or frequented Irish bars. Especially for the girls and...if you seriously haven't got to the end of this particular story by now, how the hell did you get to the end of the book?

So I hit my first bar and approached three gorgeous bits of fluff. Camcorder out, they were midst dialing 911 when I said "I'm from Home and Away, would you like your picture in next weeks paper?" and they were drooling by "away". I looked at them and knew the score and one said "Who do you want first?" I could tell they thought it was the old school way of a quick BJ and you're on page 12.

No, not this time.

I walked behind the first girl as she made her way to the ladies, holding the door open for me as we entered and we made straight for the cubicle. She unzipped me and started to kneel down before I told her to stop. I moved in, bringing her close to me and whispered long into her ear, her instructions.

She came back up and looked at me leeringly and started:

"You're better than Mulgrew, fucking Charlie? Who is he? You're a flawed genius, you are capable of things he can only dream of, free kicks? Even Stokes can hit them now and again"

We continued in this vein with all three girls and I climaxed each time. None of them noticed I still had the lens cap on.

The book launch has been confirmed for December 10th and I've got about 20 days before then.

I've recently acquired an agent and thought I'd test the water. When he signed me he asked to me write down 20 things I'd like to do. I wrote down 19 girls names and "visit Charles Manson in Prison"

Guess which one he arranged?

I flew out to California the next day, Hanford Municipal, and was in a Kings County cab on my way to Corcoran Prison before I could fix my watch.

Corcoran looks like a criminal Pentagon. Or a more criminal Pentagon.

After being bodily searched and touching my toes more times than a gymnast, I'm led through those horrible khaki corridors, with lots of bullet proof glass windows and burly guards passing me like I'm a leper. I eventually reach a room deep, deep in the bowels of the institution and the burly guards make me think of Craig Burley and how I wished that cunt was in here and I held his false teeth and controlled the menu.

I walk in the room and Charlie is there. He must be in his 70's yet he looks fantastic, far better than I do. As I go to pull up the chair, I realise it's nailed to the ground. Which means it's a tight squeeze between chair and table for my gut.

I go to speak but Charlie raises his hand

"Don't speak until you get to the point"

I think on this and say

"I wrote a story called Channeling Charlie Mul, uh, Manson and I wanted to meet you to see if I could get any vibe of leadership from you, so that I too could lead people to buy boo, I mean, kill the pigs"

Charlie looked at me and smiled, then laughed incessantly for about three minutes

Then said:

"There's nothing to it man, just make em think they need you more than you need them, it's all bullshit of course, but it works"

Then he got up to leave and I knew I had to say something, so I said

"Listen, if I can do anything for you, stamps, cigs, anything, let me know"

He shook his head and said "You can't do anything for me unless you know one of the Helter Skelter army man"

I mused this and said

"No, but I know the guy who wrote it..."

I flew back the next day, into La Guardia, so I could do my toilet run at the ex wife's house. Since I'd had a little success, she had petitioned the court to change the terms of the agreement so that I'd not only have to clean her shit stained toilet, but lick shit off her ass instead of her using toilet paper.

Unfortunately, I won.

As usual, the landing into La Guardia was bumpy. The runway is too small, but I got a solution. Demolish Citi-Field and make the fucking thing longer. I'm kidding of course, I love the Mets. Well, not love, pity mainly. Being a huge celebrity now, I thought I'd bequeath them with my presence now and again, so a couple of months back, I went down there one Sunday and I forget who they were playing but the Mets won. The reason I mention this trip, yeah trip, was I was on acid the whole day. Getting down there from The Bronx to Manhattan was no fucking joke when I had to get there by walking the whole way through treacle. On the 7 train from Grand Central we flew in and picked guys up at JFK and the train became a sort of spaceship that taught me that we are all dead with great imaginations. I got to Citi-Field and saw all the bricks and stones in front of me with the names FRANKIE FRASER, NICK LAVEGLIA, JASON HIGGINS and DAVID HARPER on them and from nothing those guys appeared in Baseball Furies outfits and started chasing me round the Ball Park. I got away from them and into the park only for Billy Crystal to run me over on a horse. I recovered from that and found my seat, only to then be transported down to make the first pitch, which I launched at Kevin James from The King of Queens and his huge head exploded. As I laughed, Jerry Seinfeld smacked me

with a golf club and knocked me out. I woke up, groggy as hell, in Bellevue Hospital the next day and realised Mike Francesa was my doctor and was screaming at me.

What a freak out that was, the Mets won a game?

When I got home, I started checking with a few people involved with the book launch. They had to know that this was my thing and no cunt better come within five time zones of even thinking of trying to upstage me. With that in mind, I needed be around egos, folk who knew how to keep people in their place, very easy In New York. Throw a stone in any direction and you'll hit an ego the size of Mount Rushmore. That makes me think, what four faces would I want on Mount Rushmore?

The first one is obvious, you have to have Francis Albert Sinatra there, are you fucking serious? is that even a debate? Don't try, Jilly will take your eye out. After that, I'm thinking Gary Busey. Does anyone, dead or alive, represent America better than Gary Busey? Here's a guy, so far gone, he thought the photos from Mars were family vacation snaps, walking round America like he has "I Feel Love" by Donna Summer on repeat in his ears and he's got more money and respect than Nelson Mandela. Also, the beauty of Busey, his face is so fucking big that he actually would not need to have it blown up to go on Mount Rushmore, In fact, he could lay on his stomach and just hang over the side of the mountain with his face up and no cunt would be any the wiser.

The third face, I'm thinking, has to be a woman. Would help keep up the pretense that men care, so I'm thinking here Betty White. The main problem being is that Betty's face is actually more craggy than the side of the mountain. Finally, you got to go with a sports guy, with that being said, as Graham Wilson would say, we have to go with Mary Decker. In true American style, when faced with a tiny bit of adversity, she reacted by being a fucking cry baby.

USA USA USA USA USA.

I take a cab into Manhattan, wasting $35 to boost my ego, and have arranged to meet Gary Haley. I was able to get him to up his payments from $800 to $1000 a month to stay away from his house due to my ever growing celebrity. I mean how the fuck can a guy like me be expected to go to a place like Port Authority Bus Station, far less, Ringwood, NJ? He's lucky I am even coming to meet him now.

I hit the Old Castle, heads turn, and I take a seat at the bar. Gary comes in right behind me, sighs, and slaps $20 on the bar. As usual, he is cussing out his work mate Glenn who, it has to be said, is a prize wanker. I laugh and go for a quick piss. I clocked a familiar face at the bar but it didn't register. It was only mid-piss that the dime dropped, it was Amanda. A shudder went through me that made me piss on my hand. Shocked, I made my way back to the bar, avoided eye contact and took my seat again before taking a long swing of part beer, part piss as then I realised I hadn't washed my hands. Amanda was that rare breed, a girl who slept me with before I was hugely famous. She was also the stupid cunt who was with me the night I met David Bowie and she hadn't fucking recognised him.

I intimated to Gary that she was in and he replied "Uh, yeah, I told you as I soon as I came in?" FUCK. I thought he had said some shit about Glenn, instead it was "I see Amanda is in again" but I had been busy answering tweets and emails. I *had noticed more and more people saying to me that I was mishearing lots of stuff and forgetting more. This made me think, was I getting too wrapped up in myself or I did a need assistant?*

I hired the assistant the day after.

I slept with Amanda again inbetween. It had come to me whilst I watched her sign the contract I made up that morning ensuring she couldn't sell the story of our sex to the papers.

The assistant was a Cuban girl who did the boat from Valadero to Key West. I could relate to this because I once walked from Silverknowes Beach to Cramond Island.

After sorting the assistant out, in a similar vein to Amanda, my whole focus was on the book launch in The Bronx.

Right after a burger at Parker Meridian. This is the best burger joint in town and I knew my order, crucial, sat down and checked the emails, there was one from Ewan Murray, the Prince Harry of Scottish journalism. He's wanting to interview me, all expenses paid and a fee, whilst playing me at golf. The cunt fancies himself a bit and also thinks he can play golf. I agree and he says we have have the pick of courses in Scotland. I'm tempted to jump straight in and say "Silverknowes" just to piss the cunt off but instead tell him that I want to play at Trump's new place. He appears incredulous and says "But it's not even open yet?" I tell him not to worry, I'm five minutes from his place in NYC right now and will go along and sort it now.

I arrive on 5th and 56th soon after and breeze in. Incredibly, his secretary has no idea who I am which I put down to her obviously being forced to watch The Apprentice 24/7. I think for a second that I would be good on that show then remember that Piers Morgan was on it so they've used up their quota for tadgers from over the water. After a wee bit shouting, I'm walking into Donnie's office and he asks me what I want and I tell him that I need four hours on his new course in Scotland. He looks at me again and says "I'll say again, you told my secretary, she told me" I start to lose it a bit when he stamps his fist on the table and says "Are you employed Sir!" Fucking employed ya cunt? He takes umbrage at my language and I get up to leave, he is screaming in the background "you're generation is over, condolences, the bums lost" and shut the door behind me. His secretary smiles and asks how things went and I say fine, Donnie told me to to tell you to book me in for fours next next week.

She types it in and hands me my booking card.

I get out onto 5th Avenue and it's a little chilly. I fancy a hot chocolate but then remember I have this book launch to get sorted. I call Graham Wilson who informs me that Jim McGuigan is bringing an arsenal. I remind him it's a Celtic book launch but realise he means that cunt is going all David Koresh on us. He explains that Jim has it in his head that bullets will be flying in The Bronx. They will be, but in his direction if he keeps this patter up.

I think about my trip back home for the golf and decide to call Jason and ask him to set up a snooker match between him, me and John. Not many people know this but Jason used to be better than John at Snooker, then John was born. I realise the golf and snooker will be the same week but beating Ewan, Jason and John will be good relaxation for it.

Speaking of relaxation, I need some now. I can't face going back to my house so call Lisa and ask her if it would be ok if I came over and diddy ride her for a bit. She agrees on the basis that I bring her three bottles of Grey Goose. She also wants two bottles of Jim Beam for herself.

I grab a cab, not literally, and before long I am heading over the 59th St bridge banging out tunes on my newly purchased I Pod. I can tell by the smiles from the driver he is loving my singing and hear him say "What a crooner", least I think he said that.

I pitch up at Lisa's and she grabs the bottles from me. She chucks them all in the fridge and comes back with two beers she had in there and unzips her top. Now you see why she is the love of my life? I pull her legs down so she is lying full length on the couch. I bring out my special diddy ride CD and put it on. Force of Nature by Oasis comes on followed by Dancing Days by Led Zeppelin. I've not yet needed to add a third song.

Deed done, she wipes herself down and that's no easy job given how backed up I was.

I stay there for a few days until it's time to fly back to Scotland, saving a fortune on the taxi fare from the Bronx. Lisa lives on Fresh Pond Road. Write your own fucking joke there.

The plane journey flies in, get it, and I am on my way Edinburgh where Ewan is going to drive us up to Trump's place, amazed that I have a booking card for it in my pocket. The drive up is boring as Ewan bores me with his tales of all the birds he's shagged, then the next minute he's going on about Hearts, who he supports to get street cred. Immediately

this makes you wonder what kind of fucking streets he grew up on.

We arrive at the course and it dawns on Ewan I have no clubs, until my assistant appears on a raft with a pristine set for me. I had her leave three weeks before me just to make sure she got there on time.

Naturally I thrash Ewan at golf, well he led all the way until the last hole when he hit a two over and I hit a five under. Some things never change.

I leave him with the bill and have the Cuban drive me down to Wishaw to teach the Higgins how to play Snooker. As a favour to both I vow to play one handed and this means I only win 9-7. Josh Gaffney referees it and is delighted that we replace all balls ourselves so he doesn't have to put his hand in a pocket once.

I make my way back to the airport and within hours I'm in a cab on the friday afternoon before the Saturday book launch. I call Chas who has had 12 crates of Morton's Rolls flown in so we are good to go. Graham is getting the train from DC, Coach is driving up with my favourite America, Jimmy The Hair and Rev is coming in tomorrow morning once he gets his allowance from his Mom. Graham has called me to say he's had to execute an Admiral on the train for continuous farting. I don't think it's either gay or drug terminology so I call Vincent The Parrot who assures me it's fine, he sailed with the guy and he was a prick anyway.

Coach arrives first. In a tank.

Jimmy The Hair and I go down to the station to meet Graham who staggers off the train after four beers. The train makes it

into the station despite having it's entire view of Westchester blocked by The Hair.

We drink the night away and carry Graham into Coach's tank so they can go to their hotel. I'd have them stay but I don't want to.

It's a beautiful morning and Chas comes to pick me up. We've been through a lot together but most of those girls went home. We arrive at The Celtic House and I am greeted like Frank Sinatra at Madison Square Garden, folk ask me if I've ever considered a wig and am I too old for all this.

Everyone shows up but no one more than Fraser Forster who saves a last minute penalty and me from being battered.

I look around and think about Francis Albert and those words "if you can make it here, you can make it anywhere"

I made it.

My motto in mind

It's harder than you think...

Right, Lisa?

Slainte

This book could not have been written without the love and support of, in no particular order, Chas Duffy, Kevin Devine, Liam Power, Graham Wilson, David Harper, Phil Mac Giolla Bhain, Evan Watson, Simon Donnelly, Joe McKenna, Jason Higgins, Jim McGuigan, Jimmy The Hair, Gary Bodnar, Chris McGuigan, Tam Donnelly, Joe Clark, Jane Hamilton, Suzanne and Tim King, Steph O'Neill, Joe Chalmers, James Cameron, Josh Gaffney, Stephen Monaghan, Kenny Millar, Ewan Murray, Albert Kidd, John Paul Taylor, Angela Haggerty, Jamie O'Neil, Mike Boyd, Jim McGinn, Stephen Holzenthal, Stephen Rodgers, RoseAnn Fleming, Average Joe Miller, Frankie Fraser and, of course, Gary Haley.

There are lots of people out there who have enhanced my life in the last few years but but none more so than Sam McLeod, Kim Petrie, Paul Montgomery-Wade, Robert Ryan, Nicola McGinley, The Carluke Bhoys, Dermot Hill, Lauren McCloskey and Leeanne Laird.

There are a few people I can't ever seem to shake off like Allan Hosey and Paul O'Neil. Whilst Mark O'Neil is out less than the olympic torch.

There are many more out there I love, why shouldn't I? I'm a people person, just never a "we are the people" person...

Printed in Great Britain
by Amazon